Going global with a brand is one of th[e]
issues facing brand managers today. [But]
how do they ensure that their brand [reaches]
its full potential as it stretches across
multiple cultures and markets? How do they
balance the differing requirements of
ensuring that the brand meets local needs
with the desire to maintain global brand
consistency?

In *Global Brand Strategy,* Sicco van Gelder
tackles this central issue head on. He shows
how both global and local brand
management need to agree a common
basis for their brand strategy and planning.
Drawing on his extensive experience, he has
created a unique framework – the Global
Brand Proposition Model – which enables
them to analyse their brand's sensitivity and
vulnerability to specific internal and
external influences across a multitude of
diverse markets and societies.

The model, which combines the strategic
planning cycle with the brand environment,
provides a powerful and practical tool that
can be applied both globally and locally.
Following the structure of the model, and
filled with real-life global examples and case
studies, the book comprises three parts.
Part I shows how to undertake an internal
analysis, Part II looks at the external
analysis, and Part III covers the central issues
of global brand strategy, such as:

• taking a brand global;
• harmonizing a global brand;
• extending a global brand;
• creating a new global brand.

For all those involved in global brand
management, the local management of a
global brand, or the management of a local
brand faced with foreign competition,
Global Brand Strategy provides not only a
robust framework for analysing the
complexities, but also much fresh and
original thinking. For students of
international business and marketing,
it will aid their understanding of our
multi-cultural world and help them to
discard any ethnocentric thinking.

Global Brand Strategy

Unlocking Brand Potential Across Countries, Cultures & Markets

SICCO VAN GELDER

KOGAN
PAGE

London and Sterling, VA

To Helga, David and Joost, for their love

120 Pentonville Road
London N1 9JN
UK
www.kogan-page.co.uk

22883 Quicksilver Drive
Sterling VA 20166–2012
USA

ISBN 0 7494 4023 6

British Library Cataloguing-in-Publication Data

A CIP record for this book is available from the British Library.

Library of Congress Cataloging-in-Publication Data

Van Gelder, Sicco, 1964–
  Global brand strategy : unlocking brand potential across countries,
cultures and markets / Sicco Van Gelder.
      p. cm.
Includes bibliographical references and index.
  ISBN 0-7494-4023-6
  1. Brand name products--Planning. 2. Brand name products--Marketing.
3. Brand name products--Management. 4. Export marketing. I Title.
  HD69.B7V357 2003
  658.8'27--dc22
                          2003016216

Typeset by Saxon Graphics Ltd, Derby.
Printed and bound in Great Britain by Creative Print and Design (Wales), Ebbw Vale

Contents

Preface

Globalization was the battle cry of the last decade of the 20th century. This phenomenon is not new or unique to this period. In the 19th century, colonialism was a potent force of globalization and created a multitude of cross-border trading links. For the first time, goods bearing a brand name were sent abroad in large quantities. Many of the cross-border trade links bearing branded goods, however, were limited to directly neighbouring countries and to the countries' colonial empires: British brands found their way to India, French branded goods to Indochina and Dutch brands to the Netherlands' East Indies. The reasons for exporting these branded goods lay in the demand that existed in the foreign markets for quality goods – especially among the colonial populations – and the ability of manufacturers to produce goods at a low enough unit cost to be able to transport their wares halfway around the world. This was the effect of mechanization of both the means of production and transportation, and resulted in low marginal costs for each additional unit produced and shipped.

The next big spur for globalization came after the Second World War when, often in the wake of US military forces, new consumer brands came to Europe and Asia. The difference with the colonial era was that although these were foreign brands, production facilities were largely located in the markets that they served, as were the companies' subcontractors. The reasons for arranging matters in this way were that because of increased affluence among the general populations in Western Europe, Japan, and urban areas in East and South-east Asia and Latin America, there was such a demand that a local presence became not only affordable but also necessary. Branding also became very much a local phenomenon, as the local representatives were responsible for marketing the brand.

The third big push for branding came in the wake of the erosion and subsequent demise of communism. The fall of the Berlin Wall opened up previously inaccessible markets to foreign brands, not just in Eastern and Central Europe, but also markets that had previously been off-limits due to political sensitivities, such as Chile and South Africa. However the biggest impetus came from the opening up of China, which is not only a massive market, but also a massive production location for US, Japanese and European brands. Deregulation of markets has allowed for flexible production and has led to increased competition. Spurred on by logistical and IT developments, manufacturers constantly seek configurations that best suit their production needs. This has lead to a fragmentation of once monolithic company structures. Branding has become separated from other company functions. The closure of local production facilities often also leads to company management questioning the need for supporting brands locally. These developments have put pressure on companies to rationalize their international brand portfolios, to harmonize their international brands, to co-brand or even merge with other global brands.

The effect that this intensified globalization has had on brands has been spectacular. New brands are seemingly born global, or at the very least experience a quick roll-out from home or lead countries into other markets. Many traditionally local brands are sold, phased out, or face transition to a new regional or global brand name and subsequent harmonization. Brand portfolios that have been built up through decades of acquisitions are rationalized in order to focus attention and resources on a limited number of strategic brands. Long-established brands have enhanced their dominant positions across the globe, threatening less marketing-savvy local brands, but are also encountering stern opposition from local brands that find ways to fight back. Some of the global brands manage to become local institutions by filling a local role in the societies where they operate, while others dominate their category as global monoliths.

Debates have also flared over the supposed supremacy of global brands and the inadequacy of (multi-)local brands. In his seminal manifesto for global brands, a 1983 *Harvard Business Review* essay entitled 'The globalization of markets', Levitt argues that consumers across the globe are becoming more alike, require the same mass-produced products at reasonable prices, and that brands should not bother with adapting to local needs and cultural preferences. Levitt's prime example is the way Japanese car manufacturers were able to trounce European and American car makers in the 1980s because of their lean production technologies. The Japanese were able to produce better cars at lower cost, something that American and European consumers were happy to lap up. However, the past decade has shown the adoption of lean manufacturing and quality control have made non-Japanese car makers competitive again and that, particularly in Europe, issues such as design, prestige, national pride, excitement and so on have become of primary importance. The rather bland Japanese cars have not been able to keep up, and their market share has slipped.

This book argues that Levitt's conclusions that consumers are becoming more similar are incorrect. Far from homogenizing, markets have fragmented over the past decade, and people around the world have asserted their local identities and idiosyncrasies. This has happened not despite, but because of globalization. As people interact more with the outside world, they become increasingly sophisticated in their attitudes and behaviours, not content to take foreign brands at face value. This book also argues that each individual global or international brand has specific opportunities and limitations when it comes to standardization or localization. Only a thorough understanding of a variety of factors that influence brands in their global and local contexts helps determine the best course for them.

SENSE AND SENSITIVITY

One of the key issues facing the management of brands today is how to deal with a brand as it stretches across multiple societies and geographies. This is not just a question of management scope (How do we control and monitor the brand?), but of reaching the full potential of a brand in diverse markets. There is often a tension between finding an optimum fit of the brand with local circumstances, and the desire to obtain brand consistency across markets. More often than not, decisions are made on the basis of organizational constructs rather than on the basis of an understanding of the brand and the various internal and external influences on it. This leads to tensions between global and local brand management that can result in power struggles about the ownership of the brand.

Instead, global and local brand management need to understand each other's viewpoints on the brand and the resulting need for adaptations, the possibilities for obtaining sustainable competitive advantage, and the opportunities for standardization. In the end, a compelling brand is in the interest of all those affected by it. The first thing that global and local brand management need is a common basis for their brand strategy and planning work. This common basis needs to provide a shared language, definitions, interpretations, assessments, and most importantly a clear understanding of the relationships between the factors that shape a brand in its global and local contexts.

The past decade has seen the increasing popularity of brand standardization among brand management. Brand standardization can reap huge benefits in terms of economies of scale: centralized production, increased leverage over distribution partners, one advertising campaign across markets, the same brand extensions everywhere, reductions in brand management staff and so on. This has made brand standardization into brand management's holy grail. For many brand managers, their brands can only be considered truly global if they are the same in every aspect everywhere. In reality, however, this leaves precious few brands to claim such a title. Brand management started asking questions such as 'Should all brands be standardized across markets?', 'In how many markets must a brand be present to be considered global?', and 'How much revenue must a brand generate before you consider it to be a global brand?' These are, however, the wrong questions to ask.

At the same time other voices emerged lambasting global brands for their detrimental effects on the environment, on workers in developing countries, on local brands, on the mental well-being of children, on public spaces and so on. Global brands are being portrayed as the epitomes of degradation, exploitation and manipulation. Anti-globalization activists started asking questions such as 'Are global brands forces of destruction in the Third World?', 'Should local brands be protected in order to defend local culture?', and 'How can global brands be stopped?' Again, these are the wrong questions to ask. In fact, Anholt (2003) claims that developing countries do not need to be the victims of globalization. If they can learn to use the classic rich-nation tricks of branding and marketing, they can turn the forces of global markets to their advantage.

What then are the right questions to ask? This book rests on the premise that each brand has its own specific potential for standardization across and adaptation to culturally and structurally diverse markets. One of the right questions to ask is, 'How can a brand best provide value to its stakeholders, those (directly) affected by the brand, dispersed across countries, markets, societies and geographies?' Do consumers value the brand enough to buy and use it? Do employees value it enough to want to work for it? Do distributors value it enough to carry it? Do shareholders value it enough to invest in it? Do communities value it enough to welcome it in their midst? Who these stakeholders are and how they relate to each other may differ by brand and also by location where the brand is present.

As for those critical of global brands, this book agrees with them that transgressions have taken place in the name of brands. On the one hand, to blame branding for these wrongdoings is to overestimate the role of this discipline in most global corporations. How many branding experts do you find on the boards of Fortune 500 companies? On the other hand, it is to misunderstand the discipline. This book considers branding to be a deeply humanistic discipline seeking to connect the various processes of an organization, in order to get people to rally around the purposes and principles of the brand and provide unique value to stakeholders.

This book focuses on how the unique characteristics of a brand can best be extended across societies by understanding that brand's sensitivity or vulnerability to particular factors, both internal and external to the brand's organization. Although each brand is unique, it is possible to categorize brands in a manner that helps us to understand to which factors certain types of brands are most susceptible. This kind of understanding is useful not only to all those corporate managers eager to make a success of their brand around the globe, but also to those who are responsible for a local brand that is faced with seemingly better endowed global competitors. In fact, this kind of knowledge can be useful to everyone with a vested interest in particular brands, such as governments, non-governmental organizations (NGOs), employees, distribution partners, suppliers, local communities and even anti-globalization activists.

In this book, global brands are defined rather loosely as brands that are available across multiple geographies, without setting any specific lower limit or any continental requirements. The revenue these brands generate also does not matter, nor does the manner in which they present themselves in each society. The term 'global' is used in this book as shorthand for brands with varying degrees of globalness. Some may be present in dozens of countries across all continents, while others may be active only in a more regional setting.

Although it would be possible and worthwhile to address the brand from the perspective of various stakeholder groups, this book focuses squarely on the perspective of consumers. In the end, it is they who decide whether they value a brand enough to spend their time and money on it. Also, addressing each type of stakeholder perspective is outside the scope of this book. Readers are encouraged to use their own judgement when applying the thinking presented here to stakeholder groups other than consumers.

Acknowledgements

When I started work on this book, various people asked me why I wanted to write a book on branding, an area already so cluttered with titles. There was clearly nothing that had not been written already on the subject, and what hope did I have of adding anything of consequence? These remarks bemused me. I had, for a while already, been trying to find books that did not deal with global branding as an academic or elevated pursuit, or in a one-size-fits-all manner. The thing I felt was missing was a book that considered global branding in a practical way without unduly reducing the complexity of the subject matter.

My own experience, as a commercial researcher and consultant to global and international clients and as a geographer by training, had taught me that no two brands and no two countries are ever the same, and that it takes persistence, genuine curiosity, honesty and creativity to do branding well across multiple geographies, societies and marketplaces. That same experience taught me about the factors that determine whether one gets global branding right or not. This understanding, acquired through years of talking to and listening to people talk about specific brands, forms the foundation of this book. A lot of additional reading, and even more pondering about what I had heard, read and had seen in the world around me, have shaped this book. Creating this book has been a demanding task, my head spinning frequently from trying to put the words together that would make sense to others, but it has been well worth the time and effort. I believe that, although far from being perfect, this book does meaningfully increase the knowledge about global branding.

I want to express my deepest gratitude and love to my wife Helga for her patience and unwavering support during the two years that it took me to write this book. I would not have been able to complete this personal project without it. My deepest appreciation also extends to both our parents who have lovingly given up their own time to look after our children week after week. My father deserves a separate mention for reviewing and commenting on practically every incarnation of this manuscript. I am also extremely grateful to Guus and Rik at Groenholland who so graciously offered me a place to work and all manner of office conveniences. My thanks also extend to all other people at Groenholland who have provided me with assistance and a chance for conversation. There are a number of people who have reviewed my (all but) final manuscript and have provided their commentary to help improve it. I want to thank them wholeheartedly for their valuable time and counsel. They are Simon Anholt, Nicholas Ind, Chris Macrae and Jack Yan.

Introduction

THE STRATEGIC PLANNING CYCLE

Defining a brand is not something that is generally left to chance. A brand is a construct and not a living and breathing organism, as some would have us believe, and as much of the language employed in branding, including some of the terminology in this book, suggests. Brands are created, stimulated and applied by people working in organizations seeking to create worthwhile experiences for their customers that will induce behaviour beneficial to the organization. This calls for some careful preparations and planning. The various stages of the strategic planning cycle are shown in Figure 0.1.

First, the business strategy

The strategic planning for a brand starts with an understanding of an organization's business strategy. Strategizing for business is not something that is exclusive to the business world. Not-for-profit organizations also have a need for this type of activity, particularly those that are dependent on donations from the general public. The business strategy is aimed at achieving particular consumer behaviour. Only if consumers actually purchase, use goods (more often), pay a higher price or donate (more) will the objectives of a business strategy be met. These objectives may include a larger market share, increased returns, higher margins and increased shareholder value. Brands are designed to persuade consumers to exhibit

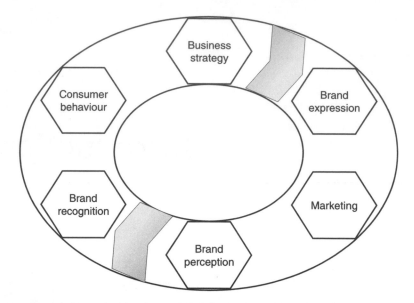

Figure 0.1   *The strategic planning cycle*

the behaviour that will make these objectives come true for the organization. Thus, the influence of business strategy upon brand strategy is direct and compelling.

Then, the brand expression

It is the task of brand management to translate the business strategy into a brand expression. Most brand managers usually consider this to be 'the brand' without fully realizing the influences on the brand as it winds its way towards the consumer. However, the brand expression does contain the materials with which brand managers are able to shape their brand. It is imperative to obtain a good understanding of one's ammunition, so to speak, to determine what kind of battles can be fought with the brand. This means getting a complete view of all the elements of the brand expression, then choosing which to use and emphasize in the brand's manifestations. It is important to realize that these manifestations do not consist merely of advertising and promotions, but that they encompass the full experience that consumers have of the brand.

Finally marketing

The marketing mix in its turn aims to translate the brand expression into actual products or services, with a specific price, to be sold at specific outlets, to be promoted through specific communications activities and channels, and to be supported by a specific service. The influence of the marketing policy is indirect, in that the correct translation of the brand into the marketing mix determines whether consumers are provided with the correct experience of the brand. The marketing implementation consists of the actual production and delivery of the products and services, their accompanying messages to consumers, and the actual product or service experience. The implementation eventually determines whether consumers experience what the brand strategy sets out to provide. The marketing implementation may make or break a brand at the moment that is of most importance to consumers: for instance when they actually experience the brand through advertising, promotions, purchase, usage, and after-sales service.

It does not end there

Having translated the business strategy into the brand expression, which in turn has guided marketing activities, brand management would seem to have done its job. Managers could be forgiven for leaning back and waiting for well-deserved acclaim to erupt. However, all the hard work put into devising and executing the brand may still flounder on the perception of the brand among consumers. Much of the central argument in this book focuses on how brand perception is influenced not only by the policies and actions of the organization, but also by the lenses through which consumers observe these activities. Understanding which lenses affect the consumer perception of a particular type of brand helps brand management to determine the brand's potential among consumers in a particular market.

The subsequent brand recognition is far more than simple awareness of the brand. It is rather the way in which consumers discriminate (or not as the situation may be) between the brand and competitive brands. In addition, it consists of how consumers see the relationships between the brand and other brands. Other brands may be part of the same organization (such as a master brand or extension brand), but can also be brands that are related through partnership, endorsement, co-branding or as a branded element. These forms of brand recognition are also considered by consumers through particular lenses that need careful consideration.

Finally, the brand must be appreciated by consumers to such an extent that they happily part with their money and are satisfied in the process. If this is the case, such behaviour will generally fulfil the business strategy. However, in most cases, the organization's management will likely see the results as the basis to reassess the assumptions, policies and activities to try to improve performance in one way or another. This starts off a new cycle of planning.

THE BRAND ENVIRONMENT

More factors influence a brand than the business strategy and the subsequent efforts of the organization and its affiliates to bring about the brand, as described in the previous paragraph. A brand operates in an environment consisting of, on the one hand, the elements of the strategic planning cycle, and on the other hand, organizational conventions, competitive forces, market structures, cultural factors, consumer motivation and media attention: the lenses and filters through which consumers perceive and experience the brand. These factors combined constitute the brand environment (see Figure 0.2).

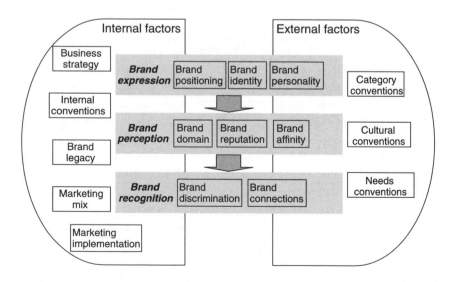

Figure 0.2   *The brand environment*

Factors that influence the brand

The brand environment consists of the brand itself – expression, perception and recognition – surrounded by internal and external factors that have an influence on the brand. Only by taking these factors into consideration can management understand the entire brand proposition, and how it is affected in different markets. Some factors affect some brand elements more than others, some types of brands are more sensitive to particular factors, and the effect may vary according to markets and consumer segments.

The problem facing brand managers is how to unravel all these elements and turn their insight into policies that will unlock the full potential of their brand in a particular market, and across multiple markets at the same time. This requires a common framework that can be used across markets in order to obtain equivalence of brand analysis. A framework ensures not only that global brand management talks the same brand language and follows the same procedures as local brand management, but also that it becomes clear which internal or external factors are uniquely influencing to particular societies or even segments of societies.

Global and local brand management

Global brand management needs to understand how various markets compare on these issues in order to determine how best to manage the brand globally. Determining communalities and differences in business strategy, brand expression and marketing provides insight into the extent to which the organization's policies and activities regarding the brand diverge, as well as the causes and rationale for divergence. Doing the same for the situational factors, the brand perception and the brand recognition provides an understanding of the extent to which the brand is perceived differently across markets, and what causes these differences. A complete analysis offers brand management an appreciation of the core elements of the brand, as expressed and perceived around the world. This type of information forms the basis for shared strategizing and planning for the branding process by global, regional and local brand management. Decisions regarding brand extensions, harmonization, rejuvenation, portfolio rationalization, alliances and acquisitions depend on a thorough understanding of a brand and its environment.

THE GLOBAL BRAND PROPOSITION MODEL

This book introduces a unique framework for equivalent and comparable brand analysis across multiple markets and societies, the global brand proposition model (see Figure 0.3). The model combines the strategic planning cycle with the brand environment into an analysis tool that can be applied both globally and locally. It allows global and local analyses to be linked together seamlessly. The model consists of two main parts, an internal analysis and an external analysis.

The internal analysis

The *internal analysis* is essential for gaining an understanding of how the brand's global and local organizational constructs shape the brand expression or multiple brand expressions, as the case may be. Issues such as business strategy, corporate culture, organizational structures, the brand's significance to the organization and the relationships between global and local brand management teams all play a role in shaping brand expression elements. These individual elements, in their turn, should guide global and local marketing activities. The way the brand defines its advantages over competition, its legacy and principles and its character have a specific influence on issues such as product and service development, channel choice, advertising, staff demeanour, delivery and supply chain management. Most important is to gain an understanding on how well these processes connect up in order to provide consumers with the required brand experience. Although there is a certain hierarchy between the processes analysed, it may well transpire that a requirement in a lower order process compels a change in a higher order process. For example, to realize a specific brand expression may require a rethink of the organizational structure by which the brand is managed.

The external analysis

The *external analysis* focuses on how local conditions act as lenses through which consumers – or particular consumer segments – observe the brand, and how these circumstances affect consumers' understanding of the brand by itself, and in relation to other brands. Specific situational factors affect brand perception elements in a particular manner, thereby influencing brands that are perceived as being especially adept at individual elements. The resulting brand recognition relates the perception of the brand to those in its environs, both competitive brands and related brands, either brands within the same organization or others that provide enhancement to the brand.

The findings from the external analysis provide new input for the internal analysis. The analysis of the brand perception, in particular, provides a starting point for further strategic planning. As the brand perception holds the meaning and significance of the brand to consumers, it is the main area that global and local brand management will want to influence. As a result, the model functions as a constant and consistent feedback loop. Each iteration of the process will help refine or redefine global and local brand propositions.

THE ROAD MAP

This book largely follows the structure of the global brand proposition model. This helps the reader to understand the flow of the analysis process, and also clearly defines the setting of the analysis. However, this book is not intended as a manual on how to do global brand strategy. Rather, the intention is to provide the reader with an understanding of the issues he or she is faced with when dealing with a brand in a global context. In addition, the book provides insight into the connections between various business processes and their subsequent interpretation by consumers, viewing these activities from their own local standpoints.

Part I: The organization, brand expression and marketing

The first part of this book discusses the internal analysis, and consists of three chapters dealing with the global branding context, and the analyses of the organization, the brand expression and marketing. This section examines globalization and its impact on branding, as well as how organizations shape their brands through their policies, cultures, structures and actions. An appreciation of how these differ between global and local brand management, and vary from country to country, lays the foundation for a global brand strategy.

The Preface provides a short discussion of the phenomenon of globalization: the increasing economic, social, technological, regulatory and political interaction between societies across large parts of the globe. This process is not new, but the pace at which globalization develops certainly intensified during the final decades of the past century. The impact of

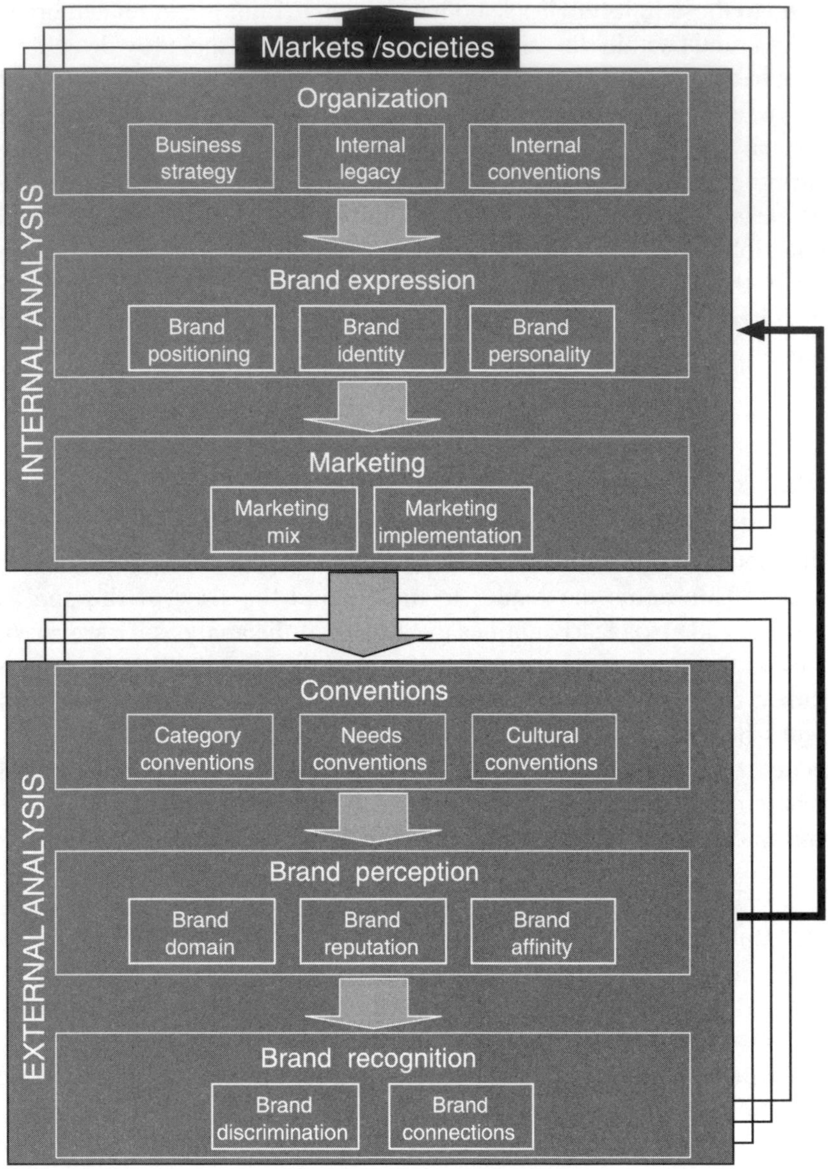

Figure 0.3   *The global brand proposition model*

globalization on branding has been profound, and debates about both the assumed superiority and supposed immorality of global brands have flared. This book holds that neither globalization nor branding are inherently good or bad, and that each brand has its own particular potential for extending across countries, cultures and markets.

Chapter 1 delves into the organizational issues relevant to global brand strategy, namely the business strategy, the internal conventions and the internal brand legacy. The business strategy is broken down into its inspiration, justification and substantiation elements. The inspiration of the business strategy consists of a view on the future of the business in terms of vision, mission and ambition. The justification of the business strategy is concerned with its goals and the soundness of the strategic reasoning. The substantiation of the business strategy deals with the resources, competencies and motivation required to realize the strategy. The internal conventions of an organization can be summed up by the oft-heard phrase 'That's how we do things around here'. Internal conventions have to do with the organization's culture, structures, systems, routines and practices. These conventions can be formalized through policies and diagrams, but are often non-formalized beliefs, customs, stories, symbols and the like. Finally, the internal brand legacy determines how the brand is regarded by the organization: who founded the brand, its milestones and its role for the organization.

Chapter 2 discusses the brand's expression, and introduces three brand constructs that enable management to mould the brand, namely brand positioning, brand identity and brand personality. This trio can be considered the prime materials for shaping the manifestation of the brand. Positioning is about being different and better than the competition. Identity is what the brand stands for and where it comes from. Personality is what the brand wants to be liked for. These constructs will differ between brands in terms of their availability and richness, and for the same brand they may also differ between countries. It is, however, essential that the brand expression that is created is congruent with the objectives of the business strategy.

Chapter 3 is the last chapter in this section, with marketing being the final activity an organization undertakes to set the brand loose on the public. This chapter deals with the policy making of marketing as well as its execution. Both are essential to generate the required consumer experience and the subsequent behaviour that the business strategy set out to achieve. Both marketing planning and the implementation deal with the products or services that are offered by the brand, their pricing, their promotion, their distribution and their servicing. However, the distinction between the two activities is that defining the marketing mix still largely deals with intangibles, while implementation makes the offer concrete to consumers. At these so-called customer touch points, the brand experience is brought to life. Both marketing policy and implementation can differ from region to region and from country to country because of local circumstances, and thus affect the brand's manifestations.

Part II: Conventions, brand perception and brand recognition

The second part of the book considers the external analysis. In other words, it looks at what happens to the brand once it is set loose on the public. A brand's management can have painstakingly devised a brand expression and can have methodically managed the marketing, planning and execution activities, still to find that the brand is not understood by consumers as was intended. The same brand may be perceived in totally different ways by consumers around the globe, because of various local circumstances. It is therefore imperative for brand management to know how the brand is perceived, what external factors are affecting the brand, and what this means for fulfilling the brand's potential.

This is generally the most demanding part of global branding, and getting it right can mean the difference between success and failure. This section, therefore, goes into quite a lot of detail. It considers the factors that are outside the direct control of global and local brand managers, but that they can try to understand and learn to work with. In many ways this is the core section of the book, because it describes and analyses the parameters within which the brand's potential can be unleashed. The extent to and the manner within which this can be achieved are unique to each and every brand. Nevertheless, there are sufficient communalities to allow us to identify the external factors that impact most on particular types of brands.

This part of the book contains five chapters. Chapter 4 introduces three kinds of situational factor that brand management will encounter in any marketplace, namely category, needs and cultural conventions. These conventions are discussed in considerable detail to assist the reader in understanding them. The effects of these conventions on the various elements of the brand perception are discussed in the next three chapters. Chapter 5 examines the brand domain, the perceived offer to consumers by the brand in terms of what goods and services the brand provides, how it communicates with consumers, where the goods and services can be obtained, and what solutions the brand provides to consumers. Chapter 6 considers the brand reputation, or the way consumers perceive the brand's background, its achievements and the company the brand keeps. Chapter 7 examines the brand affinity, or the motivations of consumers for feeling an attachment to or affection for the brand. This affinity can be based on various kinds of binding factor, ranging from purely practical efficacy to arousing sentiments and passions rooted in national pride, ethical principles, compassion, involvement and the like. Chapter 8 deals with the resulting brand recognition, with a discussion on how a brand relates to competing and non-competing brands in the eyes of consumers.

Part III: Typical global brand strategy issues

The first two sections of the book are – by necessity – rather preparatory, because it is imperative to identify and understand all the issues that go into developing a global brand strategy, as well as to appreciate how these aspects interact to ultimately shape a brand experience for consumers. The last part of this book attempts to illustrate the use of the global brand proposition model with typical global brand strategy issues. Chapter 9 looks into the difficulties of taking a brand global, discussing the issues that brand management faces when introducing a brand in one or more foreign countries. Chapter 10 examines the issue of harmonizing a global brand, dealing with the opportunities and difficulties that accompany the (partial) standardization of a brand in multiple countries. Chapter 11 considers how to extend a global brand, examining the concerns surrounding the introduction of product and service extensions to an existing global brand. Finally, Chapter 12 deals with the issues of creating a global brand from scratch, examining how new global brands are created, sometimes seemingly overnight.

This last part of the book demonstrates how the unique approach described in this book can be applied to a number of typical strategic global brand management issues. In practice, the situations will inevitably differ from the ones described in these chapters. However, the purpose of this section is to familiarize the reader with the methodology and illustrate its application.

PART I

THE INTERNAL ANALYSIS

1

The organization

INTRODUCTION

Not only is a brand the property of an organization, it is also an integral part of the organization in the sense that it impacts on and is impacted by the policies, activities, structures, culture, history and character of the organization. The organizational influences on the brand are both direct and indirect. As discussed in the previous chapter, the business strategy has a direct bearing on the brand, as the brand seeks to translate the objectives of the strategy into consumer experiences. Other direct and indirect organizational influences on the brand are internal conventions and the internal legacy of the brand. The internal conventions consist of the organizational status quo, which can be summed up by the oft-heard expression 'that is how we do things here'. The brand's internal legacy is formed by the stories about the brand's inception and its (historic) role for the organization. These three areas – business strategy, internal conventions and internal legacy – are the subjects of this chapter. It is not the intention to examine the way in which these three areas are formed, formulated or changed. In principle, the brand expression should follow from what is there. However, in practice, a revision of these organizational elements may result from a brand strategy process. Rather, this chapter aims to provide a brand's management with tools to understand the effects of business strategy, internal conventions and internal brand legacy on the brand.

BUSINESS STRATEGY

A brand is the translation of the business strategy into a consumer experience that brings about specific consumer behaviour. This means that a
proper understanding of the business strategy is imperative to any brand
development work. It does not necessarily mean that brand management
must be involved in the formulation of business strategy. Business strategy and brand strategy can be formulated separately, depending on the
degree of their integration. For example, the business strategy and brand
of Cisco Systems are so entwined – everything revolves around the Web –
that it is difficult to distinguish where one ends and the other begins, while
for the Mars Corporation it is clear where the business strategy ends and
the individual Mars (the candy bar) brand strategy commences. Whatever
the situation, it is still imperative that the business strategy and brand
strategy are aligned in order to create value for the organization's stakeholders, and specifically its customers.

Business strategy contains a number of elements that need to be examined in the process of brand strategy development. These elements are the
inspiration for the business strategy (what the organization's future looks
like), the justification of the strategy (what we want and why will it work),
and the substantiation of the strategy (what we need to do to achieve it).
These three elements are summarized in Figure 1.1.

Inspiration

To understand business strategy, we start by examining its inspirational
elements, consisting of the vision, mission and ambition that underpin the

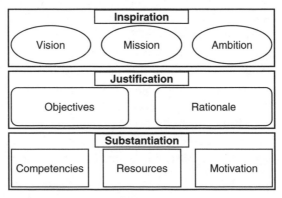

Figure 1.1   *Elements of the business strategy*

long-term view of the business. The board or management of the organization generally formulates these inspirational elements. The inspirational elements are important as they provide the perspective on the future of the organization from those who are ultimately responsible for the brand. The inspirational elements provide guidance to the business strategy, and consequently the entire strategic planning cycle. The three inspirational elements can be described as follows:

▌ *Vision* is developed to provide a business with a point of view on the future of its sector or category for a number of years to come. Typical questions to be asked are 'What are anticipated major technological, social, political, economic and regulatory developments?' and 'Who are the anticipated major players in the market and what are their positions in terms of their rank, the segments they serve and their strengths and weaknesses?' Visions seldom turn out to be accurate, and they should not be considered as predictions or prophecies. Their main function is to set the stage for strategic thinking, and they are useful because they provide the perspective within which to understand the business strategy.

▌ A *mission* is the stated sense of purpose for an organization. Typical questions to be answered are 'Who are our stakeholders, and why and how do we want to serve them?' and 'Where are we trying to get to as an organization?' Defining a mission entails management providing leadership and defining concrete indications of what stakeholders can expect from the company. Hamel and Prahalad (1994) lament that most mission statements of large industrial corporations are interchangeable, and therefore offer no sense of destiny to these organizations. These authors introduce the notion of strategic intent as a goal that demands the respect and allegiance of every employee. Such a concept combines mission and ambition, as employed in this book.

▌ *Ambition* is a statement of what the organization aspires to. This may involve a desire to be the dominant player in an industry, to be recognized as the most desirable in a category by consumers, to be available in more countries than any competitor, or to be considered the most socially responsible corporation. Whatever the aspiration, it is important that this ambition is based on the notion of providing value to stakeholders and is not just a management pipedream.

Justification

To take the understanding of the business strategy a step further it is essential to determine what the strategy actually sets out to accomplish, and whether there is sufficient logic as to how this will be achieved. This is a concrete conversion of the inspirational elements of the strategy into actual strategic objectives and a strategic rationale.

Strategic objectives

The *strategic objectives* ultimately need to define what the organization wants to achieve in terms of changed consumer mind-set and behaviour, and what needs to be done by the organization to bring these changes about. The strategic objectives must meet the following criteria:

▌ They must follow from the strategy's inspirational elements. For example, the strategic inspiration may call for an organization to become the dominant player in a particular category, based on a vision of imminent technological discontinuities that will change the way consumers interact with the suppliers in that category.

▌ They should specifically describe the consumers' attitude change to be brought about. An example of such an objective is the desire to be seen as a company that helps specific consumer segments extract the full value of technological developments.

▌ They ought to be specific as to the subsequent behaviour expected from targeted consumers, in relevant terms such as trial, repeat purchase, usage frequency, recommendation, donation, cross purchase, and use of support services.

▌ The objectives must be specific as to their magnitude: proportion of consumers whose mind-set is changed, share of consumers who will try the product or service, levels of repeat purchase, and so on. Obviously these objectives need to be attainable and need to be set within a certain realistic time frame.

▌ The objectives also need to include a description of the activities that the organization plans to deploy in order to meet them. This includes time frames for research and development, market exploration, packaging design, trials, production, advertising development, distributor development and the like. In the case of a global brand there are also decisions about the roll-out in multiple countries: will there be a lead country, will the process start with a phased roll-out, or will there be a big bang across all countries?

Strategic rationale

It is important that the reasoning behind a business strategy is sound. This means that the cause and effect chains that underpin the strategy are logical and probable. Rangan and Adner (2001) describe seven strategy misconceptions, which they apply to the Internet. Six of these also hold true for global brands.

▌ First mover advantage, which is based on the idea that the order of players' entry into a market is positively correlated with the odds of adoption by consumers. New global brands thus try to perform a kind of 'land grab' on a global scale in order to pre-empt competition. The misconception lies in the fact that being first is not the same as being the best (that is, being most valued by consumers). With switching costs for consumers low and falling in most categories and in most markets, the first mover advantage alone is unlikely to an offer compelling rationale for global brands.

▌ Reach, which rests on the premise that a firm's potential customers are often distributed in heterogeneous rather than homogeneous segments. This means that consumers belong to so many segments at the same time that it becomes important to be able to embrace more consumer heterogeneity, or go after as many consumers as possible. Thus new global brands try to address consumers around the world to maximize growth. Unfortunately, as a brand tries to address this multitude of consumers, it will have more and more difficulty in defining a brand proposition that 'fits' with these consumers.

▌ Solutions provider, or the logic that specific products and services can be complemented by additional products and services. The idea is that once a consumer has purchased one product or service he or she will be game for complementary products or services provided under the same brand name. A strategy based on this assumption may conflict with the required focus for the global brand at its inception.

▌ Partner leverage, which is about capitalizing on or creating a market opportunity by combining own-firm resources and capabilities with those of other firms. This can take the form of co-branding or component branding, whereby some of the meaning of one brand is transferred onto the other. The problem with the strategy premise is that it aligns two firms' activities, but often fails to align their interests. As one brand does not have control over the other, this strategy can be very risky.

▌ The 'born global' myth, which is the mistaken belief that as media (satellite television, the Internet) are global, all new brands must be global too. This strategy does not take into account that national and cultural borders embody real discontinuities, which are not easily eliminated. The satellite television stations most watched and the Web sites most visited are strictly local and with local content.

▌ Technology as strategy driver, which holds that technology is the benefit, rather than the purveyor of particular benefits to consumers. As this technology is universal, it must be appealing to consumers all over the planet. This is the trap that Iridium strayed into when it decided that (business) consumers would be willing to pay a hefty premium to own technology that would give them a phone in their hand wherever they are or choose to be.

There is one more misconception that seems to drive the strategy of global brands, and that is the one about global consumer segments, also known as horizontal markets (as opposed to country or industry-specific vertical markets). Kinnear (2000) defines horizontal markets as those based on common needs among consumers. Such a needs-based consumer segment can provide an organization with a multi-country market that offers sufficient potential, as opposed to several local markets with insufficient potential for a brand. The problems with this approach centre on defining common needs among consumers in various countries. Needs that are in essence similar may actually vary significantly in the way they need to be addressed. In practice many brands do not target needs-based segments, but rather segments that are believed to share common needs. An example of such a fallacy is the idea that young people around the world, being exposed to similar events, brands and entertainment, must form one almost homogenous mass of youngsters with the same needs, ideas, aspirations and motivations. There is no doubt that young people in many modern societies share superficialities, but this idea overlooks the fact that these people have been formed in their own particular cultures and at local institutions.

Substantiation

To achieve the strategic objectives, it is necessary to determine what the organization has in store to realize these. Three aspects play an important part here, namely the competencies and the resources available to the organization, and the motivation among management and employees to achieve the objectives.

Competencies

The competencies of an organization are the shared skills, technologies and talents that its management and employees must be able to apply to achieve the objectives of the business strategy. This entails having a clear understanding of the portfolio of competencies available to the organization and those that need to be acquired through research and development, training, strategic partnerships or acquisition. Hamel and Prahalad (1994) define a core competence as 'a bundle of skills and technologies rather than a single discrete skill or technology'. A core competence enables an organization to provide a particular benefit or value to customers. Core competencies can encompass areas such as miniaturization, logistics, flexible production, supply chain management, integrated media planning, service demeanour and story telling. A core competence must meet three tests:

- It must make a disproportionate contribution to consumer-perceived value.
- It must be competitively unique. This mainly means that the skills and technology involved must not be ubiquitous to a category or industry.
- It must be extendable to other new products or services.

Resources

Not only must an organization have the capabilities to execute a business strategy, it must also have sufficient and the right kind of resources, such as human and financial resources, facilities for research and development, production and distribution, and IT infrastructure. It must be clear that there are resources available and that management are willing and able to allocate them to meet the strategic objectives. Obviously, resources are always limited and they need to be used efficiently and creatively.

Motivation

Finally, the business strategy must be driven by the enthusiasm of management and staff alike. Even if all the above-mentioned elements of the business strategy are in place, lacklustre execution will still make it fail. It is therefore imperative to gauge whether the inspirational elements of the strategy spring not only from the intellect of those who formulate them, but also from a passion for their business. Also, these inspirational themes need to be understood and supported by the employees of the organization. In the same manner, it is crucial to understand the depth of belief attached by management to its strategic objectives and strategic rationale. Finally, it is important to determine whether the allocation of competencies and resources to the strategic objectives adds to or detracts from the employees' enthusiasm for the organization that they serve. As Herzberg (1987) observed, motivation does not stem from primary and secondary working conditions – what he termed hygiene factors – but rather from issues such as achievement, recognition, responsibility, advancement and the nature of the work people do. Clearly, the better motivated an organization is to fulfil the business strategy, the better the chances are of translating it into an effective and worthwhile brand.

INTERNAL CONVENTIONS

A brand is not only affected by business strategy, it is also governed by conventions internal to the organization. These internal conventions are best summarized by the comment, 'That's how we do things around here.' Such conventions can seriously circumscribe the brand expression and limit it to what is internally acceptable. Internal conventions can restrict a brand's manifestations, its communications, its distribution and its character development.

Cultural web

Johnson and Scholes (1993) describe internal conventions, what they term a cultural web, consisting of key factors surrounding a paradigm (see Figure 1.2). The paradigm is the combination of key beliefs and assumptions that are held in common and taken for granted in an organization. The paradigm develops from the following surrounding key factors:

▌ The *stories* told by members of the organization to each other, to outsiders, to new recruits and so on. These stories embed the present in its organizational history, and highlight important events and personalities.

▌ The *symbols* of the organization such as logos, offices, cars and titles, or the type of language and terminology commonly used, which become shorthand representations of the nature of the organization.

▌ The *power structures* are likely to be associated with the key constructs of the paradigm. The most powerful managerial groupings in the organization are likely to be the ones most associated with core assumptions and beliefs about what is important.

▌ The formal *organizational structures*, or the more informal way in which the organization works, are likely to reflect the power structure. They delineate important relationships and emphasize what is important in the organization.

▌ The *control systems*, the measurement and rewards systems that monitor and therefore emphasize what is important, focus organizational attention and activity.

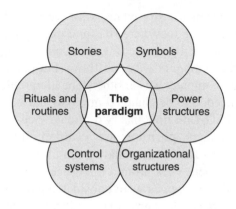

Figure 1.2 *The organization's cultural web*

▌ The *rituals and routines* of organizational life, such as training programmes, promotion and assessment, point to what is important in the organization, reinforce 'the way we do things around here', and signal what is valued.

Additional internal conventions

Two additional internal conventions need to be taken into account. The first is *organizational solidarity*, the feelings of esteem and obligation towards colleagues, which may help or hinder the brand, and the second is the *ability to hinder* specific brand developments, which can rest with employees on shop floors or at front desks. If they are not convinced by the brand they can be in a position to undermine it.

Dealing with internal conventions

It is important to determine which conventions are 'flexible' and can be challenged, and which are 'solid' and should therefore be abided by. A correct assessment of these conventions is vital for brand developments to be successful. Challenging an internal convention that is eroding can provide value to the entire organization, because employees may be glad to be rid of a drag on their activities, and management may be glad to turn an obstacle into an opportunity.

When Joost Kenemans and Frank Koster arrived in South Korea in 2000 to reorganize ING-Life Korea, they encountered an insurance company that made hardly any profit and where staff were totally demoralized. Fraudulent and sexist practices were rife, and management were abusing the company for their own gain. Setting these matters right by firing and suspending several managers was one thing, but changing the culture and structure of the company was another. The hierarchic, masculine and dogmatic system needed to be changed into one that was open, equitable and meritocratic. ING-Life now has two female vice-presidents and six female middle managers, positions are awarded on the basis of merit rather than tenure, and formal titles have been abandoned. Perhaps most importantly, management walk around the office and visit branch offices regularly. At first, these changes were considered a threat by staff. As the company has shown the highest growth rate of any life insurance company in South Korea, staff have come to accept and appreciate the changes. Local competitors now even look to emulate the success of ING-Life Korea. Kenemans admits that change did not come easily as most employees opposed it at first (Het Financieele Dagblad, 2002d).

THE INTERNAL LEGACY OF THE BRAND

Although the internal legacy of a brand is related to the issues of internal conventions discussed in the previous paragraph, it is necessary to distinguish between the organizational conventions and the organizational factors that have an immediate bearing on the brand. There are three areas of internal brand legacy that need to be explored: the birthright of the brand, the milestones of a brand and the role of the brand for the organization (see Figure 1.3).

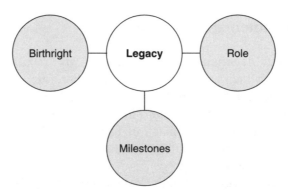

Figure 1.3 *Areas of internal brand legacy*

Birthright

Whether they are new or established, brands have a certain legacy within their organization. This legacy often goes back to the people who first developed the brand or to a single founder. A company founder, alive or deceased, can have a very dominating influence on a brand. Howard Schultz, Josiah Wedgwood, Richard Branson and Henry Ford are people that many, if not most, of us have heard of as creators of singularly successful brands. Koehn (2001) identifies a number of characteristics of successful brand creators, such as superior sales ability, profound knowledge of their products and customers, a dogged enthusiasm for their business, and being in the right place at the right time.

Even if a founder is not the face of the brand, or the brand does not bear his or her name, he or she will often still have great influence within the organization. Also individuals who were not present at the brand's conception can have a great impact on a brand. For example, Alfred (Freddie) Heineken was the third generation in charge of the Heineken brewing company, yet by turning the company into a global marketing machine he forever changed the brand. After his retirement he still loomed large over the company and the brand. It remains to be seen whether his influence will extend even beyond the grave through his only daughter and heiress.

Milestones

There may be particular events specific to the brand that are deemed especially important by the organization. For instance, at Apple Computers the introduction of the Apple Lisa, the first home computer with a graphical user interface, in 1983 was seen as a defining moment for the brand, while for consumers this defining moment occurred with the introduction of the Apple Macintosh, the more affordable version of Lisa, in 1984.

Role of the brand

Another aspect of the internal legacy of the brand is the role of the brand for the organization. This not only has to do with whether the brand is a corporate or a product or service brand, but mainly with how the brand is perceived in terms of contribution to the organization. For example, if a brand is defined internally on the basis of a matrix analysis (such as the BCG or MABA matrix), its cashflow will – rightly or wrongly – be assigned either for reinvestment or for investment in other brands in the organization's portfolio. In some cases the brand will have a particular status within an organization based on its estimated worth in monetary terms.

An essential issue regarding the brand's role is brand architecture, or how a brand relates to other of the organization's brands or to partner brands. Two issues are important here, namely levels of brands and their linkages (Macrae, 1996). Top-level, corporate and banner brands connect up the organization, strategy and leadership and work as unique organizing purposes. Low-level sub-brands target messages within product or service categories, but within a higher level organizational script. There can be many levels of brands within an organization, and subsequently many different connections between them. There has been a very clear shift towards introducing high-level brands to complement what were previously stand-alone brands, in order to leverage the qualities of the corporate or banner brand, to enhance a product or service brand and include it in a branded family. A brand architecture helps to ensure that global and local brand managers work towards similar goals for the brand, that they do not cannibalize other brands in the organization's portfolio, that they do not extend themselves too far and dilute the brand, and that they do not claim too much of an organization's resources and overwhelm higher-level brands.

Dealing with the internal brand legacy

An internal legacy can be an advantage to a brand, as it may be leveraged for purposes of company pride. However, it may also be a barrier to future development of a brand. This is one of the areas where a battle between providing brand consistency and brand vitality may rage. Polaroid filed for bankruptcy in 2001 after missing the digital imaging boat, because management banked on its mainstay technology, instant photography. Polaroid overestimated the power of its brand as an icon of cutting-edge imaging technology. Consumers had no qualms about abandoning Polaroid's instant cameras for digital cameras from Nikon, Canon and Sony.

THE GLOBAL BRAND ORGANIZATION

Currently, organizational structures largely seem to determine the manner in which brand management is organized. If an organization has a decentralized, multi-country structure, its brands are managed by numerous local brand management teams. If an organization is highly centralized, brand management is similarly organized. The premise of this book is that each brand has its own potential for successful standardization and successful adaptation. Therefore, it follows that the manner in which brand management is organized should follow the potential of the brand and not the other way around.

At Proctor and Gamble some of this realization has taken root, and brand management is more and more organized according to the requirements of product categories. For example washing powders are managed at a local level, because of the differences in clothes washing habits in different countries. Shampoo is managed on a regional basis, as habits among consumers vary less, according to Proctor and Gamble. It is a question whether this set-up is sufficiently brand aligned and fully takes into consideration the sensitivity of each brand. Kapferer (1997) describes how Procter and Gamble misjudged the sensitivity of dandruff as a social problem, worthy of sympathy, when launching Head and Shoulders in France. Its approach was to use the same advertising as in Britain and the Netherlands, with the pay-off 'Dandruff talks behind your back'. This advertising was based on the belief that one should be ashamed of having dandruff. By 1989, five years after introduction, Head and Shoulders still only held 1 per cent of the French market for shampoo. This example suggests that a regional approach to managing Head and Shoulders is not the correct approach, while it may be the right way to manage other shampoo brands that are less benefit-oriented.

Hankinson and Cowking (1996) propose that the ideal international managerial structure should satisfy three objectives, represented as an objectives triangle in Figure 1.4. This triangle reflects the inevitable tensions within any large international organization. The managerial structure must provide a system for control, ensuring that the international divisions move in the same strategic direction and achieve the desired corporate goals. The structure must also allow sufficient flexibility for individual local brand managers to contribute their inputs. Individual motivation, however, needs to be tempered by international teamwork, a sharing of knowledge and experiences, and collective responsibility arising from an ownership of adopted strategies and goals.

THE ORGANIZATION AND THE BRAND EXPRESSION

The organizational factors that have been discussed in this chapter have specific impacts on the brand expression. These effects will be detailed in

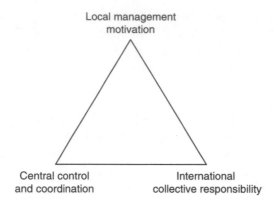

Figure 1.4   *An objectives triangle for international brand management*

the next chapter. It must be emphasized here that the brand expression is a result of the business strategy, and is a promise to consumers, providing them with expectations that need to be met or surpassed. Therefore if the business strategy is in some way flawed, the brand will never be able to deliver on its promise and will suffer a loss of credibility.

The internal conventions and the brand's internal legacy have influenced how a brand has been devised in the past. Many of the beliefs and assumptions about the brand expression are rooted in these factors. Brand management must identify those conventions that are no longer tenable and for which there will be value to the brand's stakeholders in challenging them.

Therefore, devising a new or renewed brand expression may involve getting to grips with organizational issues that are considered to have been resolved (long ago) by the organization. Conflict with management and employees may at times be unavoidable, as global and local brand management challenge the policies, beliefs, assumptions and prevalent wisdom of the organization in their quest to craft a brand expression that best fulfils the brand's potential around the world.

2

The brand expression

INTRODUCTION

The brand expression is the brand as defined and manifested by an organization. When management and employees of an organization talk of their brand, they usually mean the brand expression rather than the brand perception that has been shaped by the organization's own marketing activities and the filters and lenses applied by consumers. This is not unreasonable, as the brand expression contains those elements with which an organization can hope to mould the brand.

The brand expression receives its input from the organizational factors discussed in the previous chapter. The brand strategy defines what the brand is supposed to achieve in terms of consumer attitudes and behaviour. It is up to the brand expression to define a consumer experience that will induce the required attitudes and behaviour. The internal conventions and the internal brand legacy set parameters for the brand expression, parameters that may or may not restrict the brand's development. In its turn the brand expression provides the necessary guidance to the marketing mix and implementation activities in an effort to ensure that consumers actually are presented with the required behaviour-inducing experience.

This chapter introduces the elements that jointly form the brand expression. Understanding which elements are available, choosing elements to use and deciding which ones to emphasize are the first steps towards creating or transforming a brand. Some brands are more heavily endowed with brand expression elements than others, and this richness of meaning may vary greatly from market to market. Such differences in available instruments may need to be addressed before a truly global brand strategy can be devised.

THE BRAND EXPRESSION DEFINED

The brand expression consists of three elements: the brand's positioning, its identity and its personality. Brand positioning consists of how the brand is better than and different from its competition. It is based on fairly functional aspects of products and services. The brand identity consists of what the brand stands for and of aspects that have to do with the brand's legacy, its principles, its goals and its visual manifestation. The brand personality consists of aspects of the brand's character. These three elements and their constituent aspects are discussed in detail in the following paragraphs.

Although the same brand expression instruments are available to all brand management, some brands are historically better endowed in one area than the other. Therefore, brand strategy is dependent not only upon the current perception of the brand among consumers and how that perception can realistically be influenced, but also upon the instruments that are available to brand management or that can be developed for this purpose. Each of the three brand expression elements contain various aspects that can be selected to try to influence consumer perception of the brand, and thus achieve the brand strategy goal of delivering a specific consumer experience.

BRAND POSITIONING

Ries and Trout (1981) were the first to coin the term 'positioning'. Being advertising men, these authors saw positioning as a matter for communications. As far as they were concerned this had nothing to do with products, services or organizations themselves, but with the ability to command a position in consumers' minds, distinct from the competition. A quest for differentiation or distinctness implies having your gaze steadily fixed upon the competition and constantly striving to 'outposition' one or another competing brand. The danger is, of course, that one loses sight of consumers and is transfixed by opportunities to outwit the competition, and subsequent short-termism. Over the years 'positioning' has come to mean a lot of things, and it has occasionally been used as a substitute word for 'branding'. Kapferer (1997) considers positioning as a way of emphasizing the distinctive characteristics of the brand that make it different from its competitors and appealing to the public.

In a similar way, this book defines brand positioning as a way of demonstrating a brand's advantage over and differentiation from its competition. Brand positioning is a rather functional affair, with an emphasis on product and service features, benefits, usage, value and ability to solve problems for consumers.

Features

Emphasizing the unique features of products and services is a tried and tested way of positioning a brand. Unfortunately, features seldom provide sustainable advantages over the competition, as those features that truly add value to a brand are often quickly copied and introduced by (lower end) competitors. A number of years ago luxury cars could position themselves with the aid of safety features such as ABS brakes and airbags. In 2001 the Renault Laguna II, a mid-range family saloon, became the safest European car according to the European New Car Assessment Programme (see www.euroncap.com), well ahead of models produced by such luxury brands as Mercedes, Volvo, BMW, Saab and Audi.

Thus either features need to offer uniquely sustainable competitive advantage and value to consumers, or new features must constantly support the brand's innovative or novelty character. The latter approach requires the brand to be constantly (one of) the first to market with new features; any let-off in the pace, and the brand may be harmed.

The organizational factor with the strongest impact on features-based positioning is research and development. The availability of such resources leads an organization to put its emphasis on the development of strong product features. Philips's research and development facilities have delivered many innovations and subsequent patents to the organization. This policy has had its advantages, such as the development of the compact disc, but also its disadvantages, as Philips concentrated for a long time on turning out consumer electronics with increasingly advanced features, but with decreasing value to consumers. This example also shows that internal conventions, in this case the importance ascribed to Philips's science lab by the organization, can have an impact on the brand positioning.

Benefits

Benefits are advantages to consumers that enhance their comfort, happiness, well-being, health and the like. The value of benefits squarely lies in improving people's lives, however small the improvement may be. Therefore a benefit-based positioning has a stronger appeal than a features-based positioning. A typical benefit is convenience, which is used by brands across various categories such as frozen meals, banking and retail.

Although a benefit may be easier to maintain than a feature in the face of competitive onslaught, it is usually only a matter of time before another brand is able to match the benefit claim. For instance, in June 1999 the 'nutraceutical' Benecol was introduced in Europe with the claim that the margarine helped lower cholesterol levels. Within a matter of months, market leader Unilever's Becel (Flora in the UK) responded with its own cholesterol-reducing spread called Pro Activ. Becel seems to have gotten the upper hand in this contest, as it already possessed certain cardiovascular health benefits.

Developing benefits is often based upon a clear vision of developments affecting a category, and an understanding of the role the organization can play. Chewing gum, for example, is seeing an evolution from a sticky sweet to a so-called nutraceutical – nicotine anti-smoking gum is but one example – but gum can also carry drugs, vitamins, minerals and antioxidants. Wrigley's launched an antacid gum called Surpass in January 2002 which relieves heartburn faster and for longer than tablets. So far, however, it has not done well, as Americans see gum mainly as a breath freshener (Economist, 2002e). The internal brand legacy is important in such a case, as the members of the organization must decide whether they think the brand can support the benefits, and whether they find a changed role for the brand acceptable.

Problem solving

A problem is a matter that presents someone with difficulty or even perplexity. Solving a problem means dealing with the matter in such a manner that it takes away consumers' feelings of frustration, insecurity, helplessness or vulnerability. Some problems are mundane, such as deciding what to wear, what to eat, how to get from A to B, and how to get a stain out of a delicate fabric. Others are more intricate, such as how to transfer money safely to countries with a weak banking system, how to practise religious rituals while travelling in a foreign country, or how to ensure that the water you are drinking is safe.

Some problems present niche markets for solutions, which can sustain only one or two brands. The competitive advantages of these few brands are obvious, but leave them with limited growth opportunities. Other problems have wider market appeal and their solutions consequently attract a greater number of competitors. As competitors offer solutions to the same problem, it often ceases to be considered a problem by consumers. The first Xerox photocopier provided a solution to an intricate problem: how to replicate documents efficiently. Nowadays that problem can be solved by any number of copiers, such as those made by Canon or Océ. Xerox is clearly struggling to redefine itself, advertising itself as 'the Document Company'.

Some problems are enduring, and return again and again to trouble consumers. This is because the problem is solved only temporarily. For instance, many parents are worried about the dietary habits of their children. They eat too much fat, sugar and salt and not enough vegetables, dairy products and fibre. Offering healthy foodstuffs that are fun to eat – for instance clown-shaped cheese slices – may seem to solve the problem. However, as with many other things, such solutions do not endure as children get used to and bored by them. Some brands do seem able to persist in solving the same, seemingly trivial, problem. McDonald's restaurants all over the world solve the enduring problem of where to eat with kids. Apparently the fact that kids are so accustomed to McDonald's works to amplify the brand rather than erode it.

Although problem solving may in some cases be based on the inspirational elements of business strategy, the solutions are usually based mainly on a thorough understanding of consumers and the problems they face. In business strategy terms this is mainly a motivational issue, of whether members of the organization are willing and able to connect to consumers sufficiently. When Jeff Bezos started Amazon.com, at least part of his understanding of the problems of buying books at bookstores reputedly came from his wife, who is a novelist. In addition Bezos, who has a keen interest in computer-related matters, had a good understanding of the opportunities that the Internet offered in solving these problems: Amazon.com's core competence.

Usage

Some brands are linked to occasions, a time of day, a location or a specific use. McDonald's has a strong position as a place to celebrate children's birthdays. Snickers is a snack for those moments between meals when one feels a need for something filling. Cup-a-soup is positioned as the ideal pick-me-up for office workers at 4 o'clock in the afternoon, when it is too late for coffee and too early for a meal. The International Student Identity Card (ISIC) is strongly related to use while travelling on a budget in foreign countries. As some of these examples show, a particular usage often also entails a particular target segment with specific needs at a certain time of day, week, month, year or even life.

A credible usage-based positioning can generally be claimed by only one brand in a category. This is because a specific usage is limited to a time, place or occasion that is by its nature in limited supply. Thus claiming an occasion can only be done once, and the brand that successfully does so will own the market for that occasion, as long as it properly defends that claim.

Usage positioning is often strongly influenced by an organization's mission. The International Student Travel Confederation (ISTC), the organization that owns the ISIC brand, has as its founding mission: 'to increase international understanding through the promotion of travel and exchange opportunities among students, young people and the academic community' (see www.istc.com). The ISIC, as the principal worldwide proof of full-time student status, is the physical representation of this mission and helps promote student travel through services (such as travel information and telecommunications) and benefits (such as discounts on air travel).

In other cases, the organizational influences are more prosaic. The usage positioning of Cup-a-soup springs from a strategic rationale of market development opportunities offered by the institutional market's wish for a more varied offering of beverages to employees. A part of the brand's shift from home to institutional consumers came from the diminished role of the tired consumer brand to the organization.

Value for money

This is another tried and tested positioning. However, it is difficult to maintain unless the entire organization is geared towards offering valuable products and services at a reasonable price. Prime examples are budget airlines such as Southwest in the USA and Ryanair and easyJet in Europe. These airlines can only maintain their value position by constant vigilance over the use of resources. Another example is the Hong Kong-based retail brand Giordano, which offers jeans, T-shirts and casuals at very sharp prices. Giordano is able to do this because of the scale of its purchases in nearby China. However, a value for money positioning is not limited to low-cost or budget brands; it can also be used by higher price-tag brands. Leatherman multi-tools are fairly expensive to buy, but they come with a 25-year guarantee. The main consideration is that the balance between what consumers pay and what they get is inclined towards the latter.

A value for money positioning is not only defended at the cost side of the equation, but is also influenced by the quality of the products and services offered. Dell computers would never have been so successful if their position was built on price alone. The quality of the products and the customization service both reinforce the brand's position.

On the one hand, the inspirational elements of the business strategy have a significant impact on value for money brands: management envisions a market ready and waiting for affordable or reasonable offers, sets its sights on this market and aspires to be the leader in the category it has created. At the same time, the organization's internal conventions – its culture, structure, control systems, rituals and solidarity – must be geared towards delivering the value for money promise.

BRAND IDENTITY

Brand identity was first recognized as an important construct during the early 1990s. Authors such as Kapferer (1997) and Macrae (1996) wrote about a brand's identity: what does the brand stand for? They noted that in brand management terms, brand identity precedes brand image. It became common wisdom that it is important first of all to have a consistent self-image of the brand, in order to know how it can be expressed, and how that affects the external perception of the brand. This type of thinking made it clear that brands need to be managed for consistency and vitality, and can be damaged by marketing tactics such as price promotions, latching on to fleeting trends, and by a multitude of line extensions.

This book defines brand identity as a set of aspects that convey what a brand stands for: its background, its principles, its purpose and ambitions. In addition, a brand has a so-called visual identity, which consists of the design elements and other manifestations that help us recognize the brand, and to which we attribute specific meaning. The brand identity is the brand expression element employed to convey a brand's credentials. Unlike a brand's positioning, its identity is unique. There are no two brands with exactly the same roots and heritage, values, purpose, ambitions and visual identity. Whether or not brand managers wish to employ the brand identity depends on whether they think consumers care about such credentials.

Roots and heritage

The *roots* of a brand are defined by the circumstances of its conception: when, where, how, why and by whom was the brand created? The roots of a brand can be extremely important when conveying the meaning of a brand to consumers. The pioneering spirit of Apple computers is embodied in the company's conception in a garage. The Apple 1 was a DIY set that did not even come with a case! The romantic Latin soul of Bacardi is conveyed by its inception in Cuba in 1862, when Don Facundo Bacardi y Maso, a Spanish émigré, used a tin-roofed factory building to start a distillery. In the roof of the factory there lived a family of fruit bats, now incorporated in Bacardi's so-called bat device.

A brand's heritage is the history of changes undergone by the brand: a chronology of important life events for a brand, its role to consumers during this period, the trust it has garnered among consumers and the satisfaction it has given consumers in the past. A brand's heritage may differ from country to country, depending on whether the local heritage supersedes the global heritage. A brand's heritage consists of the following ingredients:

▌ Birthright, which aims to convey the brand's original standards.
▌ History, which help familiarize consumers with the brand and underpin its status.
▌ Narrative, which tells the ongoing story of the brand.

When McDonald's moved into Hong Kong in 1975, and into Beijing some 20 years later, it relied heavily on its roots (Americana) and its international heritage. Local McDonald's management realized that this was drawing in customers, rather than the taste of the hamburgers, fries and Coke. In fact, these products were mainly effective in supporting the brand's roots. Being one of the first US fast food chains in the territory, McDonald's could credibly defend its roots against competition. As consumers got used to McDonald's and its standard fare, the brand could start to achieve a position in the local community; introducing new and locally developed products (such as red bean sundae), becoming a refuge for school kids and women on shopping trips, and supporting local causes and community efforts (Watson, 1997).

A brand's heritage also consists of the brand's typical or symbolic products. Kapferer (1997) talks of the brand prototype being the best example of the brand's meaning. In effect these are signature products, such as McDonald's Big Mac, Volkswagen's Beetle and Golf, Apple's Macintosh and iMac, and Danone's Petit Danone children's dessert.

Obviously, an identity based on roots and heritage is strongly influenced by the organizational element of internal brand legacy. They contain similar elements such as the brand's founder and the brand's milestones, but differ in the fact that the roots and heritage are part of an externally projected narrative. The internal legacy, therefore, often has more warts to it than the roots and heritage. Also, not all issues that are relevant to the brand internally are relevant to an external audience. For instance, the opening of a new production facility or the move to a new head office is often a significant occasion for an organization, yet it does not usually feature as such to consumers. For instance, Dutch brewer Grolsch was very proud of its new brewery opened in 2002 – an animated film of the facilities is even available on its Web site (www.grolsch.nl) – yet drinkers of the beer may be excused for being underwhelmed.

Values

Values are one's deepest sense of what is right and wrong, and thus aid the choice between alternatives. Similarly, a brand's values consist of what it considers to be right and wrong. These values provide a perspective on how the brand is expected to act towards its stakeholders, including consumers. As a brand extends across societies it may become increasingly difficult to retain its original values. Many brands contain values that are common to their society of origin. For example, McDonald's (inadvertently?) carries with it the US social value of equality in the form of its service concept: everyone is expected to queue up, staff and customers are at the same height when ordering, customers need to find their own tables and they are expected to clear up after themselves. In a number of Asian countries McDonald's has had to make changes to this service concept, as consumers had difficulties understanding that they were supposed to clear up themselves. At a minimum, a brand's values must not violate the values of the consumer segments it wishes to target. In the case of a brand expression that is laden with specific values, these must connect to the consumer segments that share those values.

Even if a brand does not explicitly communicate values, consumers may still expect the brand to live up to certain standards. A case in point is the row surrounding working conditions and worker treatment at (third party) plants manufacturing products for Nike. It is thus important not only to decide which values are suitable to communicate and live by, but also to determine what consumers expect your minimum value standards to be, and to live up to those. These value standards may differ from market to market. However, this only means that customer sensitivity about such issues may differ, not that a brand should live up to different standards in each market. It may mean that the brand needs to communicate and emphasize these values more in certain places.

Some common brand values show up as recurrent themes in categories. This generally means that they represent the minimum value standards of that category. How many financial services brands around the world extol the virtues of integrity, respect, teamwork and professionalism? Probably most, if not all. Obviously this is a matter of assuring customers that their hard-earned money is in safe hands, and that those same hands are doing their utmost to make that amount of money grow.

Changing societal values (more on that subject in Chapter 4) may induce a brand to challenge the status quo. In the mid-1990s the Maximizer bra company spotted an opportunity to introduce its push-up bras to South and East Asian women, who were becoming more financially independent and more self-conscious. Traditional values in many Asian societies dictate that women should dress modestly. Although Chinese women can wear clothes that show bare legs and arms, cleavage is another matter. However, under the influence of western movies and television programmes, Asian women (particularly professional ones) became aware of the impact of cleavage and breast size. Maximizer challenged the modesty values. It used slender, dark-haired western models in its print and billboard advertising. In this manner, the values could be challenged without emphasizing that Asian female modesty was at stake. The campaign was so successful that the brand became quite bold in its advertising. I remember seeing a huge billboard above the entrance to the Raffles Place MRT station in Singapore, featuring a slight, dark-haired western model showing off her Maximizer cleavage with the slogan 'The ultimate oomph!'

A brand's values are often strongly influenced by the internal conventions of its organization. Samsung, an organization that is traditionally hierarchic and non-transparent, has shown during the last few years that it can be flexible and innovative. Characteristically, the decision to switch from developing me-too consumer electronics products to innovative ones was made by Samsung Group Chair Lee Kun Hee in 1996. However, this decision has meant untying Samsung managers from corporate red tape and allowing them to use the resources under their own roof (*Far Eastern Economic Review*, 2002b). The new Samsung brand values may be summed up as innovative, sleek, simple and creative.

The internal brand legacy influences the brand values when the brand has particular founding values that remain or become relevant again to the organization. Walt Disney's quest to provide wholesome entertainment to the family still inspires the brand's family values. The organization's activities that may not be in line with these values are undertaken under different brands, such as Touchstone for motion pictures. Touchstone produced such famously non-family values films as *Pretty Woman* ('She walked off the street, into his life and stole his heart') and *Scenes from the Mall* ('A hilarious adventure in marriage, infidelity and bargain shopping!').

Problems can occur when the internal brand legacy and the brand values diverge. Beaujolais used to be synonymous with quality and prestige French wines. The introduction of Nouveau wines, although initially very successful in most European countries, undermined these values. Beaujolais became synonymous with large volumes of young, unripe and mediocre wine. Faced with increased competition from innovative new producers in the Americas, Australia and South Africa, the Beaujolais brand lost its shine, and the wine growers were stuck with large amounts of produce that needed to be destroyed, distilled or made into vinegar to support their prices. A return to the original brand values will be difficult, and will require much more than a lament by the Beaujolais wine growers that new wine drinkers prefer 'Coca-Cola wines' over their produce (winespectator, 2002).

Purpose and ambitions

A brand expresses its purpose and/or ambitions in order to stake a (future) claim. Often purpose and ambitions are expressed using succinct tag lines, such as those used in advertising on packaging, in letterheads, on trucks and the like.

A brand expresses its purpose in order to assert its function to consumers. IBM's purpose is to provide 'Solutions for a small planet'. Renault's purpose is to be '*Créateur d'automobile*'. Hallmark is there 'When you care enough to send the very best'. AT&T encourages people to 'Reach out and touch someone'. BMW is 'The ultimate driving machine'. A strong brand purpose can also help rally employees around the brand. It is, for instance, easier to explain to new recruits what is expected of them by the organization in order to deliver the brand to consumers. It also gives employees something to be proud of.

Closely linked to purpose is a brand's ambition. According to ORC, an international marketing research agency, a brand's ambition is 'The brand's reason for being expressed as an aspiration' (www.orc.co.uk). Philips expresses its ambition as 'Let's make things better'. British Airways declared itself to be 'The world's favourite airline' as an intent rather than as a declaration of its global popularity at the time. Alternatively brands adopt consumers' ambitions or aspirations as their own, and encourage consumers to fulfil their ambitions. Nike says 'Just do it'. Apple wants people to 'Think different'. Sony urges consumers to 'Go create'.

Clearly, purpose and ambitions link back to the inspirational elements of the business strategy, vision, mission and ambition, as discussed in the previous chapter. In some cases these links are very direct, for example when the organization's purpose and ambitions translate directly into the brand purpose and ambition, as in the case of Patagonia. This outdoor wear firm takes an ethical stance of principles before profit and against consumption for its own sake (Ind, 2001).

However, more often the inspirational elements of the organization are too top-heavy, with large words to be translated directly. In addition, the purpose and ambitions of many brands are often no less interchangeable than the mission statements that spawn them. Probably most financial institutes would formulate their brand ambition something like 'To create a relationship in which we become a proactive and trusted financial partner for our customers'.

Visual identity

The visual identity of a brand is the outward manifestation of its identity in the form of logos, signatures, tunes, colours and sometimes even the brand's premises. These so-called identifiers are designed to provide consumers with:

- Instant recognition of the brand through its name, visual or audible devices: for instance McDonald's Golden Arches and the 'Intel inside' jingle.
- Legitimacy of the brand through symbols and devices that convey authenticity or trustworthiness. Grolsch beer has a specific swing-top bottle that emanates authenticity. This is appreciated in places with a beer brewing tradition, such as the UK and Canada, but is not recognized as such in a place like Hong Kong.
- Connections between the products in a brand portfolio. For example, in the case of Ola (aka Wall's and Algida) ice cream, the umbrella brand connects up all the underlying product brands such as Magnum, Solero, Calippo, Festini, Cornetto and Winner Taco.
- A badge to be worn on the brand's products, as in the case of Tommy Hilfiger and Lacoste.
- An expression of the brand's identity aspects: the brand's roots and heritage, its values, or its purpose and ambitions. Examples are Shell's shell, Nestlé's nest and Nike's Swoosh.

Thus, the visual identity can encapsulate important brand expression aspects and conjure up instant mental associations.

BRAND PERSONALITY

Along with the other anthropomorphic concepts, the term 'brand personality' is a fixture of the modern brand manager's vocabulary. The term refers to a set of human-like attributes associated with a particular brand (Aaker, J L, 2000). A brand personality is developed to enhance the appeal of a brand to consumers. To determine a brand's personality one may ask the question, 'What does the brand want to be liked for by consumers?' The brand personality can take the form of an actual person (the Marlboro cowboy), a generalized persona (the Singapore girl) or an animated figure (Ronald McDonald). However, in most cases the brand personality is a construct of the brand's underlying character (Levi's traditionally rugged character in the United States), or a transfer of user imagery (Heineken's young and cool club audience).

Consumers are able to think of brands as persons with characters, for instance during personification exercises in qualitative research. This does not mean that consumers think of brands in this manner in ordinary life. Rather, they have been stimulated to provide an allegory that marketers and advertisers can understand and make their own. In some cultures, such as the French, consumers have learnt to express themselves in this manner from early on, while in other cultures, such as the German, people find these exercises tormenting.

Brand personality dimensions

Research into personality psychology has identified the 'Big Five' human personality traits or dimensions. Similarly, research was undertaken by J L Aaker (2000) and Aaker, Benet-Martinez and Garolera (2001) to establish brand personality dimensions. The latter study focused on the stability of these constructs across three societies, namely the United States, Spain and Japan. These authors identify three broad brand personality traits that are more or less constant across the three diverse cultures. These more or less consistent personality dimensions are sincerity, excitement and sophistication. They identify one dimension that is shared by brand personalities in Japan and the United States, competence, as well as one shared by Japan and Spain, peacefulness. In addition, they identify culture-specific brand personality dimensions in the United States (ruggedness) and Spain (passion). What constitutes the shared dimensions differs somewhat between the three cultures, but the structures are similar enough. Figure 2.1 shows the dimensions and a summary of their constituent items.

This research suggests that there may be more local brand personalities that are culture-specific. The interesting thing is that, although a brand personality dimension like passion may be unique to a Latin culture, the dimension can be used by brands as long as they satisfy a Latin heritage. For instance, Bacardi with a Cuban heritage, Seat which is Spanish and Alfa-Romeo which is Italian all make use of passion as the core of their brand personalities. They do so successfully in the non-Latin societies of northern and western Europe. This confirms that brand personality is clearly a brand expression element, an instrument in the brand managers' toolbox, rather than a brand perception element.

Influences on brand personality

A brand personality can be shaped by a number of factors internal to the organization. An obvious factor is a brand's founder whose own personality

Dimensions	Japan	Spain	USA
Sincerity	Warmth	Thoughtfulness, realness	Down-to-earth, honesty, wholesomeness, cheerfulness
Excitement	Talkativeness, freedom, happiness, energy	Happiness, youth, independence	Daring, spiritedness, imagination, contemporary
Sophistication	Elegance, style	Style, confidence	Class, charm
Competence	Responsibility, determination, patience	–	Reliability, intelligence, success
Peacefulness	Mildness, naivety	Affection, naivety	–
Passion	–	Intensity, spirituality	–
Ruggedness	–	–	Masculinity, toughness

Figure 2.1   *Dimensions of brand personality*

functions as the brand's own. This is often the case with designer brands, such as Giorgio Armani, Yves St Laurent, Ralph Lauren and Paloma Picasso, yet these kinds of brand personality are uncommon in other categories.

Often a brand personality will derive from the mission and ambition defined by the business strategy, which becomes the mission and ambition for the (corporate) brand. A financial services provider that strives to be a reliable institution may develop a brand personality consisting of competence traits. A consumer electronics firm that endeavours to be innovative will probably try to develop a brand personality based on sophistication traits. A sports attire company wishing to be a leader in the youth market will likely develop a brand personality on the basis of excitement traits. A charity that wants to attract donations in order to provide nourishment and educational facilities to Third World children will doubtless develop a brand personality on the basis of sincerity traits.

In yet other organizations a brand personality will be affected more by the organizational culture, history and structures than through a deliberate design or development. Take for example Levi-Strauss, a brand that was conceived for frontiersmen and workers in the 19th century United States, and retained a rugged brand personality in that country until the end of the 20th century. In this case the brand personality grew naturally from the organization's traditions and stories. Only when Levi's were introduced in Europe did the organization deliberately develop an exciting (young, hip) brand personality, as the original US personality had no relevance to Europeans. Currently Levi's is redesigning the brand personality, based on excitement and sophistication traits, in an attempt to rekindle consumer affinity worldwide. The traits employed differ between continents and countries. Sexual tension is a key ingredient in the United States and Latin America (dangerously low jeans), Japan (sexy lady 501), and Australia and New Zealand (scenes of lesbian flirtation). In Europe, Levi's bases its brand personality on shabby expensive chic (engineered jeans with frayed pockets) (see www.levi.com).

One of the world's most well-known brand personalities, Marlboro man, was apparently initially designed to attract women smokers. Clearly, he struck a different chord and has become synonymous with individuality and freedom, and in some places has become one of the main symbols of Americana. This shows that even carefully elaborated brand personalities can be interpreted differently by consumers than had been intended by brand management.

3

Marketing mix and implementation

THE ROLE OF MARKETING

The brand expression elements described in the previous chapter circumscribe the consumer brand experience that is to accomplish the organization's strategic objectives. However, they do not deliver this experience. This important task is part of marketing's responsibilities. It is the role of marketing to define and deliver the actual products and services that are sold under the brand's banner. The word 'deliver' is used here as shorthand for making sure that the appropriate products and services are developed, produced, distributed, communicated and promoted to consumers. This means that marketing itself has two separate areas of responsibility, the marketing mix and marketing implementation. The former involves formulating the policies for new product and service developments, distribution channel choice, pricing strategy, marketing communications and customer servicing. The influence of the brand expression on these activities is the subject of the first part of this chapter.

Marketing implementation is the final step in delivering products and services to consumers, and involves such activities as production, supply chain management, logistics, employee training and motivation, advertising and promotions, and sales and after-sales service. These activities are crucial to realizing the consumer brand experience. Without proper implementation or execution the brand will trip up at critical consumer touch points, and all the careful strategizing and planning that has gone into the brand will be useless. How marketing implementation may affect the brand is the focus of the second part of this chapter.

THE MARKETING MIX

Formulating the marketing mix involves translating the brand expression into a marketing mix that contains the following elements:

▐ Products or services that best meet the brand's promise of value to consumers. This may consist of a promise of constant innovation, thereby assuring consumers that they are buying the most up-to-date product available in the category.

▐ Prices that best reflect the brand expression. A brand must be priced in such a way that consumers do not doubt its quality because the price is too low, or would not consider purchasing it because they consider the price too high. The price selected within this range is also dependent on the business strategy, that is, whether it is aimed at market penetration, price skimming, trial generation, and so on. Obviously pricing must also be set to ensure that, at some point in time, price and volume will cover operational and support costs for the brand.

▐ Communications channels are aligned with the brand expression. For example, glossy magazine advertising may be perfectly suited to a brand with a sophisticated personality, but not one with a down-to-earth personality.

▐ Channels that best convey the brand expression. A luxury brand obviously seeks out different and more exclusive outlets than does a home improvement brand.

▐ Employees who are willing and able to support the brand at its most crucial moments, namely at customer touch points where the brand experience occurs. A full-service bank will hire and train its personnel differently from an Internet bank with a limited portfolio.

These five marketing mix elements, and the impact of the brand expression on them, are the subject of the following paragraphs.

Products and services

The bases for any brand are its products and services. This is what consumers eventually buy and use. No matter how augmented a product or service, a disappointing experience is bad for the brand. Disappointment and satisfaction are functions of expectations. If a brand over-promises and under-delivers consumers will be upset. This sounds basic, but every day there are brands that promise a lot in their communications and then let consumers down when it comes to the product or service. Even when a brand does not make any explicit promises, consumers will still have certain expectations about the products and services offered. They take these cues from the brand expression. This is why products and services must be in line with the brand expression.

Brands that emphasize their positioning aspects are generally most product-focused. This is because of their confidence in the inventiveness, functional superiority or value of the products or services they offer. New product development (NPD) programmes of such brands are aimed at reinforcing these advantages. For example, Sony has a strong positioning regarding the pocketability of its portable products, going back all the way to the first Walkman, and now applied to such products as MP3 players and digital cameras. What is essentially a benefit positioning has had an immense impact on the entire brand. Similarly, Amazon.com has extended its problem-solving positioning gained in books and CDs into other categories such as toys, hardware, electronics and kitchenware. Whether these new services are successful will largely depend on whether consumers view these particular categories as having difficult-to-access outlets, with limited stock and products of more or less uniform quality.

Brands that rely on their identity as their main expressive element are often less concerned with constant NPD. Their products and services rather need to be in line with the brand's legacy, history, values and purposes. When Coca-Cola introduced New Coke in 1985, consumers felt that the new product, although it may have tasted better, was a disgrace to the brand. Coca-Cola had failed to understand that its own reliance on its identity traits, once neatly summed up by its own advertising as 'The real thing', had become deep-rooted among its (mainly US) consumers. Replacing it with 'The new thing' was counterintuitive to the values held true by its consumers. This episode scared the Coca-Cola Company into a torpor regarding new products. Apart from the introduction of Cherry Coke in 1985, it took until 2002 for the brand to introduce a new flavour, Vanilla Coke. The lesson here is not that a brand expression based around identity traits leads to brands that do not innovate, but rather that such innovation needs to take place within the context of that identity.

A brand that emphasizes its brand personality needs to develop its products and services in line with its character. A competent brand personality does not allow frivolous products. How would people react if American Express decided to offer a credit card bearing the image of a joker rather than that of a centurion? Likewise, a sophisticated brand personality is supposed to create similarly stylish products. Again, this does not mean that such brands cannot develop new or innovative products, but just that they should remain within the context even if it does sometimes entail pushing the envelope. Burberry was known as a tasteful yet staid brand offering suits, coats and its signature checked scarves. By introducing swimwear and bags decked out in the Burberry check, the brand was able to become more contemporary while remaining stylish.

Such notions also extend to packaging, which needs to reflect the brand expression. An obvious example is the packaging of luxury perfume, which has itself become an intricate part of the brand. The distinct round bottle used for Noa by Cacharel exudes simple yet precious and delicate refinement. But the importance of packaging following brand expression is not limited to luxury brands. Gateway computers packs its PCs in boxes adorned with the black and white patches of a cow, thus emphasizing its identity as the Silicon Prairie company. Even for brands that rely heavily on positioning, packaging should be aligned with the brand. For example, a value for money brand will be inclined towards simple, no-frills packaging. In many European countries, pre-paid mobile phones are sold in such quirky yet simple packs as first aid boxes, milk cartons and cans.

Products and services for global brands

For a global brand, it is a question of how products and services best manifest the brand expression locally. There are a few truly global brands that do not adapt their brand or their offerings to different markets, mainly ICT companies such as Microsoft, Dell and IBM. Coca-Cola is probably the most standardized fast moving consumer goods brand. A brand may be standardized across countries, while its products and services are not. MTV Asia is expressed in the same manner across the region, yet its music content offering is customized to fit the local markets. Conversely a brand may be locally adapted, while its products and services are not. The Parker pen company sells pens under the same name in all markets. It attempted to use global advertising, but after a slump in sales in the 1980s it restored multinational advertising to better fit individual markets. In Germany, print advertising showed a hand with a Parker pen writing the words 'This is how you write with precision'. Advertising in the United States revolved around the brand's status and image. One of the US ads had a caption saying, 'There is a time when it has to be a Parker' (Milavanovi, 1997).

Finally, the brand and the products may be both locally adapted. Melitta is positioned as a premium coffee brand in the United States, while in its home market Germany the brand is more middle of the road and aims to provide coffee enjoyment. In addition, Melitta sells distinctly different coffee blends and aromas in the United States (such as French Vanilla and Hazelnut Crème) from those sold in Germany, where it employs traditional coffee blends (although it does have a separate aroma syrup as well).

Pricing

Contrary to common practice, setting prices is an issue that follows from the brand expression. Basically this has to do with the way organizations view their prices, as either cost-based or value-based. The former entails marking up estimated costs, while the latter entails estimating the most that customers are willing to pay, then charging a little less to leave the buyer with some 'consumer surplus' (Kotler, 1999). This does not mean that an organization should not try to cover its costs, just that costs should not be the basis for pricing.

The brand expression has a specific influence on pricing. Within each brand expression element are clear indications for price setting. For example, a positioning based on usage occasions has a far better chance of charging a price premium than one based on benefits. Gatorade can command higher prices than Lipton Iced Tea. This is because occasion-related purchases are impulsive, and often so specific that consumers do not even consider alternatives. A brand identity based on values of health and regeneration is more likely to fetch a higher price than one based on values of community. In some places Evian commands a whopping US $50 per litre for what is essentially plain water, while the local tap water costs only a few cents per litre. An urban legend has it that Evian is actually 'naïve' spelt backwards. A stylish brand personality is more likely to demand a higher price than a less assuming one. A Prada handbag can fetch up to US $900, while a handbag by Mexx may set you back only US $35. This does not mean that the brand that commands a higher price is also more profitable. It is often very costly to maintain innovative, celebrated and sophisticated brands.

There are very few brands that charge the same price for their products and services worldwide, apart from local taxation, legal and exchange rate issues that affect the price. On the demand side, global brands need to deal with purchasing power that differs across and even within countries, with differing (price) competition, and with differing category significance and histories. For example, the price of a Big Mac in Hong Kong is US $1.40 while the same offer costs US $2.37 in the Netherlands, a 69 per cent higher price (Economist, 2002a). The reason for this difference is partly to be found in purchasing power: not that the average purchasing power is lower in Hong Kong, but the differences between rich and poor are far greater than in the Netherlands. Another reason is that competition in the fast food arena is much greater in Hong Kong, as McDonald's has to compete with international and local chains – such as Pizza Hut, Wendy's, Café de Coral and Hardee's – as well as a host of individual fast food outlets and food courts. In the Netherlands, McDonald's is primarily situated by or near the motorway where there is much less competition than in the busy streets of, say, Causeway Bay, Hung Hom and Mongkok. On the supply side, global brands are faced with costs of manufacturing, transportation, distribution, sales and marketing that can vary considerably between countries.

Pricing for global brands

Hankinson and Cowking (1996) describe a classification of global pricing strategies as ethnocentric, polycentric and geocentric pricing. The ethnocentric strategy is a kind of cost-based pricing approach, whereby prices vary per region or country based on the variations in freight, duty and other add-on costs. This is typically the approach of a brand that manufactures in its home country and exports its products. The strategy can be successful as long as either consumers are willing to pay a premium for an imported brand (such as Carlsberg beer in Hong Kong, or a Mini in Japan) or the add-on costs are negligible in relation to the price, as is the case with a lot of software.

The polycentric approach allows for prices to vary according to differing market and competitive conditions. Local brand management is free to set prices as it sees fit, subject to financial objectives set by the organization. The case of McDonald's described above is such an approach, which is supported by the use of local franchisees. For some brands this approach could lead to such price disparities that it induces parallel import. A case in point is Levi's jeans, which are far cheaper in the United States than in most European countries. This spurred companies such as Tesco (a UK supermarket chain) to parallel import its Levi's, leading to legal action by Levi-Strauss to prevent it. The geocentric approach takes into account local market and competitive conditions, but aligns local prices with a global pricing strategy. This approach allows prices to vary, but keeps a check on them to ensure that the brand does not get out of line in one or more countries.

Certain pressures are coming to bear on differential pricing between and within countries. There is the advent of national chain stores and supermarkets in parts of the developing world, such as Asia and Latin America, which is harmonizing prices for brands across huge and diverse countries. There is the introduction of the euro in January 2002, which has made cross-border price comparisons and shopping easier, although the effects for consumers are still limited. For example, HEMA department stores quote different euro prices for exactly the same products in their Belgian, German and Dutch stores. Finally, there is the Internet, which allows consumers to buy certain products and services where they can find them cheaper. For example, a book lover in Brussels can purchase books from a variety of online shops located around Europe, and figure out which one is cheapest including shipping charges. Airline prices are being harmonized, as more consumers book their flights online. Not only is it easier than before to compare the prices of various airlines, it is also possible to spot whether the same flight is offered at a lower price in the country of destination. Even though consumers may not be able to act on all these price differences, they are bound to feel that they are being over-charged for some brands or products. UK consumers were certainly unhappy when they heard that new cars are cheaper on the continent than in Britain.

Distribution

The choice of distribution channels for a brand is not only limited to finding outlets that will most effectively get the brand into consumers' hands. Distribution channels also need to fit with the brand expression, so as to reinforce the brand's entire proposition. The most basic choice is whether to distribute the brand's products and services directly to consumers or to do so through some kind of intermediary. Selling directly to consumers is typically done by brands with a strong value-for-money positioning. The brand saves money by cutting out the intermediary, and passes on (part of) the savings to the consumer. Examples are budget airlines, Internet banks and insurance direct writers.

For other brands, the emphasis on their brand identity aspects leads to direct selling. An example is Mary Kay cosmetics, which has a philosophy of enriching women' s lives around the world. Its method of connecting with its customers is through direct selling by women to women. Mary Kay Ash, the company founder, says it like this: 'In particular, we cherish the personal touch' (www.marykay.com). Brands that focus on their brand personality may also sell direct in order to underscore those characteristics. Cosmetics brand Yves Rocher sells its natural beauty products through its own stores, beauty centres, by mail, over the Internet and through relationship selling. The Yves Rocher brand personality is one of sincerity and caring, as can be inferred from the company slogan, 'No one respects the nature of women more'. For Yves Rocher direct selling is a way of getting closer to consumers. As the corporate Web site puts it, 'Always closer, always more accessible, always listening' (www.yves-rocher.com). Yet other brands simply require direct contact with customers through a sales representative, because the offer of the brand is so specific or so complex. This is the case with brands that rely heavily on such positioning aspects as (technical) features and problem solving. In the business market, large sales forces are still common among such tech companies as Xerox and IBM. In the home consumer market, such sales forces are still common for insurance and mortgage companies.

Obviously direct selling is not the appropriate route for every brand. Most brands rely on distributors (such as importers, wholesalers, retailers and dealers) to deliver their brand to the consumer. For brands with strong positioning aspects, such as features, benefits and problem solving, it is often advantageous to be seen and directly compared with competitive offers by consumers. This direct comparison allows such brands to show off their strengths relative to the competition. Sony's knack for design is all the more obvious when its products pose between less well-designed competitive products. Brands with a positioning based on usage are obviously distributed through outlets that are somehow linked to that usage occasion. Lucozade is sold at sports venues, Mars bars are sold in places where people tend to be peckish in between meals (such as filling stations, supermarket check-out counters and office canteens) and the International Student Identity Card is sold primarily at student travel agencies.

Brands that emphasize their identity often have to be somewhat careful with their choice of distribution channels. For example, brands with a strong heritage usually avoid deep discount formats, simply because the association with that type of store is not beneficial, and the subsequent low prices can even be detrimental to the brand. A brand such as Adidas is unlikely to choose a discounter like Aldi as a distribution partner. The example cited above of Levi-Strauss's legal battle with supermarket chain Tesco shows the same considerations.

Brands with specific personality traits will seek out outlets that, at a minimum, do not hurt those characteristics. In many cases such brands have opened their own stores to provide a fuller brand experience to consumers. Examples abound in the fashion business (for example Emporio Armani and Versace stores), but also in other categories such as sportswear (such as Nike Town), computers (Apple stores) and ice cream (Haägen-Dazs stores).

Distribution for global brands

Hankinson and Cowking (1996) describe five distribution routes that may be taken when a brand goes global. The first option is to appoint local agents or distributors in each of the foreign markets. This is a very effective way of dealing with language barriers, local buying practices and local price competition. Many products – cars, beer, computers and consumer electronics to name a few – are imported by local and international distributors who push these products down the supply chain towards the end users. Inchcape handles a large portfolio of foreign brands across multiple categories from automotive to confectionery, as it has proven to be able to handle the intricacies of wholesale distribution in complex markets such as China. However, this does mean that the choice of consumer outlets is largely dependent on the distributor. Certainly in the early stages of market entry, all marketing activities are delegated to these distributors. This can lead to two unwelcome situations. The first is that the brand diverges significantly from its original principles, to suit the wholesaler not the consumers. The second is that the wholesaler slavishly adopts the brand and misses the mark among consumers. When a local distributor is successful this may still lead to problems should the organization want to set up a own wholly owned subsidiary in the country or buy the distributor. This may lead to litigation and local hostility to the brand.

The second option is for the brand to piggyback on the distribution channel of a well-established organization, such as a parent or a partner organization. There are clear advantages to such an arrangement, as the brand can be introduced quickly and efficiently. However, there may a drawback that the brand does not receive sufficient attention from the local parent or partner organizations. Their own brands are likely to be their main concern.

The third option is to license or franchise the brand. This means that there is a contractual agreement between two organizations to manufacture and sell the products or services abroad to exact specifications. Franchising also includes adopting the entire business concept. The main advantages are an efficient roll-out of the brand and long-term commitments by the licensee or franchisee. Also, because the licensee or franchisee is a locally owned organization, it is an effective way of dealing with local cultural, language and business practices. The obvious disadvantage is that the brand owner may not be happy with the way the licensee or franchisee manages the brand. An example is the way in which Whitbread established Heineken in the UK as a value for money lager. Heineken was unhappy because the brand is a premium beer in most other places. British consumers complained about the lack of taste of the locally brewed beer. Heineken sales in the UK slumped as consumers switched to Stella Artois and Grolsch. Finally Heineken broke with Whitbread when the latter was acquired by Belgium's Interbrew.

The fourth option is to establish a joint venture between the brand's organization and a local organization for the manufacture and/or distribution of the brand's products or services. This allows the brand's organization to access global markets and local knowledge with greater control than in the case of a license or franchise agreement. A drawback can be that the joint-venture partner attains more control over the company through political connections than it is entitled to by the formal agree-ment. Another disadvantage is that the local joint venture partner may transfer the (technical) know-how it has gained from the venture to its other companies, and thus siphon off the valuable intangible assets.

The final option is that the brand's organization goes in and handles the distribution itself. However, most organizations lack the resources and expertise to control distribution channels in foreign countries, making this an unattractive option for them. In general, the more dissimilar the culture is to the organization's home market, the more dependent the organization will be on the local distributor.

Communications

The way in which the brand is communicated is logically dependent on its brand expression elements. A brand that relies greatly on its positioning aspects will emphasize those in its communications, and the same goes for brands that leverage their identities or personalities. Most global brands will make use of various forms of communication, usually with an emphasis on mass media. However, some forms of communication are particularly suited to certain brand expressions.

Most brands that accentuate their positioning aspects regularly intro-duce new products or services. Public relations are the most effective and credible way of communicating such innovations. When consumers read about a brand innovation or novelty in their newspaper or see it in a televi-sion programme they are more likely to take notice and believe the bene-fits of the product or service. Aaker and Joachimsthaler (2000) note that event sponsorship may be a necessary lever to elevate the news value of a new technology or product. Such events may also be an opportunity to showcase a new product or service. This is particularly important for brands that rely on constant innovation to keep the brand contemporary and relevant to consumers.

Brands that rely on their identity aspects seek communications channels that fit and enhance their identities. Brands with a strong heritage tend to open visitors' centres to provide consumers with a first-hand experience of learning about and (often) trying the brand. Guinness opened a new visitors' centre in Dublin in late 2000 called the Guinness Storehouse. The facility needed to capture the 243-year history of the brand, as well as breathe life into an ageing brand and reconnect it with young consumers. The Storehouse features not only exhibits that recount the company history, but also facilities such as conference rooms, an art gallery, restau-rants, bars and an event space. This makes it a place for tourists, locals and

Guinness employees to mingle. In its inaugural year the Guinness Storehouse drew 570,000 visitors (*Fast Company*, 2002a). For such heritage brands, Web sites also provide a platform to recount the brand's story.

Brands that extol certain societal values need to either create their own media (such as a Web site, folders, newssheet or magazine) or find partners that have similar principles. The Body Shop ran window campaigns against animal testing, launched human rights campaigns with Amnesty International, sponsored posters for Greenpeace and hands out its own Human Rights Award, to name a few (see www.thebodyshop.com).

Brands with strong personality traits choose communications channels that will make their personalities shine brighter. Event sponsorship is a way of ensuring that such brands are associated with the correct crowds. There are the (extreme) sports events for brands with exciting or stimulating personalities, such as Red Bull. There are music events for brands that wish to be associated with a particular genre or a certain crowd. For example, Chevrolet sponsors the Country Music Awards in Nashville, Tennessee. A Web site is also a perfect place to stage the brand personality. For instance, Mentos has a Web site featuring Freshworld, a virtual cruise ship where Fresh People can come chat, meet and play. Promotional activities can also contribute to the brand personality by leveraging some of the sophistication, excitement or coolness from the promotion offered. Finally, a competent brand personality may be helped along with venue sponsorship. For example, there are FedEx Field in Washington, DC, ANZ Stadium in Brisbane, and Eircom Park in Dublin (Karolefski, 2003).

Communications for global brands

Global brands are faced with the dilemma whether they should use the same communications and the same channels across countries. Standardization is tempting to global brand management, because of the economies of scale involved in making one advertisement and choosing the same communications channels everywhere. De Mooij (1998) finds that international advertisers tend to target international audiences with their home country's value systems. The problem, as she sees it, is that unless the sender and the receiver of the message have a shared culture, the receiver will interpret the advertisement incorrectly. The cost savings of a standardized campaign are easily offset by the loss caused by a less effective advertising message. Part II of this book deals with the potential for brands to be successfully standardized or adapted, which has an obvious influence on the ability to standardize communications.

Apart from the question whether to standardize the message, there is also a matter of whether to use the same communications channels around the globe. Currently this issue is most potent when it comes to the Internet, simply because its penetration and usage differ across countries. According to the OECD (2002), in Europe Internet penetration as a percentage of the total population differs between a high of over 50 per cent in Sweden to little more than 5 per cent in Portugal. Obviously this makes an integrated media campaign across the entire continent a bit problematic, to say the least. But then it is merely a matter of time before southern Europe shows similar Internet penetration rates to the north.

More significant is that media consumption patterns also differ due to more stubborn local circumstances. An example is Hong Kong, where most people tend to spend most of their days and evenings away from home. This is partly because of their rather cramped living quarters and partly because of the local habit of going for dinner and shopping with friends and family after work; and people tend to work late already. This means that in Hong Kong, people generally spend far less time in front of the television than in Europe, let alone the United States. Important media channels in Hong Kong are newspapers (there are more newspaper titles per inhabitant than anywhere else in the world), the Mass Transit Railway (MTR) underground stations, signage on buildings (there are a lot of very tall ones) and the Star ferry that plies between Hong Kong Island and the Kowloon Peninsula, to name just a few. This shows just how singular media consumption can be. So even if the content of the advertising is the same, the means needed to get the message across may differ significantly.

People

Once overlooked as a means for marketing products and services, employees' roles as providers of consumer service have been acknowledged in recent years. This is probably due to the growth of service industries in most developed countries, as well as a propensity among manufacturers to add services to previously non-serviced products. In fact, this is nothing new. Treacy and Wiersema (1995) explain that IBM's rock-solid business in the 1970s was actually based on the depth and range of services that IBM offered to its customers, rather than on the reliability or inventiveness of the products it offered them.

When discussing employees (or human resources as some prefer to call them) in the context of branding, we touch on a number of related issues that extend beyond the marketing function. First of all, employees often embody the brand. This applies not only to customer-facing staff – such as sales reps, front desk and call-centre staff – but to everyone ranging from the CEO to the delivery truck driver. Recently a lot of attention has been paid to internal branding, whereby employees are encouraged to 'live the brand'. The idea is that when employees fully understand and appreciate their brand they will be better able to provide the desired brand experience to consumers. Three influential books on this subject were written by Ind (2001), Kunde (2000) and Pringle and Gordon (2001). Internal branding focuses on ensuring that employees relate to and share the brand's values, purpose and ambitions. Internal branding is aimed at creating an organization that is able to live up to and exceed the expectations that consumers have of the brand. Den Engelsen (2002) identifies four schools of internal branding: the mission school, the strategy school, the communications school and the organization school.

The *mission school* asserts that organizations must have a corporate belief, extolled by visionary management, that functions as an internal bonding mechanism and strategic directive. Typical examples of such brands are Virgin and Harley Davidson. The *strategy school* prefers brand-based strategic management, in which the brand is the leading organizing principle of a corporation and drives all corporate activities. Macrae (1996) has coined this the brand learning organization. Examples are Singapore Airlines and Ikea. The *communications school* sees branding as an internal and external communications strategy which is aimed at educating staff and customers alike about the brand. A case in point is IBM's eight-page print ad in the *Wall Street Journal* launching its e-business campaign, which was aimed at employees and customers alike. The *organization school* aims to establish internal conditions that allow employees to deliver the correct brand experience to consumers during so-called moments of truth. This thinking stems from the disenchantment felt by consumers with brands that over-promise and under-deliver, and the subsequent frustration of service staff who have to deal with these issues. These are typically issues for such service industries as banking, telecommunications and hotels.

The brand expression has a specific influence on the activities that staff undertake, and therefore on human resource activities such as hiring and training. A courier company may have a positioning based on such features as fast, accurate, first-time right and secure service. For most of its employees, whether they are dispatchers, truck drivers or call-centre operators, this means that they do mainly routine work. Training will be aimed at performing the tasks required to make the company's operations run smoothly. The employees need to derive their work satisfaction and company pride from the fact that they are able to deliver on the positioning aspects. This implies that employees need to be hired who exhibit traits such as conscientiousness, meticulousness and deference. Free agents should not apply. An example of such a brand is TNT Express.

A DIY retailer that bases its brand on solving its customers' problems will encourage its staff to be knowledgeable, caring, attentive and unhurried. Employees will be expected to carry out a lot of non-routine tasks such as trying to unravel a customer's problem, searching for correct materials and instructing the customer on their application. Staff training will focus on giving the employees a good understanding of the materials on sale, on DIY skills and on interpersonal skills. Such a retailer will want to hire sales staff who are by nature caring, open and self-assured. An example of such a brand is Nordstrom in the United States.

A brand with an identity based on specific values or principles will need employees who underwrite these and convey them to consumers. Their daily activities will be shaped by these values. The sandwich chain Pret a Manger states that it is 'Passionate about food', and it claims to go to extraordinary lengths to avoid the chemicals, additives and preservatives common to much fast food. Whatever is not sold when the shops close goes to local charities to help feed those who would otherwise go hungry. About their employees Pret a Manger has the following to say, one of the clearest statements regarding hiring people on the basis of their personality rather than on other characteristics:

We are equally passionate about the people we employ. We're incredibly privileged that so many creative, hard working and talented young people have chosen to work for us. We're often asked about the secret of our customer service training. There is no secret – in fact, there's no customer service training. Instead, we employ people with personality who we think have the potential to give genuinely good service – people who like mixing with other people, who are good-humoured and like to enjoy themselves. (www.pret.com)

Then what do brands do that rely mainly on their brand personality? Should employees' personalities match the brand's? Obviously, it is impossible to hire employees with exactly the same personalities. However, they must possess skills that will enable them to bring the brand personality to consumers, and the organization must encourage and train its employees to make the best use of these skills. For example, Porsche has an exciting brand personality. It even proclaims itself to be a genuine 'Excitement company' (www.porsche.com). Apparently Porsche hires its workers on the basis of their creative abilities and courage, and nurtures this through a company culture of being small, being customer-centred, being open to opportunity, and through continuous training. And these are mostly employees that seldom if ever meet a customer face to face!

Peters (1999), and more recently Gad and Rosencreutz (2002) have focused on the branding of oneself. The idea is that in today's transparent and networked world people need to adapt and reinvent themselves. To quote Peters, 'In today's wild wired world, you're distinct ... or extinct.' An example of such a constantly reinvented personal brand is Madonna. Gad and Rosencreutz focus more on the development of personal identity: in short, knowing what you stand for will make you stand out. In addition, Gad is also active in the alignment of company management's personal interests with (aspects of) the corporate brand. The issue of personal branding is rather controversial, as it begs the question whether an organizational construct can and should be applied to individual humans.

People and global brands

The main issues facing global brands when it comes to hiring and training employees in various countries are variations in skills and cultural differences. The differences in skills have to do with the level and the types of education people enjoy in particular countries. In most parts of Asia, a lot of the education is aimed at learning or cramming information rather than critical thinking. This is due partly to East Asian character-based scripts which require cramming, but is more the effect of the importance that is attached to perfect reproduction and recitation. The level of education of employees is often dependent on the general level of development of a country. In China, there used to be a dearth of graduates, and those who were qualified often had few foreign language skills. For this reason a lot of Taiwanese, Hong Kong and Singaporean expatriates were hired to work in China. However, expatriates are normally only hired for management level jobs. For the other levels companies need local employees, who often need extensive training before being able to perform the required tasks.

The local culture is an issue that transcends job levels, and needs to be well understood before organizations are able to work effectively in foreign countries. One of the first to explore the influence of local culture on organizations was Hofstede (1980). On the basis of research conducted among IBM employees in 56 countries, he identified the following four cultural dimensions:

▌ *power distance*: the extent to which less powerful members of society accept and expect that power is distributed unequally;
▌ *individualism versus collectivism*: people looking after themselves and their immediate family only, versus people belonging to in-groups that look after them in exchange for loyalty;

▍ *masculinity versus femininity*: achievement and success versus caring for others and quality of life;
▍ *uncertainty avoidance*: the extent to which people feel threatened by uncertainty and ambiguity and try to avoid these situations.

Michael Bond of the Hong Kong University found an additional dimension to Hofstede's four on the basis of a Chinese values survey (Hofstede, 1991):

▍ *long-term orientation:* the extent to which a society exhibits a pragmatic future-oriented perspective rather than a conventional historic or short-term point of view.

Hofstede and Bond's value dimensions provide insight into broad societal themes which explain interactions between members of the same society, and frictions or misunderstandings between members of different societies. The most important issue is to realize and recognize that employees' cultures differ from that of the brand's home market, and that things like training, policies and procedures cannot simply be transplanted into an organization in a different society. For instance, demanding initiative and creativity from junior staff members in countries with high power distance is unlikely to have effect. These people are generally used to doing what they are told, and rely on orders from their superiors.

MARKETING IMPLEMENTATION

How a brand is experienced and perceived is probably most affected by consumers' contacts with the brand. Some of this contact will be passive, as in the case of advertising, while other instances will be active, for example when consumers buy and use a product or service offered by the brand. If the marketing mix is badly implemented this will adversely affect the brand, and will render all careful branding work fruitless. Marketing implementation includes such activities as producing advertising material, undertaking promotions, manufacturing products, logistics, sales, customer service and loyalty programs. Discontinuities in these activities can badly hurt a brand: stock outages, damaged products, inconsistent promotions, bad sales staff manners, badly administered coupon or loyalty card activities, incorrect translations, badly designed Web sites, and so on. There are a number of common implementation mistakes which are discussed here.

Products and services

Products or services that do not meet consumers' expectations are probably the main implementation problem to plague brands. Shoddy production is the most deadly of sins. It brought infamy to once venerable British automobile brands such as Triumph, Austin and Morris. In a similar fashion, badly executed service concepts may harm a brand. By the end of the 1990s, the Wireless Application Protocol (WAP) promised mobile phone owners mobile Internet access in the palm of their hand. Unfortunately, WAP could never live up to this promise, because of slow connections, few services and high costs. Part of the problem was that WAP had been over-hyped by service providers, but a lack of usefulness to consumers left the service practically stillborn. Boo.com, a now defunct online fashion retailer, put so much heavy flash and shockwave software on its cutting-edge site that any mere mortal with a dial-up connection went stark raving mad waiting for the Web pages to download. Not surprisingly, Boo.com had very few customers ordering any clothing.

Yet even a well researched and manufactured product can lead to a brand disaster. An already classic example is the introduction of Omo Power (Persil Power in the UK) in 1994. Unilever introduced this washing powder as a revolution in stain removal. Thanks to a manganese substance, dubbed an accelerator, practically any stains could be removed at low temperatures. Unilever had thoroughly researched and tested the new product before launching it with a lot of fanfare. Unfortunately Unilever had failed to test the product at temperatures other than those recommended to consumers. Used at higher temperatures, Omo Power not only removed stains effectively but also destroyed fabrics efficiently. Procter and Gamble, who got wind of this product fault, were quick to advertise the destructive force of Omo Power with ads showing shredded pieces of clothing that had been washed in Omo Power. Sales of Omo Power collapsed, and it took Omo several years to regain ground lost to Procter and Gamble's Ariel.

Even when on the face of it a product or service is not shoddy, the experience can still fall well below expectation. Chello, the broadband Internet division of United Pan-European Cable (UPC), introduced its television cable-based services with a promise of speeds well in excess of dial-up modems. When customers started using the service in 2000, they found that at certain times of the day – particularly during evenings and weekends – the speed of the connection dropped significantly. This turned out to be because of the way the cable system worked. Instead of a one-to-one connection with an Internet server – as is the case with telecommunications networks – the cable network functioned as a large loop carrying the communications of all users to the Chello Internet server. During busy times, the packets sent over the cable network formed a traffic jam waiting to be handled. This led to various negative reports in the media. Chello's handling of the matter did not help. Instead of owning up to the problem, it decided to blame its users. Chello claimed that some of its customers were using too much bandwidth and thus clogging the cable, and decided that it would restrict bandwidth usage by allowing the use of only so many megabytes a month. Customers countered by saying that they had been attracted to the service because it promised vast capacity and had never set restrictions regarding usage.

Badly designed packaging can also harm a brand. External design or imagery may put off consumers. A classic example is Gerber baby food, which sold its products with a label of a cuddly white baby (the same as in the United States) in Africa. When sales did not meet expectations, Gerber sought to find the cause. In Africa, consumers are used to labels portraying the contents of a pack, since many people are illiterate. The white baby definitely sent the wrong message. Packaging design can also upset local sensibilities. McDonald's put the 24 flags of countries participating in the 1998 Football World Cup on millions of Happy Meal bags, including the Saudi flag. The Saudi flag includes a passage from the *Koran*, which is not to be used for such a profane purpose as a bag that is eventually crumpled and thrown away. The Saudis complained and McDonald's removed the bags.

Packaging can also be badly designed for the use it is put to. Faulty packaging can lead to spillage and subsequent damage. An interesting case is a Dutch soft drink called Exota which was very popular in the 1970s. According to a television news report the glass bottles used by this brand were unsafe as they tended to explode without warning, sending pieces of glass flying. Footage of an exploding bottle was shown on television and the brand's sales plunged. The company that owned the brand denied all charges, and after a 25-year legal battle it finally emerged that the television programme makers had shot a bullet through the bottle to make it explode. The programme makers were ordered to pay compensation, but the brand had long expired. This example shows that even the threat of faulty packaging can make consumer desert a brand.

Pricing

Although pricing is clearly a marketing mix issue, it is possible for a brand to trip up over pricing tactics. The most basic problem is a simple pricing blunder. Compaq Australia accidentally promoted its Presario laptop computers for one cent online. The company blamed the price on a Web site systems glitch. One customer who spotted the incredibly low price posted it on an Internet news group. This posting apparently led to a flood of people wanting to take advantage of the offer. Some purchased 10 laptops at a time. As the Compaq Web site actually printed out a receipt for the one-cent transactions, customers felt they had the right of purchase. Compaq did not feel duty bound to honour the transactions, and claimed that it had not processed the credit card payments (ZDNet, 2002a). Later Compaq admitted to having processed the payments and refunded the buyers, but refused to honour the transactions, because it was an obvious error (ZDNet, 2002b).

Another serious mistake is to experiment with pricing outside a controlled environment such as a marketing research study. Amazon.com had to make a public apology when customers found that they were being quoted different prices for the same DVDs. Amazon.com had been conducting a random price test to test the price elasticity of DVDs, with discounts of some 30 to 40 per cent. The company agreed to give consumers who had purchased any of the DVDs in question during the five-day test period the lowest price quoted (E-Commerce Times, 2000b).

However, generally only brands that sell directly to consumers have complete control over sales prices. Most brands are sold through some type of intermediary, which means that the intermediary sets the prices. Kotler (1999) explains that in the car industry, discounting is so rampant that hardly any buyer pays the list price nowadays. Therefore pricing mistakes are made that are outside the control of brand management. Car manufacturers provide their dealers with a list price for a model, but that is considered to be a starting point for negotiations by dealers and consumers. Apparently, actual prices paid for new cars are currently so low that dealers do not make any money on sales.

Communications

The most publicized implementation problems are those surrounding brand communications, as these provide the most evident mistakes. These include such blunders as brand names that do not travel or are badly transliterated, or tag lines that are badly translated. Mitsubishi has a 4x4 vehicle called the Pajero, which means 'masturbator' in Spanish. Colgate introduced toothpaste in France under the brand name Cue, incidentally the name of a notorious local porn rag. The slogan 'Pepsi brings you back to life' was translated into Chinese as 'Pepsi brings your ancestors back from the grave'. Swedish white goods manufacturer Electrolux advertised its vacuum cleaners in the United States with the slogan: 'Nothing sucks like an Electrolux'. Advertising gaffes can also be downright hurtful. In August 2002, as the military and political tensions between India and Pakistan ran high, Cadbury-Schweppes ran a newspaper ad for one of its chocolates on India's Independence Day with the catch line, 'I'm good. I'm tempting. I'm too good to share. What am I? Cadbury's Temptations or Kashmir?' This caused an uproar from Indian politicians and citizens. Cadbury's India apologized (Guardian, 2002).

Communications blunders are not confined to advertising; they are also often the result of ineffective public relations. Abercrombie and Fitch offered a range of T-shirts that made fun of racial stereotypes. One of its T-shirts read 'Wong Brothers laundry service – two Wongs can make it white', and showed two men with slanted eyes and conical hats. The company actually believed the T-shirts would be popular among Asians. Ford USA and Bridgestone/Firestone were embarrassed, to say the least, by the dangers posed by Ford Explorer SUVs equipped with Firestone tyres. The tyres had the tendency to shred and the cars to roll over. First of all the two long-time partners spent a lot of time accusing each other over the matter, before acting and recalling 13 million tyres. It appears that especially Bridgestone/Firestone's denial of the problem has raised hackles among US consumers.

Anti-smoking campaigners reacted furiously when Philip Morris delivered a report to the Czech government stating that the country could save as much as US $147 million in 1997 as the result of smokers dying before being able to make use of housing and healthcare for the elderly. 'Following that logic, the best recommendation to governments would be to kill all people on the day of their retirement,' Czech public health campaigner Eva Kralikova said. Philip Morris subsequently denied that it was trying to present a positive side to smoking (BBC News, 2001).

Distribution

The most clear distribution embarrassment stems from products being out of stock or not available at all. Haig (2003) describes how Virgin Cola failed to gain distribution comparable to its main competitors, Coca-Cola and Pepsi, who were able to block Virgin from getting crucial shelf space in half the UK's supermarkets.

Out of stock situations often occur when a brand is being introduced and is more successful than was anticipated. In some cases this may actually strengthen the brand by demonstrating its desirability. Harley Davidson motorbikes and Morgan sports cars production levels are deliberately held at levels lower than demand. However, in most cases stock-outs are detrimental to the brand, not only because consumers will switch to another brand – with the resulting loss in revenue to the brand – but also because a brand that does not get into the hands of its consumers fails to convey the required brand experience.

Especially in large developing markets, such as Indonesia, brand distribution relies heavily on independent local distributors. A natural conflict exists between a manufacturer and an independent distributor: the manufacturer wishes to build a brand, while the distributor is interested only in short-term profits. This may mean that a brand ends up in retail outlets where it was never intended to be. In Indonesia, for example, small shops or kiosks called Toko Obat usually sell ethical drugs, although they are not licensed to do so (Castle, 1995).

Particularly difficult to handle is the distribution of foodstuffs that require refrigeration, such as ice cream, fresh fruit juice and dairy products. These products need to remain frozen or refrigerated until the moment of purchase, which means a need for reliable refrigeration during transport and stocking. Rasna, one of the leading soft drinks companies in India, experimented with a fizzy fruit drink called Oranjolt. The fresh product required refrigeration. Indian retailers, however, tend to switch off their shop refrigerators at night, leading to quality problems with Oranjolt (Haig, 2003).

People

As discussed in the previous paragraph on the marketing mix, the people behind brands have over the years become increasingly important. Everyone will have a good or bad service experience that has influenced the way they consider a brand. In fact, people have become so important to brands that a failure on their part is probably the worst possible thing to happen to a brand. This is not only the people failure that we experience through bad service, but also the failure of people to uphold the values that the brand embodies or should embody. The case of Arthur Andersen's complicity in concealing Enron's massive debts – further complicated by the refusal of the company's chief auditor at Enron to testify before a Senate committee – quickly destroyed Arthur Andersen's reputation around the world.

Recent incidents, such as homemaking sage Martha Stewart's fall from grace in 2002 for alleged insider trading (Economist, 2002d) and talk show host Rosie O'Donnell's break with the magazine bearing her name after a battle for editorial control with publishers Gruner + Jahr (AdAge,

2002), throw up questions about how closely tied founders and corporate brands are, and whether the latter can survive the departure, demise or tarnishing of the former.

A 'lowly' customer service rep can also ruin a well-defined brand proposition if he or she fails to see the relevance and applicability of the brand to him or herself. No brand is more aware of this danger than Disney. The Disney orientation programme teaches the cast of Disney theme parks about the heritage, the history and the quality standards of the organization. The most important thing they learn is to 'create happiness' (Pringle and Gordon, 2001).

PART II

THE EXTERNAL ANALYSIS

4

Local conventions

INTRODUCTION

Whatever is devised and undertaken by an organization – in terms of business strategy, brand expression and marketing – to provide a specific consumer experience, will pass through a number of filters and lenses which shape the way consumers perceive the brand. These filters and lenses can cancel, distort, amplify and reduce certain elements of the brand. This chapter looks at those factors that influence the brand when it is released into the outside world. We introduce three important influencing factors that circumscribe the opportunities for a brand to reach its full potential in various markets and societies: category conventions, needs conventions and cultural conventions. This chapter is mainly concerned with describing the conventions rather than relating them to branding. Therefore, this chapter has a rather introductory character.

In this book the word 'convention' is used to describe unwritten rules that govern people's perceptions of and decisions about a brand. When a convention is considered to be *solid*, consumers are unwilling to accept an alternative, and there is little alternative than to adapt the particular aspect of a brand to this convention. When a convention is *flexible*, the convention is undergoing development or erosion in consumers' minds, and there is an opportunity to challenge such a convention, and to obtain differentiation from competitors and offer distinct value to consumers. Judging the solidity of a convention is dependent upon the following issues:

▌ *Ubiquity.* How widely is something practised by competitors or consumers?

▌ *Uniformity.* Does every competitor or consumer behave in exactly in the same way or think exactly the same about this matter?

▌ *Stability.* Has the convention changed much over time? Has it begun to show changes recently?

▌ *Significance.* Does the convention have a particular relevance to competitors or consumers? Do they feel that they could do without it?

▌ *Depth.* Is the convention rooted in the fabric of the category or in the society? How valuable do competitors and consumers consider it to be to them?

Often, judging these issues will be a matter of making a judgement call on the basis of competitive analysis and consumer research. The most important consideration is whether adhering to, or conversely challenging, a convention will provide sufficient additional value to consumers. Brand adaptation for fear of upsetting consumers is just as mistaken as challenging them purely for differentiation purposes. A well-executed challenge can provide consumers with new and worthwhile experiences. A classic example is Volkswagen, which challenged US car design conventions when it introduced the Beetle there in the 1960s. Evidently the small and quirky car struck a chord among many (young) Americans looking for an alternative to cars the size of battleships, decked out with ostentatious fins and bulging fenders.

This chapter is intended to introduce the three kinds of convention (category, needs and cultural) that influence the perceptions that people have of brands. The actual way in which they influence the brand perception is discussed in Chapters 5 to 7, which deal with the three brand perception elements: domain, reputation and affinity. The reader will have to suffer the hardships of induction before being offered any insights into the influence of these conventions on the brand. The author apologises for any discomfort caused by this approach, but he sees few alternatives to providing the reader with an adequate understanding of local conventions.

CATEGORY CONVENTIONS

In every product or service category, there are customs and unwritten rules that most if not all players abide by. These conventions generally have a particular value to these players, and in many cases even to consumers. For example, why do Dutch beer drinkers abhor the idea of drinking or even pouring their brew from a plastic bottle? What is the value of a glass bottle to them apart from the fact that they are used to it?

These category conventions, so coined by Morgan (1999), are mainly determined by the major market players in a category. Therefore they have most often developed, not as a response to consumer demands, but rather as a response to internal demands such as production, logistics and advertising. Morgan distinguishes three types of category convention:

▌ *Conventions of representation* which surround how and where a brand portrays itself. These consist of such factors as advertising, packaging, brand name and logo.
▌ *Conventions of medium* which concern the way a brand is delivered, both physically and emotionally. This includes distribution as well as message delivery.
▌ *Conventions of product experience* which have to do with the product offered and the surrounding experience it delivers. In this book we also include price as one of the conventions of product experience. Morgan is not entirely clear about how he sees the role of pricing.

Category conventions are often the first to be challenged, as they often lack a demand-side logic. In addition, they are the most clearly observable and recognizable of the three types of conventions discussed in this book. Morgan provides the example of how Swatch challenged not only the conventions of product experience by offering a plastic watch as a fashion accessory, but also conventions of medium by hanging a great big Swatch off the Commerzbank building in Frankfurt. The three types of category convention are discussed in more detail below.

Conventions of representation

Conventions of representation influence advertising, packaging, brand name and logo. By challenging these conventions a brand wishes to distinguish itself from the way its competitors manifest themselves. Whether this challenge is successful depends on the solidity of each convention and the value it provides to consumers.

Advertising

Advertising is full of conventions, which make it easy for consumers to understand and relate to adverts. Powerful players or market leaders in a category will generally write the rules regarding advertising concepts. In Japan, television commercials for beer – for example for Asahi Super Dry – tend to finish with a scene of a man downing a glass in one go with audible gulps, followed by a loud 'Ahhh'. The scene is actually rather off-putting to non-Japanese, but appealing to Japanese consumers. The scene to them conveys the refreshing and drinkable qualities of the particular beer brand.

De Mooij (1998) provides the example of television advertising for detergents, which generally feature mother and daughter pairs. In southern European ads, the elder woman usually instructs the younger one, while in northern Europe, the roles are usually reversed. De Mooij ascribes these differences to a value dimension called power distance, first described by Hofstede (1991) as the degree to which less powerful members of a society accept that power is distributed unequally.

Packaging

Packaging has two main functions, to protect and to communicate what is inside. Even mundane products are subject to conventions that affect the design, the material and the format of their packaging. For instance, in the UK round tea bags are generally packed in large carton boxes with light colours, pictures of fresh green tea leaves and Indian heritage designs. In the Netherlands sachets of tea with a string and label are packed in small cartons with dark or warm colours, emblazoned with English heritage designs.

Some packaging conventions have a very practical background, related to the distribution or usage of a product or to consumer spending power. For example, a value for money washing powder brand in the United States will generally be in a rather blandly coloured, large box to signify economy – no money spent on frivolous design and a discount for bulk purchase. In India or Indonesia, a value for money washing powder brand will be packaged in a brightly coloured sachet. The colour signifies that the consumer is buying a modern product (as opposed to old-fashioned soap bricks) and the size of the sachet makes the product affordable to those with little spending power. Cavin Kare, an Indian consumer goods firm, even introduced 0.4 millilitre sachets of its Spinz brand of perfume in order to provide rural consumers with the opportunity of using a fragrance (Far Eastern Economic Review, 2003).

Challenging packaging conventions can do more than simply provide a novel experience to consumers. It can signify an organization's values and beliefs. The Body Shop challenged the conventions of representation governing the packaging of cosmetics and personal care products, by offering these products in simple and reusable containers. This demonstrated to consumers the brand's commitment to environmental issues, in particular recycling and waste control.

Brand names and logos

Apart from such legal issues as trademark registration, brand names and logos are also governed by local conventions. For instance, German beer brands are named after their founders, often families or religious orders, or the town or area where the brand originated. This convention was carried to China in the 19th century by brewers in the then German enclave of Qingdao or Tsingtao, as the brand name is spelled. In many parts of Asia beer manufacturers tend to use animals for brand names, such as Kingfisher, Cobra, Tiger and Singha (Lion).

A challenge to a brand name or logo mainly signifies that a brand wants to differentiate itself from competition. Morgan (1999) gives the example of Goldfish, a credit card which came to the UK market when there were already 400 brands on that market. With a user base of 600,000 in its first year, 80 per cent awareness and users that use it more often than any other card, the challenge appears to have been effective.

Conventions of product and service experience

Conventions of product and service experience govern the way a product or service is designed, the features and the benefits it offers. This can differ markedly between societies. For example, in the United States cookies are assumed to be moist and chewy, while in Singapore they are expected to be hard and crunchy. In 1995 Goh Lek Oon took on the Mrs Fields Cookies franchise in Singapore and Malaysia. When she opened her first store in Singapore's Holland Village, she found she had to battle the local mind-set. 'In Singapore, a cookie is expected to be hard and dry. When people bite into [a] Mrs Fields cookie, it is soft and soggy, and many thought the cookies were not fresh,' said Goh. The first few months were spent introducing this new taste to the public, enabling the 'taste to sell itself' (SME IT Guide, 2001). A similar preference for hard and dry biscuits exists in the Netherlands. This is probably partly because of the Dutch fondness for dunking their biscuits. According to consumer research conducted by Verkade, a Dutch brand of cookies and chocolates, posted on a dedicated Web site (www.soppen.nl), one in three Dutch men and women dunk their biscuits, primarily in tea (69 per cent) and coffee (55 per cent).

Such conventions also exist for certain media. In Finland, it is quite normal for the front page of a newspaper to be filled entirely with advertising, something that would be considered unacceptable by consumers in most other countries. Apparently the Finns do not mind as long as it means that their newspapers are affordable.

Similarly, services are influenced by conventions of service experience. Many seasoned business travellers will at some time bemoan the tedium of hotel service uniformity worldwide: the similarities between check-in service, room design and furnishings, breakfast buffets and sand-filled ashtrays in the corridors, to name but a few. By challenging such conventions of service experience, boutique and designer hotels have managed to thrive in major cities worldwide: for example the Hudson in Manhattan, the Sanderson in London, the Montalembert in Paris, the Manor in New Delhi and the G@llery in Singapore.

Successfully challenging service conventions is not limited to traditional service industries such as banking and hotels. Retail brands can also challenge such conventions. Ikea has challenged the conventions of service experience with its self-service stores and self-assembly furniture, previously unheard of in most places in the world.

Free Internet access, offered by the likes of Internet4Free in the United States, Freeler in the Netherlands, Freeserve in the UK, Libertysurf in France, Starhub in Singapore and TuTopia in Brazil, is the clearest case of a challenge to pricing conventions. However, such challenges to pricing conventions can also consist of how a product or service is charged. An example is an insurance refund plan on consumer durables after a set period of years.

There are also conventions of price promotions that differ between countries. In the UK a typical promotion will be 'Buy one, get one free'. In the Netherlands a typical promotion will consists of 'Get three, pay for two'.

Conventions of medium

Media channels

The conventions of medium govern which media channels are considered to be appropriate for brands within a category. These conventions can differ from country to country. For instance, in many western countries shampoo brands rely heavily on magazine advertising, which often includes sample sachets. In Indonesia, shampoo brands use promotional teams to offer samples at such venues as cinemas. In France, roadside billboards advertising nearby supermarkets and hypermarkets are a very common sight. In the Netherlands this kind of advertising for supermarkets is unknown, and supermarkets use door-to-door folders to draw customers. In Hong Kong luxury watch brands, such as Piaget and Jaeger le Coultre, use the television as their main medium. In most European and North American countries, these brands advertise mainly in upmarket magazines.

Advertising agencies are constantly looking for new ways of communicating with consumers, and thus often challenge existing media conventions. There was a time that product placements in television series and movies were such a challenge, as well as branded events. One of the newer ways of bringing consumers into contact with a brand is stealth marketing, whereby seemingly innocuous people turn out to be pitchers in disguise, drawing attention to a certain brand. These types of activity do prompt many to debate their ethics.

Distribution channels

The conventions of medium also govern the choice of distribution channels. These can differ from market to market, as can be witnessed in the washing powder sector. In many poorer Asian countries, such as Indonesia and the Philippines, washing powder is distributed through tiny kiosks and corner stores, which generally sell daily necessities in small units.

Western supermarket chains have found that challenging distribution conventions in Asian countries can be very difficult. For instance, the conventions governing distribution of fresh groceries – consumers tend to shop for these in the so-called wet market – are a lot more durable than was expected, even among the so-called middle classes. As for the poorer consumers in these societies, they have too few means to contemplate visiting a supermarket or hypermarket: no car and too little money for the purchase of large quantities of groceries.

Challenges to distribution conventions are sometimes very creative, as in the case of Pepsi's use of students in the western Chinese city of Chengdu selling cups of cold Pepsi from space age coolers strapped to their backs. The students pace crowded shopping areas dispensing cups at 5 renminbi apiece to thirsty young shoppers. Stored at 2 degrees Celsius, the soft drink stays cool and fizzy in the backpack's 3 gallon insulated tank. The students have a cup dispenser on one shoulder strap, a money belt and a dispensing gun snaking around from behind (Far Eastern Economic Review, 2000a).

Challenges to the conventions of distribution can take the form of unusual partnerships, such as the one announced by Philips and Ikea, whereby Philips consumer electronics feature and are for sale in Ikea stores (Het Financieele Dagblad, 2002a). Apparently, the idea is that Ikea customers will associate Philips with Ikea's contemporary design, and will decide to purchase their consumer electronics to match the furniture they buy.

The distribution of services is also affected by conventions. For instance, traditionally airline tickets are sold through ticketing agents. Low-cost carriers, such as easyJet, Ryanair and Buzz, have successfully challenged this particular convention by selling tickets only over the telephone and via the Internet. The easyCorporation has adopted the same distribution strategy for its easyCar rental brand. Such a challenge to distribution conventions may not succeed in a place like Japan, where people are generally loath to provide their credit card details over the telephone or the Internet.

Another example is the advent of online share trading, which became possible due to the combined development of the Internet and the popularization of shareholding. Established stockbrokers failed to respond adequately to the challenge to their conventional mode of operations, and thus lost a lot of their business to online traders such as Charles Swab.

NEEDS CONVENTIONS

Consumers sift through their brand experience with an eye to their personal needs. These needs are also governed by conventions which determine how needs are manifested. This means that, although a particular need may be common to all people, this same need may be satisfied in a different manner in different societies. For example, a basic need for early morning nutrition may be met by eating bread and sausage in Germany, eggs and toast in the UK, rice and fritters in China and a muffin in the United States.

As long ago as the 1950s Maslow (1954) recognized that there are specific types of needs that are common among people the world over. He also believed that there is a universal hierarchy to these needs, starting with the most basic physiological needs and extending to self-actualization needs. Pinto (2002) identifies an alternative hierarchy of needs for so-called high-context societies, mainly non-western countries, where the need for honour is topmost in the hierarchy.

When considering brands, it often transpires that various types of needs are in play at the same time, and that a hierarchy is often impossible to establish, if not counterproductive. In addition, the importance of these needs may vary widely across societies. For example, in the United States a visit to a restaurant belonging to a well-known fast food chain may primarily meet consumers' needs for security and convenience: they are sure of what will be on offer and what the service will be like. In Russia, a visit to a restaurant belonging to the very same fast food chain may primarily meet consumers' needs for status: they wish to be seen entering and sitting in this modern and smart restaurant.

This book identifies the following types of need, without wanting to ascribe any kind of ranking to these needs:

■ physiological needs, sustenance, health and regeneration;
■ security, our need for safety, protection and certainty;
■ social or affiliation needs, our need for belonging, to fit in and feel right;
■ esteem, our need to be valued, respected and appreciated, honour;
■ cognitive, our need to know, learn and experience;
■ self-actualization, our need to be someone and be self-confident;
■ aesthetic, our need for beauty, creativity and imagination;
■ transcendence, our need to do good for others, advocacy.

Another typology of needs may be equally useful to brand management. The key issue is not what needs exist and whether or not they are universal needs, but how the manifestation of needs differs between countries, and how this is governed by conventions. It is for this reason that the following paragraphs examine needs conventions rather comprehensively. It is not the intention to revisit Maslow's needs typology – any serious student of marketing will know it by heart – but to describe how seemingly similar needs translate into (sometimes radically) different consumer behaviour.

Physiological needs

Physiological needs are not just about food, clothes and shelter, but also about health and regeneration. Physiological needs are subject to conventions which vary between societies. For example, in East Asia there is a strong need for eating rice on a daily basis. Many Asians start feeling uncomfortable when they do not obtain their daily dose of the staple. Similar needs exist among many Europeans when it comes to foodstuffs such as bread. This does not mean that these consumers are unwilling to try something new or exotic, but it does mean that uncommon foods are valued more for the experience they provide than for their innate ability to satisfy physiological needs. A case in point is the rising interest in coffee among young Asian urbanites. These new coffee consumers are more interested in the refinement of coffee than in the buzz the beverage provides. It will likely be many years before Asians gulp down coffee as their European counterparts do. Even in Europe coffee needs differ significantly, with Scandinavians consuming 12 kg of coffee per capita annually versus only some 2 kg for Britons, Spaniards and Greeks (www.coffeeresearch.org).

Security needs

Although at a basic level security needs all involve protection from physical and mental harm, the definition of basic security needs can differ between countries. Apparently, German drivers trust properly functioning brakes to ensure automotive safety, while French drivers prefer a powerful engine to ensure their safety. In most cases, however, it is not the definition of the security need that differs between markets, but the manifestation of a specific security need. For example, in many developing countries there is little knowledge and interest among consumers about health and safety hazards. This can be compounded by fatalistic attitudes to life. In many Asian and African countries there is little interest in road safety, as consumers tend to believe that when their time has come, their time has come.

Other higher-level security needs can be based on particular cultural or structural traits of a country. For instance, in Belgium there is a strongly felt need to save money in case of eventualities such as accidents and illness. In the neighbouring Netherlands, no such urge is felt, even though both countries have similar social security and insurance systems, as well as comparable income levels. This is because Belgians are highly uncertainty avoidant, while the Dutch are low uncertainty avoidant (Hofstede, 1991).

Social and affiliation needs

Social and affiliation needs differ considerably across countries. On the one hand, this is because of cultural issues such as collectivism and caste systems; on the other hand social or affiliation needs can be based on nationalism, socio-economic class, religion and ethnicity. A sense of belonging does not always have to stem from one's own socio-cultural background. Some people like to identify with other nationalities or ethnicities, as in the cases of Francophiles and Anglophiles the world over. Another example is the strongly increased popularity of South African wines in the Netherlands, since the end of apartheid. The Dutch consumers seem to be rediscovering some of their kinship with Afrikaners now that it has become politically acceptable to do so again.

Brands can build on such needs for affiliation. Obvious examples are nationalist and patriotic sentiments that surround flag carriers, often nationalized airlines. However, consumers in other countries generally do not have such sentiments towards a foreign flag carrier. This implies that a flag carrier brand has a totally different meaning abroad than it does in its home market.

Brands can also be influenced by the prevalent need to belong to a particular in-group. In-groups tend to vary among societies, and may consist of family, friends, peers, colleagues and so on. Although the importance of family is generally considered higher than that of friends worldwide, the relative differences are large between societies. For example, family is considered equally important in Spain and the Netherlands (82 per cent very important), while the importance of friends in the Netherlands (63 per cent very important) is much higher than in Spain (45 per cent very important) (Inglehart, Basañez and Moreno, 1998). An indication how brands use such affiliation needs is provided by Amstel beer. The brand has run a long campaign in the Netherlands featuring the life and times of three best mates. The same brand, albeit under the brand name Aguila Amstel, is sold in Spain. The Spanish advertising shows the quintessential young and hip, and uses a slogan that goes something like, 'Amstel 100 per cent, malt 100 per cent, people 100 per cent, Aguila Amstel 100 per cent!'

Esteem needs

There are two types of esteem need. There is self-esteem, which results from competence or mastery of a task. Self-esteem needs are reflections of a desire for strength, achievement, adequacy, mastery and competence, confidence in the face of the world, and independence and freedom. The other type of esteem is the attention that comes from others, or the desire for reputation or prestige, status, fame and glory, dominance, recognition, attention, importance, dignity or appreciation.

How self-esteem is expressed differs between societies. In some the expression takes the form of the very visible display of wealth, including related luxury and status brands. For example, in China high-powered business dinners are often accompanied by a bottle of Remy Martin XO brandy. This habit has not come about because successful Chinese businessmen have developed a particularly discerning taste for spirits.

Esteem needs may differ between societies. For instance, in the United States retail customers want active regard by store employees. This takes the form of – in many non-American eyes outlandish – manners, such as profuse greetings, 'Hi, how are you today?', and feigned humbleness: 'How may I be of service?' Many Americans in their turn find most European sales staff to be discourteous, and most Asian sales staff shy and detached. Several US service and retail companies have had to tone down their service styles in societies where such gregariousness is not understood or appreciated.

Cognitive needs

Cognitive needs span a wide variety of different knowledge, learning and experience needs, such as a need for news and information, a need for learning a language, a need to experience specific events and a need for entertainment and thrills. Brands that specifically cater to such needs are Early Learning Centre, Reuters, Lonely Planet, Linguaphone and Disneyland.

Obviously in countries that have low levels of development, cognitive needs manifest themselves mainly in the form of needs for basic education, for traditional forms of entertainment and ritual events. The more developed a country becomes, the more sophisticated and specific these cognitive needs become, such as a general need for further education, a need for instant news, and a need for unique once-in-a-lifetime experiences.

The conventions surrounding cognitive needs differ between generations and cultures. One of the clearest examples is that of the rites of passage that every adolescent experiences. In some societies these rites are formalized into rituals – for instance, circumcision – while in others they are unwritten yet clearly understood – for instance, the first holiday without mom and dad. Some brands cater for coming of age. For example Unilever's Axe (aka Lynx and Ego) brand of deodorant aims to boost young men's confidence by implying – albeit with a dose of absurdity – that they are more attractive to the opposite sex when they use the brand.

Self-actualization needs

Self-actualization needs are based on people's desire to achieve what they are capable of, being able to exploit their own potential. Self-actualization needs differ between countries, because of the existing possibilities – for instance educational and economical – but also because of the appreciation accorded to the manner in which someone exploits his or her talents. In societies where religion plays an important role, it is likely that a significant number of men and women will choose a religious vocation – becoming monks, nuns or priests – in order to fulfil their self-actualization needs. In societies with more secular attitudes, people will be more likely to choose careers as a way of self-actualization.

Self-actualization needs clearly differ between societies, and this is already apparent at a young age. Lindstrom (2003) writes that in worldwide research carried out among so-called tweens (aged 8 to 14), some 90 per cent of Indian youngsters dream of becoming famous, while less than 30 per cent of Japanese youths have the same desire.

Self-actualization can take the form of overcoming obstacles or outdoing oneself. Nike's motto of 'Just do it' is perfectly suited to those who put great stock in physical exercise as a way to self-improvement. One might argue that so-called lifestyle brands are the epitome of self-actualization.

Aesthetic needs

What is considered beautiful or pleasing can differ significantly between countries and cultures. Clear examples are the definitions of what constitutes female beauty, pleasing music, and fine arts. Most western ears are unlikely to appreciate traditional Chinese opera, and conversely most Chinese will not be thrilled by western opera.

Aesthetic needs also impact such mundane merchandise as furniture, as witnessed by the differing tastes in furniture between Scandinavia – ascetic, natural designs – and Italy – intricate stylish designs – not to mention the lavish furniture tastes in Saudi Arabia, a style that is sometimes disparagingly referred to as 'Louis Farouk' (viz Louis XIV).

In Japan, a lot of stock is put in perfection. This is an aesthetic need that encompasses many aspects of Japanese society, ranging from manufacturing to sports and from religion to food. Examples of brands that try to cater to this need for perfection are Lexus automobiles (tag line: We pursue perfection, so you can pursue living) and Shiseido cosmetics (the Shiseido 'meme': beauty and technology). Coca-Cola apparently even introduced a brand called Perfect Water in Japan in 1997.

In many western societies, creative thinking and imagination are considered to be very important and pleasing. This aesthetic need also reaches far and deep into society, as witnessed by the import placed upon creative concepts in education, advertising, business models, fashion and so on.

Transcendence needs

Transcendence needs are a desire to do good for others. These others can be anonymous (such as the poor) or people in one's vicinity (such as children and neighbours). These others can consist of actual persons (such as a sick relative), groups (for example women, children in the Third World), organizations (a local sports club or a church) or constructs (like society and the environment).

Transcendence needs can differ between countries because of structural factors, such as economic and social development, and cultural factors, such as what are considered appropriate benefactors. In cultures that show strong communalist characteristics, it is more likely that the beneficiaries of good deeds will be part of a person's in-group, such as friends, family and clan, while in individualistic societies beneficiaries are more likely to be anonymous, such as the Red Cross and Greenpeace.

The form that such assistance takes will also vary. For instance, in the Netherlands it is common for people to donate limited amounts of money across various charities, usually collected at the door. In the United States it is more common to donate fairly large sums of money to a limited number of organizations, such as a university, a church or a charitable foundation.

Transcendence needs can be driven by motives such as altruism, social obligation or expectation, self-interest, the ability to help, or a combination of these. Needless to say, the import and form of such motives also differ from country to country and between cultures. For instance, in southern Spain shopkeepers tend to give candy to small children, probably based on a combination of altruism – love of children – expectation – it's what shop-keepers do – and self-interest – customer loyalty. In northwest Europe shopkeepers generally do not give candy to children, as parents are horri-fied by the dental health implications for their children, but may accept a piece of sausage or cheese offered by the relevant retail establishment.

CULTURAL CONVENTIONS

Culture is a system of shared beliefs, values, customs and symbols that the members of a society use to cope with their world and with one another. Each society develops specific cultural conventions, which influence the way in which the members are supposed to think and behave. Branding activities are also viewed by consumers in a particular society in the context of cultural conventions.

Beliefs

Beliefs are points of view that members of a society hold to be true. Some beliefs are ancient and typical to a culture, while others are of more recent times and may be shared across a number of cultural groups. The follow-ing types of belief and their associated impacts are relevant to branding.

Religious beliefs

Religious beliefs are mainly concerned with the purity and well-being of the soul. These types of belief often affect consumption – such as kosher and halal foods – hygiene – such as feminine hygiene or personal cleanliness – and communication – for example, prohibiting the depiction of dogs or scantily clad women in advertising.

Beliefs about destiny

There are also beliefs about destiny, which affect ideas about the ability to influence fate and fortune. A good example of such beliefs is the application of the principles of feng shui – a set of traditional Chinese beliefs about influencing fate – to the design of offices, stores and housing. A building that is designed according to these principles, for example the direction of its entrance, will bring good luck to its occupants. The Bank of China tower in Hong Kong is a good example of a building that was not designed with these Feng Shui principles in mind. The angular, reflecting structure is considered inauspicious by the locals, because it seems to cut the air like a knife. The building did little to assuage the existing local apprehensions about this mainland institution.

Beliefs about health

Furthermore, there are beliefs about physical well-being and health, such as the Chinese belief in eating a diet of cool (yin) and hot (yang) foods. A balance of these elements is thought to help keep the body in equilibrium and ward off disease. The classification of foodstuffs as cool or hot is only partially based upon the characteristics of the food. For example, milk is considered cool, while chocolate is considered hot. Thus, the Milka cow is a rather odd symbol for chocolate in such a context.

Social beliefs

In addition, there are social beliefs that affect people's position in society. Good examples are the hereditary caste system in India and the American dream, a belief that anything is possible as long as one tries hard and often enough. Such beliefs have an influence on how people think about themselves and how they behave towards each other. Many US brands are infused with that country's social beliefs, yet they also operate outside their home country where such beliefs are not as strong or are even absent. Harley-Davidson is an epitome of US social beliefs regarding personal freedom, pioneering spirit, independence and adventure. Outside its home country Harley-Davidson's following consists mainly of people who are attracted to such beliefs.

Beliefs about emotions

Everybody has emotional beliefs which affect our views of such issues as happiness, frustration, anger, fear, guilt and shame. In the Philippines, it is widely believed that an unmarried woman cannot be happy. This belief often turns into a self-fulfilling prophecy, because unmarried women feel terrible for not meeting society's expectations.

Economic beliefs

There are economic beliefs that can affect brands. For example, since Deng Xiaoping proclaimed that 'Getting rich is glorious' this has been a commonly held belief in China. No doubt this was supported by China's traditionally materialist values. Brands catering to ostentatious demonstrations of wealth became popular, from foreign brandy to luxury cars. Interestingly, the Chinese also generally believe that thrift is a quality to be encouraged in children (Inglehart *et al*, 1998).

Beliefs about consumption

Whole product and service categories can be influenced by beliefs about consumption. These types of belief affect the usage of particular products or services, such as a general belief in East Asia that only a meal based on rice or rice products (such as noodles) constitutes a decent meal. Western fast food is seldom considered to comprise a meal, but rather a snack which does not fill you up. In South Korea, McDonald's local management had serious discussions about the name for its value meal. The local word for meal, *siksa*, was not acceptable as it connotes a meal based on rice. Finally, management settled on using the English word 'set' (Watson, 1997).

Beliefs about our world

Different societies have differing world views. This translates into conventions revolving around such issues as beliefs about societal progress, beliefs about racial superiority, beliefs about other countries, societies and religions, and so on. These types of belief affect the manner in which consumers view and experience brands. The most typical example of this is the so-called country of origin effect. Consumers often have a set of beliefs or myths about a country which can have a positive or negative influence on how they consider a brand from a particular country. For example, Germany is often associated with engineering excellence, France is associated with romance, Italy is associated with design flair, China is associated with cheap quality products, and so on.

Values

A value system is a learnt organization of principles and rules to help one choose between alternatives, resolve conflicts, and make decisions (Rokeach, 1973). Values are generally somewhat less deep-rooted and unyielding than beliefs, which is shown by the fact that people's values tend to change as they get older and as they get richer. Values also change under the influence of social and economic development, such as industrialization, urbanization and globalization.

In a comparative study among 64 nations and five minorities across all continents, Schwartz (1999) identifies three broad dimensions of values:

▌ autonomy versus embeddedness, which straddles the extremes from broadmindedness and pleasure to obedience and respect;
▌ egalitarianism versus hierarchy, running from equality and honesty to authority and wealth;
▌ harmony versus mastery, running from peace and environmental protection to ambition and daring.

Figure 4.1 shows the prototypical structure of these dimensions. Although these are universal value dimensions, cultures differ in the degree to which they embrace each value type. Schwartz's value typology is based on overall personal values for societies worldwide. Countries or communities can be placed within this framework to show their prevalent values. However, these values are often (somewhat) different for specific product or service categories. For instance, the prevalent values in Germany are egalitarian, but when it comes to beer the most commonly held value is that of respect for tradition. This shows in German beer advertising, which often stresses the history and tradition of beer brands. Until recently, Germany even had a so-called *Reinheitsgebot,* a law that ensured traditional brewing methods were followed. This law was repealed under pressure from the European Union, which considered it to be too protective of German brewers.

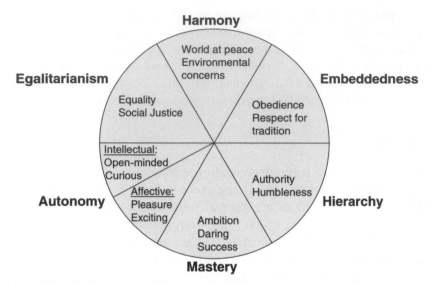

Figure 4.1   *Dimensions of values*

Customs

Customs dictate what is considered acceptable behaviour in societies. As such they can have a strong impact on brands, especially service brands. Ignoring or even offending local customs is probably one of branding's deadly sins. An advertising campaign for jeans that portrayed Buddhist monks as fashion models offended Thais, as monks are supposed to wear only their orange robes. There are various customs that affect branding. These are discussed briefly below.

Rituals and practices

The most obvious types of customs are rituals and practices, as they are clearly observable. Rituals and practices involve ceremonies and rites, but also everyday activities such as greeting. In Japan, business people present their business cards by holding them with both hands, bowing slightly when handing them over, and studying the cards that they receive intently. Practices also include such manifestations of culture as dress, jewellery, organized marriage and housing designs.

Habits

Less obvious, but still clearly evident are habits, such as eating with chopsticks, drinking coffee in the morning and tea in the afternoon, and sleeping on a tatami mat. A television commercial for Asahi beer that was tested in Vietnam left respondents bemused. The characters in the commercial were drinking beer out in the sun. In a tropical country like Vietnam people rather drink their beer in the shade or after sunset when it is cooler. Haig (2003) describes how Kellogg's attempted to introduce Cornflakes in India in 1994 – spending US $65 million in the process – only to find that many Indians have the habit of starting the day with a bowl of hot vegetables. In fact Indians partake of a wide range of break-fasts, such as *paraatha* (wholewheat unleavened flatbread filled with cooked ground meat or a vegetable mixture) and *dosa* (a savoury crepe), depending on their regional background. Not only did Kellogg's need to promote Cornflakes, it also needed to create an entire category in the subcontinent.

Manners

Somewhat more difficult to fathom as a foreigner are local manners. For instance, it is considered rude in Thailand for someone to point a foot, and especially the sole of the foot, at someone else. In the United States, it is the custom that someone helping you in a store smiles profusely at you, while in East Asia a smiling store attendant is considered to be rude: he or she clearly knows something the customer does not!

Conduct

Related to manners is the area of conduct, which is effectively public manners. Conduct prescribes how one is supposed to behave as a member of society. Examples of conduct are refraining from littering, not spitting in public places, showing no emotion in public and queuing up. In fact, there is an urban myth in Hong Kong that McDonald's taught the local population how to queue up when the restaurant chain entered the then colony in 1975 (Watson, 1997). Queuing up was deemed necessary for McDonald's service system to work. The customary free-for-all that ensued in those days at bus stops and ticket windows in Hong Kong would have wrecked McDonald's chances of success in the territory.

Symbols

Symbols not only provide instant recognition, more importantly they contain specific meanings. Some symbols that are perfectly acceptable in one culture are totally unacceptable in others. One of the most apparent symbol conflicts exists between the western interpretation of the swastika as a symbol of Nazi hatred, and the Buddhist interpretation, where the swastika (depicted in mirror image) is considered to be a symbol of love.

Images

A symbol can consist of an image, such as a painting, statue, drawing or photograph. Throughout history, images have been used as symbols. Shiva, the Hindu god of destruction and fertility, is often depicted as a *lingam*, either in the form of a realistic phallus or in the more abstract form of a pillar. More recent and mundane images can also bring out all sorts of associations. In some countries, the image of a smokestack is a symbol of progress, while in others it is a symbol of degradation. Benetton used strong images in its print and billboard advertising, such as those of a dying Aids patient and of a victim of a mafia hit, as a form of consumer provocation.

Persons and icons

Other symbols are actual persons or icons. Saint Valentine is considered a symbol of love in Anglo-Saxon countries. Increasingly, the habit of celebrating Valentine's Day is being take up in other countries, however without recognizing the saint's religious background. Che Guevara was a popular symbol of rebellion in the 1960s and 1970s, and massive amounts of merchandise bearing his photo, taken by Cuban photographer Alberto Diaz Gutierrez (aka Korda), were moved during this period. The Japanese mouthless cat called Hello Kitty is a very popular symbol of young female innocence in large parts of Asia. Young women across the region wear backpacks, use pens and diaries adorned with Hello Kitty, and have little Hello Kitty dolls on their desks. A similar rabbit-like character, called Nijntje in its home country the Netherlands and Miffy elsewhere, is accorded a similar status in Japan. However, in most countries it is considered a symbol of child-like innocence.

Animals and natural elements

Symbols also include animals and natural elements. Crickets in China are a symbol of prosperity, cranes in Japan are symbols of fidelity, prosperity and longevity, lions are traditionally considered a symbol of strength in the Netherlands, mountains and rocks are often considered symbols of steadfastness, bamboo a symbol of perseverance, and a star a symbol of hope. La Vache Qui Rit uses a laughing cow, as a symbol of nature and abundance. The cow symbol has different meanings in various societies. To Hindus the cow is a sacred animal. To the Masai cows are a symbol of wealth. In Argentina, the cow is now a symbol of lost past riches.

Sounds

Sounds can also be symbols, for example, the sound of a train whistle symbolizing the romance of travel, the sound of a sledgehammer symbolizing progress, the sound of rain and wind symbolizing tranquillity, and particular mobile phone ringtones represent disturbance. Sounds have long been used to identify brands, such as the Intel four-tone jingle and the fizz of Alka-Seltzer.

Colours

Colours also have powerful symbolic meanings which differ between cultures. Blue symbolizes confidence and solidity in many western societies. It is not surprising that dependable IBM chooses blue as its corporate colour. Red and gold (or yellow) symbolize good fortune in East Asia. Shanghai Tang, which has set out to become the first global Chinese lifestyle brand, uses these colours generously in its stores and collections.

Language

Language is probably the ultimate conveyor of symbolism. Symbolism is particularly evident in written language, as the characters used can each have their own meaning, which is particularly true in oriental character-based languages such as Chinese and Japanese. Korean script itself is a potent symbol of national independence and achievement.

5

The brand domain

INTRODUCTION

The situational factors discussed in the previous chapter have a profound impact on how brands are perceived by consumers in different societies. This and the following two chapters deal with the way in which brands are perceived. Each chapter introduces a specific brand typology that is formed in the minds of consumers, because of particular brand expression and marketing activities. In addition, these three chapters deal with the sensitivity of each typology to particular conventions which were introduced in Chapter 4.

The brand perception is defined as the total impression that consumers have of a brand, based on their exposure to the brand. This consists of both the image that consumers form of the brand and their experience with the brand. Obviously not each person gets the same exposure to a brand, and some brands have a strong mental image among consumers without generating much experience – for example luxury brands – while the perception of other brands – for instance household cleaners – will be more experience-based.

This book argues that the brand perception is actually the starting point for branding strategies, rather than the brand expression. This is because the brand expression is merely concerned with manifesting the brand, while the brand perception consists of the consumers' experience, which is supposed to accomplish specific behaviour among consumers that will realize the business strategy. It is therefore imperative for brand management to have a clear understanding of their brand's perception among specific groups of consumers in various societies, as well as an appreciation of the lenses and filters that help shape those perceptions. When a brand is introduced into a foreign society, brand management must define the desired perception and must try to anticipate the situational effects on that perception.

THE BRAND DOMAIN DEFINED

The brand domain is an element of the brand perception. The brand perception is formed by consumers' experiences with a brand, effectively their experience with the brand expression, its subsequent translation into the marketing mix and implementation activities, and consumers' examination of the organization's activities through the lenses and filters formed by the various types of conventions that were discussed in Chapter 4.

Brand domain aspects

The brand domain is defined by what consumers understand the actual offer of the brand to be. In other words, the brand domain consists of:

▪ *What* the brand offers. This concerns the products and services provided under the brand name, including all the product and service attributes.
▪ *How* consumers learn about the brand. These are the various forms of media and events employed to communicate about the brand, as well as word of mouth.
▪ *Where* the brand can be obtained. This has to do with the distribution channels or outlets that help get the brand into the hands of consumers.
▪ *Which* solutions the brand offers to consumers. This involves the way in which a brand resolves problems or deals with inconveniences with which consumers are faced.

Figure 5.1 shows the brand domain as a set of axes along which extensions or contractions of the domain dimensions take place. A development on one axis does not necessarily entail a development on another axis. More often than not, developments (such as product innovations, new service concepts, communications integration, online purchases) take place on one dimension at a time. For example, when a bank introduces online banking services it seldom introduces new products at the same time.

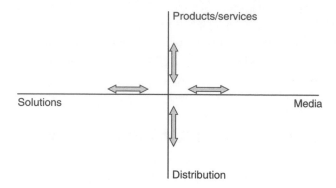

Figure 5.1   *Dimensions of the brand domain*

Brand domain specialists

Brand domain specialists are perceived by consumers to be experts on one or more of the domain's dimensions, namely products and services, media, distribution and solutions. A brand domain specialist consistently tries to pre-empt or even dictate particular domain developments. This requires an intimate knowledge, not only of the technologies shaping the category, but also of pertinent consumer behaviour and needs. The lifeblood of a brand domain specialist is innovation and creative use of the brand's resources.

Domain specialists are under constant pressure to offer consumers innovation or novelty. This requires these brands to place a great emphasis on research and development, and the subsequent road to market of innovations. The cost of many product and service innovations is on a scale that transcends most geographic boundaries. Product and service specialists are almost forced onto a global stage, and business strategies reflect this: global product roll-outs, global alliances and worldwide technology standards.

The focus on innovation means that these brands seldom put much stock in their internal legacies and conventions. Brand managers know from experience that intransigence spells decline for their brands. A lack of significant innovations in the pipeline is a major vulnerability for product and services specialists. Domain specialists therefore need to either establish new conventions themselves (through a successful challenge) or not enter a particular market at all. Information and communications technology (ICT) companies have had the advantage of establishing conventions without having to challenge existing category conventions.

They have had the opportunity to shape their category. This is why many ICT companies have been able to establish highly standardized global brands.

Consumers will typically classify domain specialists as leaders, contenders, also-rans and flankers – not that they will necessarily use these terms. However, consumers perceive one (maybe two) *leaders* in categories that are dominated by domain specialists, and many will opt for such a winner, such as Nokia, Sony, Amazon and Visa. *Contenders* are those brands that seem to offer similar products and services as leaders, but never quite make the mark for various reasons. Contenders are, however, within consumers' evoked set of brands, and are considered and regularly purchased. Examples are Ericsson, Philips, Barnes and Noble, and Amex. *Also-rans* are those brands that appear not to be able to provide products and services that are up to the standards of the leaders and contenders, such as Sagem, Aiwa, Bertelsmann Online (BOL) and Diners Card. *Flankers* are often brands that come from an adjacent category and offer products and services that are dissimilar to those of the established brands in the category.

Microsoft is acting as a flanker by moving into the mobile phone market with its PocketPC, a move aimed at establishing Windows CE as the standard operating system for third-generation mobile phones instead of Symbian. Mobile phone operator O2 already offers an XDA, which is combination of a PocketPC and mobile phone specifically designed for O2. Intel is trying to enter the digital portable audio category with the Pocket Concert , which boasts four hours of music and USB PC connectivity among other things. Walmart.com is trying to extend its philosophy of a wide selection of products and everyday low prices to the Web. Paybox offers consumer payment services at retailers by mobile phone in Germany, France and the UK.

The influence of brand expression on the brand domain

Being considered as a brand domain specialist is often the result of a brand expression that rests heavily on positioning. Matters such as features, benefits, usage, problem solving and value for money largely shape the perceived brand domain. The other two brand expression elements, brand identity and brand personality, can enhance the positioning but retain a secondary role in forming the brand domain. However, brand identity is becoming an increasingly important form of brand expression for domain specialists. This is because there is a growing interest among consumers about the company behind a brand, and because domain specialists increasingly extend their brands across several (adjacent) categories in order to capitalize on the efficiencies of scope offered by a single brand name. This means that consumers look beyond the product or service offered and more at the background, the principles, the ambitions and the symbolism of the brand.

Domain specialists often are seen to excel on one or more of the domain dimensions, and therein rests their value to consumers. The following paragraphs look at these focused strategies and the situational factors that impact upon them.

PRODUCT AND SERVICE SPECIALISTS

Product and service specialists are the classic examples of brand domain specialization. These are brands that are perceived by consumers as providing a constant stream of new and inventive products and services. These new products and services function as a kind of constant reiteration of the brand, and ensure that the brand retains vitality in the eyes of consumers. Research and development into new products and services are all-important to such brands, as is an exceptional understanding of consumers' needs regarding the category. The heavy investments involved mean that a product specialist needs sufficient scale to be able to offer innovations at reasonable prices.

Gillette is the dominant razor brand, because of its superiority in research and development of new razors, coupled with its in-depth understanding of shaving needs. The ability to offer regular innovations provides the brand with a decisive edge over much smaller competition such as Wilkinson. Iridium, the mobile satellite phone operator, did not have this kind of consumer knowledge and failed miserably when it introduced a service that few felt a need for. Most people already had excellent alternatives to the expensive and unwieldy system.

If a product specialist lacks sufficient scale to dictate industry standards, it needs to cooperate with competitors. This often means that the effects of innovations for the brand are diluted. A case in point is Philips, a company that has produced many innovations in consumer electronics, but was unable to capitalize fully on its expertise. Philips needs to share its inventions with Sony and Matsushita in order to ensure that industry standards are agreed and systems are interoperable.

There are also service specialists which concentrate on constantly providing new and innovative services. Singapore Airlines is well known for its service innovations, such as mobile flight information, its first class

Sky Suites with turn-down service and down-filled duvet, its advance Book the Cook menu selection, and free SMS services for all passengers.

A special form of product specialization is a focus on value. Value specialists are determined to consistently offer consumers quality products or services at budget price points. The budget airlines such as Southwest, easyJet and Ryanair are such value specialists. Consumers can be sure that when they book with any of these they are paying one of the lowest airfares (if not the lowest) on a particular route. Innovation for value specialists concentrates on offering increased value at the same or lower price points, or by offering additional budget offers, such as low-cost car hire and hotel accommodation.

Brand expression and product and service specialists

The brand expression of product and service specialists is strongly dependent on positioning, and drives a marketing mix that focuses on the product or service features and benefits. Motorola recently introduced the V70 mobile phone, which twists open rather than flips open. This is a major design innovation offering unique style and refinement to the fashion-conscious, or so the company wants us to believe. It remains to be seen whether consumers think so too, and whether twisting your phone open is really such a spectacular novelty. Product specialists, certainly in a highly competitive and saturated category such as mobile phones, are prone to heralding minor product adjustments as major innovations.

Although adding features to a product may provide value to consumers, it seldom provides a brand with lasting advantage over the competition. However, by consistently offering new features a brand can reinforce the entire brand proposition. A case in point is Nokia which, by continuously offering new features, reinforces its brand proposition centred upon innovation. In 2001 Nokia launched 15 new products. In 2002 this number doubled to 30. Nokia also moves faster than its competition in introducing new features such as a built-in camera, which was introduced six months ahead of competition in the fiercely competitive European marketplace (Fast Company, 2003).

Another brand positioning aspect employed by product and service specialists is *benefits*. For example, Procter and Gamble's Head and Shoulders shampoo offers the benefit of controlling dandruff. Benefits positioning offers better possibilities for brand value and sustainable advantages over competition. This is because consumers are generally more interested in the benefits rather than the features of a product or service, and because a benefit that has been successfully claimed is not easily copied by a competitor. Unless the competitor can successfully up the claim, its brand is likely to be seen as an also-ran.

Usage is a positioning aspect employed for products and services that have a particular connection with an activity or time of day. A typical usage positioning is that for Gatorade sports drink, which is used as a body liquid replenishment during physical exercise.

Value specialists typically use *price* or *value for money*, which are tried and tested positioning aspects. The advantage of price or value positioning is that claiming a (relative) price point or value for money is difficult to achieve in the long term. For instance, a low-cost airline such as easyJet is only able to maintain this positioning by gearing the entire organization to this purpose. Not only does easyJet communicate its budget prices, it also ensures that the customer touch points communicate this budget proposition. Bookings are done solely over the Internet and through a call centre, passengers are provided with a booking code instead of a ticket, mostly secondary airports are used, no meals are served on board and drinks are charged for.

The brand identity aspects of *roots and heritage* are used to infuse product and service specialists with a corporate mythology. For example, the Apple computer brand is well known not only for its innovation, but also for its founding history of two geeks in a garage. The mythology enhances the brand and helps cement brand loyalty with those averse to the Wintel monopoly.

Values are employed to augment a brand's corporate responsibility. BP not only manufactures and distributes hi-tech oil products but also cares about the environment, and thus also invests in renewable energy sources. Unfortunately most values extolled by domain specialists ring somewhat hollow, and quickly sound surprisingly similar: professional, ambitious, caring, result-oriented, inventive and so on.

The brand personality aspect of *competence* is used by product and service specialists. Competence is the trait that many product and service specialists feel most at ease with, because it expresses their mastery of their particular domain dimension. HP expresses this personality trait by adding 'invent' to its corporate logo and with its slogan of 'The new power of invention'.

Product and service specialists often challenge conventions of *product and service experience*, as this is within the main area of their competencies. Dyson challenged such conventions by developing a vacuum cleaner that had continuous suction power and did not use dust bags. The dust and fluff swirl around in Dyson vacuum cleaners for the user to see. This challenge was very successful in the UK. Dyson held a 30 per cent market share by volume in the UK by 2001. UK consumers, used to the upright

Hoover models which had limited suction power, had been ready for a new type of vacuum cleaner. Dyson's first model, the DC01, conformed to conventions by being an upright model but showed much better perform-ance. In continental Europe, consumers are more used to sleigh model vacuum cleaners. Upright models are considered old-fashioned and diffi-cult to handle. Dyson could not successfully challenge these fairly solid product experience conventions on the continent.

Conventions and product and service specialists

Product and service specialists are often susceptible to *beliefs* surrounding their categories. Such beliefs are particularly apparent in traditional cate-gories such as foodstuffs, detergents, washing powder, personal care and automobiles. Kapferer (1997) describes how Procter and Gamble misjudged the sensitivity of dandruff as a social problem, worthy of sympathy, when launching Head and Shoulders in France. Procter and Gamble's approach was to use the same advertising as in Britain and the Netherlands, with the slogan, 'Dandruff talks behind your back'. This advertising was based on the belief that one should be ashamed of having dandruff rather than eliciting sympathy.

Service specialists are prone to local *customs* which dictate how customers should be served. A new service concept needs to take into account what is acceptable behaviour by sales and service staff, what are correct appellations on printed matter and Web sites, and how much personal responsibility staff are expected to take during customer critical incidents. The familiar 'Hi, how are you today?' approach by US service staff is considered unbecoming by most Europeans, and in East Asia such staff are supposed to perform their tasks with determination rather than a smile. In the early days in Hong Kong, McDonald's sales staff demeanour had to be adapted from service with a smile to service with a frown in order for customers not to feel uncomfortable with them (Watson, 1997).

Because of their focus on innovation and novelty, product and service specialists often appeal to consumers' *cognitive needs*. In most cases, this is an appeal to a need for new experiences. Singapore Airlines is very good at consistently introducing service innovations in order to provide new experiences to its regular passengers.

Value specialists are perceived as catering to one cognitive need only, namely affordability. At the same time, value specialists are particularly susceptible to *security needs*. Consumers want to see these satisfied before trying the value specialists' product or service. For instance, any doubts about budget airlines' safety will keep consumers away. In the case of distributors' own brands, it is the brand equity of the distributor that allays such fears. Obviously, the significance of the security needs depend on what consumers stand to lose in terms of money, time, temper, illusions, health and life.

MEDIA SPECIALISTS

Media specialists have a rather unusual kind of domain specialization, namely one that involves communicating with consumers in new and novel ways. Media specialists are brands that regularly seek ways of innovating and integrating the media they use to communicate with consumers. Media specialists succeed in stimulating consumer engagement. For this, they need to have a thorough understanding of available media, the manner in which consumers use and perceive these, and creativity in the use of these media.

Heineken is one of the major global beer brands due to its innovative use of various forms of (integrated) media. Although Heineken strives for a global brand proposition, the brand is largely tailored to local circumstances. Heineken's marketing mix and media use are defined by global brand management only in general terms, modified for each of the brand's development stages: anchor, build and star stage. This requires hands-on involvement of local brand management to define the marketing mix and manage implementation. During the Sydney Olympics, Heineken staged an award-winning integrated media campaign involving television, radio, posters and stickers to promote the Heineken Green Line, a free bus service through the city centres of Sydney and Melbourne. The service ran for 16 weeks around the time of the Olympic games. In Hong Kong, Heineken managed to register more than 33,000 members on a Web site encouraging people to collect Heineken crown corks at bars and restaurants. Members could bid for limited Heineken memorabilia using their collected crown corks.

Brand expression and media specialists

Brand expression elements used can vary considerably between media specialists. Even the same brand may use varying elements in different markets. Usage, in the form of a link between the media employed and the place where the brand is consumed, is common. In the case of the Heineken Music Hall in Amsterdam, the medium itself is a place of consumption.

Media specialists often employ brand personality traits such as *excitement and sophistication* in order to move the brand beyond the often-generic product and service attributes. Beginning in the United States in 1985, Camel introduced the 'Cool Joe Camel' cartoon character in a multitude of media: magazines, billboards, T-shirts, hats, lighters, matchbook covers and so on. The campaign, devised by New York ad agency Mezzina/Brown, was eventually discontinued in the United States because of pressure from the Food and Drug Administration (FDA) on parent company R J Reynolds. The campaign continues abroad.

Conventions and media specialists

Media specialists are by nature particularly sensitive to conventions of *media*, as these determine which media channels (and their combinations) are acceptable to consumers, and the value consumers attach to such media. For example, different societies attach differing value to particular types of sports, and therefore to sports sponsorship. This does not mean only that brand management need to choose sports that carry particular relevance in a society (such as rugby in Ireland, or cricket in India) but also that the sponsorship reinforces the brand proposition. In China, where football (soccer to the US reader) is a relatively new sport, it is associated with modernism. Pepsi is the sponsor of the Chinese National Football League to reinforce its proposition as being the choice of a new generation. In England, football is deeply rooted and carries connotations of tradition. The English Premiership is sponsored by solid financial services brand Barclaycard.

In striving to provide specific brand experiences, media specialists need to take into account consumers' *cognitive needs*. Unlike product and service specialists, media specialists are not always looking to provide novel experiences, but rather seek to reinforce the brand experience through reiteration. In its various guises – television, Internet, print advertising – CNBC Europe seeks to reassure consumers that it is a prime source of financial news coverage.

DISTRIBUTION SPECIALISTS

Distribution specialists are constantly seeking new ways of getting their products into the hands of consumers. They know that the availability of their brand is the driving factor for consumers to use it. A brand can only be considered a distribution specialist if consumers perceive the brand to be available at all relevant outlets or locations.

Mars is a typical distribution specialist. Some 70 per cent of confectionery is bought on impulse, which means that the purchase is unplanned. Thus, the distribution of such products needs to be far and wide. Mars and its sister brands Bounty, Snickers and Twix are available in outlets ranging from supermarket check-out counters to news stands, tobacconists and filling stations. In addition, Mars provides all sorts of venues with vending machines free on loan in return for a share in the profits. In fact, Mars Electronics International (MEI) developed the first electronic coin validator in the late 1960s in response to a need for reliable machines to vend the Mars bar. Mars currently has one of the world's largest installed bases of vending machines.

By rebranding its local banks, such as Midland Bank and Hong Kong Bank, HSBC clearly wants to emphasize its worldwide network. Its advertising, aimed at demonstrating local knowledge, albeit in a whimsical fashion, has the tag line, 'Never underestimate the importance of local knowledge'. This is aimed at convincing us that HSBC is 'The world's local bank'.

A special form of distribution specialization is that of payment cards. It is imperative that a card brand is widely accepted for it to be successful. Credit card companies put a lot of effort into persuading retailers to accept their cards, and to demonstrate that fact by prominently displaying the credit card decal. Seeing the decal and finding that the card is indeed accepted makes such a card brand worthwhile to consumers.

Brand expression and distribution specialists

Usage is often the main positioning aspect employed by distribution specialists. Many snack food brands are promoted to be eaten in between meals, which is underpinned by their wide availability. Credit card brands also tend to position themselves on usage. Visa uses numerous tag lines around the world for this purpose: 'How the world pays', 'It's everywhere you want to be', 'The world's best way to pay' and 'All it takes'.

Visual identity is an important aspect of distribution specialists' brand expression, as they often rely on instant recognition. That is why the logos of such brands are so ubiquitous around the world: Coca-Cola, Mars, Ola/Wall's, Kodak, Visa and the like.

Conventions and distribution specialists

Obviously, distribution specialists need to be sensitive to conventions of *distribution*, the acceptability or value to consumers of certain forms of distribution. Stockbrokers long imagined that consumers would be unwilling to trade equities through an impersonal medium. Charles Schwab showed that consumers did not value the conventions of distribution as much as was expected, and were rather keen on the new form of online trading. However, the value that consumers attach to specific distribution channels does differ between societies. CNN distributes its news services through various media, such as satellite television, radio, the Internet and mobile phones. The willingness of consumers to partake in each of these channels differs from country to country. For instance, Internet penetration and usage is lower in southern than in northern Europe.

SOLUTIONS SPECIALISTS

A solution specialist is able to bundle its products and services, media and distribution in such a way that these solve specific problems for consumers, which the individual products and services, media and distribution cannot. Combining the three other domain elements to provide consumers with hitherto unheard-of solutions means that solutions providers have strong business strategy skills. These involve a very clear vision on the market, a very compelling definition of the company mission and a very strong ambition, coupled with the competencies and resources to make it all work. The case of Amazon.com shows that being able to combine these qualities can quickly lead to building a world-renowned brand. Amazon.com also shows that first mover advantage is important for solutions specialists, as imitators spring up quickly. However, being first to market is not enough to stay in the lead. A solutions specialist must also be able to keep on providing value over and above the competition. Amazon does so through its large and ever-expanding selection of products, its online customer reviews and simply through delivering the goods as promised.

Microsoft is the dominant computer software brand, because it provides unrivalled solutions to both consumers and business users. Microsoft is seldom the first to develop a specific software application, but is very good at replicating and incorporating applications that others have devised. By doing so, Microsoft provides an all-important interoperability solution to users: files that can be shared, similar interfaces that require little additional learning, drag and drop copying between applications, ease of installation. In fact Microsoft mainly provides users with peace of mind, as they do not need to worry about their choice of software.

eBay bills itself as 'The world's online marketplace' and states its mission as follows: 'To help anyone trade practically anything on earth' (www.ebay.com). By combining such services as access to its online auction, billing services, shipping services, fraud protection and dispute resolution eBay offers a complete trade solution.

Sikkens Car Refinishes, a brand of chemical and pharmaceutical corporation Akzo Nobel, offers not only innovative automotive paint, but also advice on how to improve the efficiency and hence the profitability of body shops. Only if body shop owners are convinced that these improvements will increase their profitability are three to five year contracts signed for Sikkens' car paint. In addition, Sikkens offers training to body shop staff – car spray painters and management – at over 60 Car Refinishing Instruction Centres (CRIC) worldwide (Het Financieele Dagblad, 2002b).

Brand expression and solutions specialists

Solutions specialists typically employ *problem solving* as their primary form of brand positioning, which is in fact the narrow definition of a solution. Examples are Tide's stain removal properties, the convenience offered by Bird's Eye frozen ready-to-eat meals, and the ease of no maintenance offered by Acuvue disposable contact lenses.

The brand identity aspects *purpose and ambitions* are used by solutions specialists to demonstrate that a brand has a vision of the future and a role to play in that envisioned future. Microsoft not only brings us new and improved Windows and Office software, it also has a vision about the future of home and office computing: the dot Net initiative.

Conventions and solutions specialists

All solutions specialists are prone to *security needs*, as consumers need to have confidence that the brand will indeed deliver on its pledge. Once a solutions provider has won consumers' confidence its position can become extremely strong. Microsoft thrives on security needs, as few consumers or business decision makers dare opt for another software provider, because of the anticipated cost of switching, the incompatibility of files and applications, the relearning of software skills and the like.

However, in some societies consumers are more risk averse than in others. In Japan 7-Eleven expanded its e-commerce offerings with the launch of a Web site called 7dream.com. According to the company, 7dream.com shoppers can browse through more than 100,000 items, including music, flowers and photo supplies, place their orders online, then go to their local 7-Eleven stores to pay for and collect their purchases.

Other Japanese e-commerce ventures have established a system that allows consumers to purchase items over the Internet and make payments in cash at convenience stores. BOL Japan, the Japanese Internet subsidiary of Bertelsmann AG, offers that option to its Web bookstore shoppers, and also transacts credit card sales on its site (Enos and Blakey, 2001).

Solutions providers can also be susceptible to other *needs conventions*. For instance, McDonald's is in many ways a solutions provider by offering a way to indulge your kids (transcendence needs), by offering uniformity of products to travellers (security needs), by offering a modern experience to consumers in developing countries (cognitive needs), and by being a hangout for Asian young women (social needs).

CONCLUSION

The brand domain is a particularly important part of the brand perception, as it is probably the most transparent element for consumers. This is an area where consumers can judge quality and novelty of products and services, where they can gauge the brand's communications, where they can sample the brand's distribution strengths and where they can decide whether a brand truly offers a solution to one of their inconveniences. Being perceived as a master of (parts of) the domain can provide a brand with a clear advantage over its competition. It is no wonder that domain specialists are among the world's largest and ubiquitous brands.

The next two chapters deal with the two other brand perception elements, reputation and affinity. These elements can provide value to consumers and competitive advantages in their own way by exploiting 'softer' aspects of the brand.

Case: Station 12 (currently Xantic)

As the satellite communications division of Dutch telecommunications company KPN, Station 12 traditionally offered various Inmarsat services, mainly to the maritime sector, the military (or peacekeeping) sector, aid organizations and governments. These services included analogue and digital voice, telex and data services. With its own Land Earth Station (LES) at Burum in the Netherlands, and a partnership with KDD of Japan for the use of its LES, Station 12 was able to provide worldwide access through geo-stationary satellites, which retain a fixed position in relation to a place on earth. These satellites orbit a few hundred kilometres over the Equator. Station 12 was primarily known for the reliability of its LES, which is a function of operational dependability, speed of connections, voice quality and few interruptions. The name, Station 12, was derived from the numerical position of its LES on the dial of Inmarsat satellite terminals: 12.

Gaining increased independence from KPN in the mid-1990s, Station 12 decided to strike out on a route of innovative services. In the beginning these innovations concentrated on bringing in new, or enhancing existing, Inmarsat services. In the maritime sector this meant offering Inmarsat-based services such as high-speed data links for large-volume data, light and cost-effective terminals for smaller ships, and e-mail and messaging solutions. In the (newer) land market, innovations included Inmarsat mobile satphones, and tracking and tracing services for truck fleets.

Shifting the brand perception from what was essentially one based on reputation to one that was domain-driven proved to be difficult and dependent on local circumstances. Station 12's brand perception was especially entrenched in the maritime sector, where it had a long and successful history of dependability. This brand perception was not as prevailing in the land-based market, because of a limited exposure to the brand. It was Station 12's explicit aspiration to gain ground in the land-based market, as this segment was largely untapped for satellite services.

Studies were conducted into the potential of the various innovative products and services. In the maritime sector these studies focused mainly on offering new value-added services, such as online billing, fleet-wide e-mail and various ways of reducing satellite communications costs. One piece of research was into a so-called two-stage access service for shore to ship communications. This service works roughly like the callback services for fixed line telephones which sprang up in the 1990s as a way of reducing international calling costs. As Inmarsat satellite communications can be prohibitively expensive, the idea seemed appropriate. The study consisted of interviewing decision makers in a number of countries, among them Germany, Singapore and the United States.

In Germany, decision makers wondered whether Deutsche Telecom would allow them to use the service. They worried that, by circumventing the national telecoms company, they would risk being denied service altogether.

German respect for authority was getting in the way of innovation. In Singapore, decision makers were delighted with the prospect of saving money on their satellite communications. The practical materialist attitude of Singaporeans was conducive to service acceptance. In the United States, a fair number of the decision makers interviewed revealed that they were using regional satellite services rather than Inmarsat. This was in part because many US merchant and cruise ships never stray far from the continental United States. The regional satellite operators were offering continuous online services at a fixed cost irrespective of traffic, rather than the Inmarsat dial-up services with a connect and time charge. From a perspective of cost control, this made a lot of sense to the decision makers. The conventions of service experience were therefore totally different from what Station 12 had to offer.

In the land-based market, the studies concentrated mainly on new products and services such as tracking and tracing, remote measurement, messaging and various means of communications from remote sites, such as construction sites, oil exploration rigs and manufacturing sites in developing countries. One such study was into the potential for Station 12's Altus satphone. This phone was small and light by the standards of the time, being the size and weight of a laptop computer. This made it possible for the first time to carry a satphone rather than being consigned to a vehicle. The cost of the terminal (approx US $2,000) and the traffic charges (approx US $2 per minute) were low compared with other satellite services.

Again the study was conducted through personal interviews with business decision makers in a number of countries, including the Ukraine and Indonesia. In the Ukraine, the decision makers were impressed, or to be more precise overawed, by the Altus. This was because fixed-line services were largely unavailable and unreliable, even in the capital Kiev. The gap between shoddy communist-era telecommunications services and the Altus satphone was simply too wide to be crossed in one go. The Ukraine decision makers decided they would first await the advent of mobile phone networks in their country. The challenge by Station 12's Altus to the conventions of service experience was too much for the Ukrainians.

In Indonesia, the businesspeople interviewed felt little need for such an expensive and unwieldy contraption as the Altus. This was because they had the impression that their mobile phones already offered complete worldwide coverage. They meant that they spent almost all their time in urban areas in Indonesia or other Asian countries, and had excellent mobile phone coverage there. These wealthy Indonesian urbanites did not feel the least inclination to venture into the countryside if they could help it. Indonesia's hierarchic society proved to be one obstacle on Station 12's path.

These few examples show that Station 12 had a struggle on its hands when trying to introduce innovations around the world. Even in such a relatively young and fast-changing industry as satellite communications it was faced with various local beliefs, customs and conventions of service experience which hindered the development of brand's desired perception into that of a specialist service provider. By widening its offer of satellite services to include non-Inmarsat services, as well as concentrating more on providing solutions (such as private networks and content distribution) and satellite broadband Internet access, Station 12 did manage to become recognized as one of the most innovative players in its industry.

In 2001 Station 12 merged with the satellite division of Australian telecoms company Telstra and with SpecTec, an enterprise resource planning (ERP) software developer for the maritime industry, to form a new entity called Xantic. On the announcement of the merger Knut Reed, the company's then CEO, commented, 'Today sees the birth of the world's leading provider of satellite-based business solutions of connection, content, consultancy, applications and transactions, one that brings more of our customer's worlds into range. Through providing innovative and reliable services to customers across the world, we expect Xantic will be the number one choice for organizations across the globe.'

(Taken from Xantic press release, 19 March 2001)

6

The brand reputation

THE BRAND REPUTATION DEFINED

In Chapter 5 the brand domain was introduced to define the brand's offer as perceived by consumers. The domain is only part of the entire brand perception, which is formed by consumers' experiences with the brand. In this chapter, we discuss the brand reputation, or – in plain English – what consumers perceive the brand to stand for. A brand's reputation provides it with authenticity, credibility or reliability. A brand reputation consists of certain qualities that consumers ascribe to the brand.

Types of brand reputation

There are three types of reputation qualities, namely those that are:

▌ *Contextual* to the brand. These aspects consist of matters such as the brand's birthright, its lineage, its past or current locality, and its creator or founder. The importance of such contextual traits rests on their ability to provide legitimacy and assurance to a brand.

▌ *Intrinsic* to the brand. These are qualities or strengths that the brand has developed over the years and that form the basis of expectations of – or even outright promises by – a brand.

▌ *Associative* to the brand. These are qualities that are attributed to the brand through its association with others, such as experts, famous persons or particular groups of consumers, as well as other brands. Qualities are either sanctioned by or rub off from these third parties on the brand.

Then there are reputation qualities that are specific to a product or service category, while other qualities can transcend category boundaries. The latter kind of reputation allows brands to extend their product or service offers beyond their category, although not all brands in such a position choose to do so. Figure 6.1 provides an overview of the six types of brand reputation that arise from the combination of the reputation qualities of a brand.

Brand reputation specialists

Brand reputation specialists use or develop the specific qualities of their brands to support their authenticity, credibility or reliability over and above that of competitors. A brand reputation specialist needs to have some kind of *history, legacy or mythology*. It also needs to be able to narrate these in a convincing manner, and be able to live up to the resulting reputation. A brand reputation specialist has to have a very good under-standing of which stories will convince consumers that the brand is in some way superior.

Reputation specialists are a diverse bunch, some of whom rely heavily upon their pedigrees while others leverage their connections to celebrities, and yet others build on a promise that they have demonstrably been able to keep. Reputation specialists are often good at tweaking their brands to ensure relevance to consumers in specific societies. This often means that brand management needs to be largely localized, with a guiding task for global management. It also means that competencies such as consumer understanding and narration need to be available locally.

Among the brand expression elements, the brand identity has the most influence on the brand's reputation. The choice of which aspects of the

Relation	Qualities		
	Contextual	*Intrinsic*	*Associative*
Category specific	Pedigree brands	Quality brands	Endorsed brands
Category transcendent	Origin brands	Promise brands	Personality brands

Figure 6.1   *The six types of brand reputation*

brand identity to emphasize needs to be based on the current reputation among consumers, and the direction in which brand management wishes to steer the reputation. This direction may differ between markets, or brand management may want to harmonize the reputation and bring diverging reputations together.

The following paragraphs discuss the six types of brand reputation specialization and the impact that situational factors can have on them.

PEDIGREE BRANDS

Pedigree brands have reputations circumscribed by their particular contexts, or backgrounds that are specific to the brands' product or service category (see Figure 6.2). Pedigree brands are often connected to a region, a legacy or a founder. The pedigree implies to consumers that the brand has special qualities that cannot be matched by competition who lack that specific background. A pedigree can extend to various brands in a geographic area, such as the Champagne region in France. The geographic background ensures that brands such as Moët & Chandon, Veuve Clicquot and Bollinger have a reputation unmatched by sparkling wines from other regions and countries.

A brand's legacy can also provide it with a pedigree that makes it desirable over other brands in its category. Ferrari's legacy of motor racing provides the brand with an authenticity that cannot be matched by other supercar brands such as Maserati, Lotus and Aston Martin, not to mention more common brands such as Mercedes, Honda and Toyota, although these also (successfully) participate in Formula One racing.

Relation	Qualities		
	Contextual	Intrinsic	Associative
Category specific	**Pedigree brands**	Quality brands	Endorsed brands
Category transcendent	Origin brands	Promise brands	Personality brands

Figure 6.2   *Pedigree brands*

A brand's founder can also ensure that consumers prefer it above all else in the category. This is certainly the case in the fashion industry, where designer labels work as magnets. Take for instance Yves St Laurent, Giorgio Armani, Hugo Boss and Ralph Lauren. Whether the designer is still involved in the actual designs or even the company does not seem to matter, just as long as his or her legend is attached to the brand.

The above description of pedigree brands may suggest that this is the realm of luxury or fashion brands only, yet there are plenty of examples of mainstream brands that very effectively leverage their pedigrees. Take for example Bacardi with its Latin spirit, Grolsch beer with its swing-top bottle, KFC who have Colonel Saunders and Levi-Strauss who are the inventors of blue jeans.

Core competencies for pedigree brands are narration and embellishment of their heritage, legend or mythology. Many brands find it hard to grow beyond a certain point, because they consider their pedigree to be restrictive. Therefore a pedigree specialization is often gained in the earlier branding stages, while ensuring the authenticity and credibility of a brand to consumers. The pedigree is thus used as a basis for further branding activities which build further layers of meaning on top of the brand's pedigree.

Brand expression and pedigree brands

A true pedigree brand is formed by an emphasis on its roots, the unique qualities it inherits from its founder, those that are bestowed on it by its birthplace, or those that are inherent to its date of birth. As discussed above, the qualities emphasized will be unique to the product or service category. Brand managers must therefore scrutinize the brand's roots and heritage to see which information these contain that will provide sustainable differentiation and value to consumers. A pedigree brand's reputation may become trivialized over time. The question then is whether the reputation provides sufficient differentiation to make an attempt at rekindling the pedigree worthwhile, or whether the brand will need to shift its reputation. The closest shifts are towards an origin brand and a quality brand.

Pedigree brands often employ an actual brand personality, for instance a company founder such as Yves St Laurent (the fashion label of the same name), David Tang (Shanghai Tang) or Kan Yue-Sai (Yue-Sai cosmetics and dolls), or an iconic figure such as Colonel Saunders (KFC) or the Don (Sandeman sherry).

Conventions and pedigree brands

Pedigree brands are strongly influenced by the brand's internal legacy and internal conventions. The strength of a pedigree brand is often derived from a founder, and his or her inheritance, which permeates the organization. Such a legacy can inspire management and employees to produce the finest quality products and services, and needs to be protected against fads. However, when the legacy is set in stone it may stifle necessary innovation. Many French wine brands consider their regional *appellation controlé* system to be sacred, and are dismissive of modern winemaking techniques introduced by winemakers from other regions such as the Languedoc, Rioja, the Barossa Valley, the Cape Region and the Napa Valley. This has been detrimental to the development of many French wine brands.

Generally held beliefs usually provide the main strength for pedigree brands, in the form of a mythology surrounding a brand. Luxury brands especially tend to thrive on this type of belief, with consumers paying top dollar to own a part of the designer mythology. In a similar fashion, consumers tend to prefer liquor brands with specific backgrounds because they believe that such brands are more authentic than competitors from places lacking the same fabled setting. For example, European consumers will most likely prefer Glenfiddich whisky and Hennessey cognac over Old Tavern whisky and Golconda brandy, both Indian liquor brands.

Closely linked to this is the symbolic value of many a pedigree brand. The meaning of such consumption symbols can differ markedly across cultures. Before the Asian crisis, many urban women in the region were more than happy to pay hefty prices for Louis Vuitton and Gucci handbags in order to be accepted by their in-groups. In most western societies, such a purchase is generally for self-expressive purposes. This shows that pedigree brands are influenced by esteem and self-esteem needs, depending on the societal context.

Pedigree brands sometimes leverage social needs, in most cases a need for belonging among ethnic groups, and most specifically among their diasporas. The improbably named Tough Guys brand of cigarettes appears to be popular among the Armenian diaspora in Los Angeles. The Welsh Whisky Company anticipate that their exclusive The Penderyn brand whisky, the first genuine Welsh whisky for over 100 years, will prove popular in Wales, but also among the Welsh scattered worldwide.

ORIGIN BRANDS

Origin brands derive their reputation from their contexts or backgrounds, just like pedigree brands. However, origin brands differ from pedigree brands in that the source of their reputation is not directly product or service category related (see Figure 6.3). In other words, the same reputation can be employed by brands in different categories, or by the same brand across categories. The origin can be a city, a region and most often a country of origin. German brands such as Deutsche Bank, Siemens and Audi can all benefit from the perception of German thoroughness, dependability and (engineering) quality.

Typical examples of city of origin brands are DKNY, Chicago Town Pizza and L'Oreal de Paris. Such brands draw on the repute or mystique of these places to declare their authenticity to consumers. Regional origin brands are fairly rare, because there are few regions in the world that inspire consumers' trust in a brand. An example is California, which binds together such disparate brands as Sun Maid, the Beach Boys, O'Neill and UCLA.

There are hosts of fake origin brands, such as a Dutch pizza delivery service called New York Pizza. Australian Home Made Ice Cream is actually an initiative of a Belgian entrepreneur called Frederik van Isacker who established a store in the sea-side resort of Knokke in 1989. The chain of stores has been expanded through franchising to the Netherlands and Spain. In Asia the fashion chain Giordano, founded by Hong Kong businessman Jimmy Lai, suggests an Italian origin.

A special case of an origin brand is when a brand claims to represent more than its country, city or region of origin. For example, Cathay Pacific Airways claims to be 'the heart of Asia', thereby leveraging Asian service

Relation	Qualities		
	Contextual	*Intrinsic*	*Associative*
Category specific	Pedigree brands	Quality brands	Endorsed brands
Category transcendent	**Origin brands**	Promise brands	Personality brands

Figure 6.3   *Origin brands*

perceptions, Asian values of respect for tradition, and its home location at the busiest airway intersection in Asia.

An origin brand is formed by an emphasis on the unique qualities that are bestowed by consumers upon its birthplace or the place that it currently calls home. Brand management must therefore scrutinize the brand's roots to see what information these contain that will provide sustainable differentiation and value to consumers. An origin brand's reputation may be improved or damaged by events that affect its home. Until the 1950s anything produced in the UK was considered of superior quality. However, the decline of the British Empire, and subsequently its economy and industry, gave British brands an aura of shoddiness. The most logical shifts that a damaged or exhausted origin brand may undertake are towards a pedigree, quality or promise brand.

Brand expression and origin brands

Origin brands will often express personality traits in line with those attributed to their backgrounds: for example competent and serious (German), sophisticated and stylish (Italian), rugged and independent (United States), perfectionist and balanced (Japan), passionate (Spain), mysterious (India), romantic (Paris), exciting (New York) or cool (London).

Origin brands tend to carry in them elements of their native lands that have been incorporated into their organizational cultures. These customs, values, traits, traditions and beliefs permeate the organization and influence the brand, often to its advantage. Many German and Japanese brands flourish because of their attention to detail, French and Italian brands benefit from their sense of style and romance, British brands are often blessed with a sense of humour, Dutch brands benefit from their open culture and their focus on common sense, many US brands are imbued with a sense of freedom, adventure and leadership, and many Swedish brands have humanistic principles that empower them. Such internal drivers are often also historical. Well known are the nationalistic strategic intents of Japanese brands to overtake US ones, and similarly for Korean brands to overtake Japanese ones.

Conventions and origin brands

Origin brands are very sensitive to commonly held beliefs about their countries of origin. These beliefs can take the form of stories, myths, expectations and even propaganda. It is no secret that countries are viewed differently by various peoples, and this means that an origin brand can differ significantly in meaning across countries. An origin specialization can last as long as the brand's specific origin remains relevant or appealing to consumers. This is the case when beliefs about the brand's origin have a bearing upon the quality perception of the products or services offered, and as long as consumers are convinced that the quality is guaranteed, for instance through import. Local production often means that a brand's origin becomes meaningless. For example, BMW now manufactures in so many countries around the world that the brand's German roots have begun to lose their impact.

These beliefs about a brand's origins can also affect how the brand is perceived as a symbol for its native society. Brands such as Coca-Cola, Nike, McDonald's and Marlboro are considered as symbols of Americana in many societies. Such an origin can be boon to a brand, but can also be restrictive or even a liability – as in the case of US brands in Islamic countries. It is not surprising that brands spring up that seek to capitalize on perceived American imperialism, such as Mecca Cola, created by French Muslim entrepreneur Tawfik Mathlouthi.

Shifting perceptions in a society can also undermine an origin brand. For instance, the sense of modernity that foreign brands provide in developing countries can fade, as consumers get used to the brands and as local brands improve to such a point that the differences become insignificant. The latter situation can be intensified by (re-)emerging nationalist or regionalist sentiments. An example is Future Cola (tag line: Chinese cola of our own!), a brand of China's Wahaha Group, which sports a red label with three yellow stars, similar to the flag of the People's Republic. So far Future Cola does not seem terribly successful in China's cities, but it appears to fare much better in the countryside, partially because it has better access to distribution channels there than its foreign competitors. The company claims a 15 per cent share of the mainland's carbonated soft drinks (CSD) market (see http://future.en.wahaha.com.cn/softdrinking.shtml).

QUALITY BRANDS

Quality brands derive their reputation from the appreciation of consumers for their product or service excellence, and subsequent consumer loyalty. Quality brands are dedicated to a specific product or service category, as this is the arena they know best. Figure 6.4 shows the position quality brands take among the six reputation types.

Relation	Qualities		
	Contextual	*Intrinsic*	*Associative*
Category specific	Pedigree brands	**Quality brands**	Endorsed brands
Category transcendent	Origin brands	Promise brands	Personality brands

Figure 6.4 *Quality brands*

A quality brand has earned a reputation as offering services or products that are of exceptional quality. This is however not the same as being a product or service specialist (see Chapter 5). A quality brand is not necessarily innovative, nor does it rely on a continuous stream of brand extensions for its relevance to consumers.

Volkswagen builds on a reputation for the quality, durability, reliability and resale value of its cars. The average Volkswagen apparently has six owners and lasts 20 years. There is limited pressure on Volkswagen for constant innovation. Most of its models evolve. For example, the Volkswagen Golf is in its fourth incarnation since 1974. Volkswagen only needs to demonstrate innovation when entering a new product class, such as with the Lupo mini car (3 litres of fuel for every 100 km) and the Phaeton luxury limousine (built to achieve speeds of 300 kph).

Quality brands offer a safe choice to consumers. The saying used to go that no one would ever be fired for buying IBM. The same thing may currently be said of brands such as Hilton, British Airways, AT&T and Toyota.

Core competencies for quality brands are to consistently convince consumers of the quality and contemporariness of their offering. This is more difficult than it sounds. It is clear that the differences in quality between the products and services of various brands have decreased dramatically over the years. In many categories – at least in developed countries – there are no longer clearly inferior or superior products and services. This means that quality brands are often defending increasingly smaller turf. Those that fail to defend that turf suffer badly; witness Opel (Vauxhall in the UK), which lost its quality reputation through shoddy workmanship in the mid-1990s. Apparently the Opel Sintra was so bad that it was pulled from the market, and the 4x4 Opel Frontera was still getting dismal results in consumer satisfaction surveys conducted by J D Power in the UK in 2001.

A quality brand may also lose its contemporariness and thus become unattractive to (attitudinally) younger consumers who are looking for something besides a quality assurance. In Europe, the retail chain C&A has suffered because it lost touch with consumers, despite offering quality merchandise. Many consumers looking for affordable, fashionable clothes were willing to compromise somewhat on quality, and found such offerings at Hennes & Mauritz instead.

Another risk to a quality brand is that it overplays its premium pricing based on its perceived quality. Quality brands are particularly at risk of being overtaken by value specialists (see Chapter 5), which are able to offer acceptable quality at affordable prices. This is what is currently happening in the airline industry and in stock brokerage. Such challenges suddenly show up the price premiums charged by quality brands, and even previously loyal customers decide to try the value for money offer.

Many quality brands decide to move on in order to pre-empt these kinds of difficulty. Volvo, with its reputation for automotive safety, realized that downmarket competitors were closing the gap with it on this matter. Thus Volvo put more emphasis on the design of its cars, and introduced new special models such as the V70XC (cross-country). This has helped make Volvo a more appealing and prestigious brand.

Quality brands are often the pride and joy of a manufacturing company's technological and production departments. These types of brands will often extol the virtues of total quality care and zero defects. For service brands the pride is usually based on notions of professionalism.

Brand expression and quality brands

A quality brand is often expressed by employing the following brand identity aspects: *values, purpose and ambitions*. The values expressed will usually centre on issues such as professionalism, hygiene, friendliness, safety and personal attention. The purpose and ambition issues addressed will generally deal with consistency and continuous improvement. The main erosive event for a quality brand is when other brands catch up or overtake it on the elements upon which its reputation was built. Quality brands make little use of personality traits as a form of expression, and when they do, the kinds of traits employed are most likely a derivative of sincerity and competence. The aim is to garner as much reliability and trustworthiness as possible. This often makes quality brand personalities rather bland and one-dimensional.

Conventions and quality brands

Quality brands are particularly susceptible to consumers' cognitive needs, as they expect a certain quality experience from such brands. How long can Volkswagen continue to produce multiple car models on the same platforms – such as the Volkswagen Passat, Audi A4 and Skoda Superb – without causing cognitive dissonance among buyers? In this case, consumers are paying vastly different sums of money for what appear to be rather similar cars. Apparently the same applies to the Ford Mondeo and the Jaguar X-type, two cars of a totally different class. Quality brands are also susceptible to consumers' security needs, as this is one of the driving forces behind the popularity of quality brands. As long as this assurance is in place a quality brand can charge a price premium over the competition. If the assurance is undermined, a quality brand can make a dramatic plunge. Arthur Andersen was considered one of the mainstays of the solid accounting profession when it got caught up in the Enron accounting scandal. Within a matter of months Arthur Andersen had ceased to exist, not only in the United States where the scandal broke, but worldwide.

Some quality brands do not seem to travel well. For example, white goods brand Maytag has a strong quality reputation in North America, but hardly features in Europe, where Miele is the dominant quality white goods brand. In Asia, National fills this quality slot. This is due to conventions of representation which dictate product design in this category. For example Miele builds frontloading washing machines, as is common in Europe. Maytag manufactures large toploading machines, which are the norm in the United States. National produces compact toploading washing machines, as Asian homes are small and space comes at a premium.

PROMISE BRANDS

Promise brands build reputations that transcend their original category. These reputations are based on attitudinal, behavioural or ethical promises by the brand, or at a minimum, the expectations that consumers are allowed to have of a brand. Such expectations or promises are not limited to a specific category, but have a bearing on issues that are social, educational, environmental, developmental or even political. Figure 6.5 shows how promise brands relate to other reputations.

Relation	Qualities		
	Contextual	*Intrinsic*	*Associative*
Category specific	Pedigree brands	Quality brands	Endorsed brands
Category transcendent	Origin brands	**Promise brands**	Personality brands

Figure 6.5   *Promise brands*

Virgin's challenge to competitor complacency has provided the brand with a reputation for being exciting, irreverent and bold. This reputation provides Virgin with the credibility to enter a category where it thinks there are complacencies to be challenged. Or as Virgin puts it on its corporate Web site (www.virgin.com), 'We believe in making a difference. In our customers' eyes, Virgin stands for value for money, quality, innovation, fun and a sense of competitive challenge.'

The Body Shop promises to act against environmental degradation, social injustice, animal abuse and unfair trade, thus promising its customers that the personal care and hair products they purchase are ethical. The Body Shop backs this up by supporting campaigns by Non-Governmental Organizations (NGOs) such as Greenpeace, actively participating in fair trade, not testing its products on animals and so on.

Promise brands are in an enviable position to extend into various (unrelated) product or service categories, but as the examples of Virgin and the Body Shop show, some brands do take advantage of the opportunity and others do not. Richard Branson always had the intention to branch out into other businesses and thus chose his brand name Virgin to indicate his freshness to these businesses. By choosing to name her business the Body Shop, Anita Roddick apparently wished to indicate that she had a core business she would stick by.

A promise brand needs to be able to deliver on a pledge beyond instrumental and emotional product or service values. This means that consumers can count on a promise brand to provide an experience without cognitive dissonance. When one of the Body Shop's first stores in the United States had difficulties with garbage disposal, consumers started doubting the entire ethical stance of the brand. Promise brands are vulnerable to small disappointments, because they themselves create such high expectations among consumers.

Charities and causes are a special form of promise brand. The promises can involve a single cause (such as Greenpeace, Amnesty International or Oxfam) or multiple causes based on one pledge (as with the Red Cross). With their pledges linked to good causes, charities are vulnerable to public disenchantment. The American Red Cross experienced this when it decided to funnel excess donations from its 11 September 2001 fund to other purposes.

Brand expression and promise brands

To be perceived as a promise brand, the values expressed by a brand will need to encompass matters such as social, environmental, ethical, lifestyle and attitudinal issues. The purpose and ambitions that will be expressed are related to improving people's lives, providing them with what they deserve, improving the environment, workers' rights and so on. A promise brand's reputation may be eroded by social, economic or political developments. For instance Bacardi used to be a promise brand, based upon the middle-class dream of spending a holiday on a sunny palm-fringed island. The fact that more and more consumers were able to realize such dreams eroded the Bacardi brand. Bacardi was successfully rejuvenated by emphasizing its Cuban roots, its heritage as a rum maker and the bat device for its visual identity.

Promise brands express brand personalities that are in line with their pledge to consumers. They can use their founders as brand personalities who embody the brand promise. Anita Roddick is a caring activist; Richard Branson is a daring, irreverent entrepreneur. Promise brands can also express their personalities without an actual person. The Red Cross is competent and caring, Greenpeace is exciting and Amnesty International is earnest.

Conventions and promise brands

Promise brands are susceptible to such cultural conventions as *beliefs and values*. These beliefs and values centre on the relevance of the core pledge or promise of the brand. Virgin's reputation as a challenger to incumbent brands connects well with the general British distrust of major corporations. Whether the same will work for Virgin in the Far East is doubtful, as consumers there tend to trust major companies and their brands more than contenders.

In addition, promise brands are vulnerable to consumers' *social needs*, their senses of belonging. In different countries, people wish to belong to different kinds of in-group. Most notable are the differences of wanting to belong to a society, which is the expression of western social needs, or to want to belong to a family or clan, which is the expression of social needs in much of the rest of the world. This goes a long way to explaining why promise brands built on societal issues have done so well in the United States and Europe, while they have not encountered similar resonance in Asia.

ENDORSED BRANDS

In the minds of consumers, endorsed brands are associated with third parties that are relevant to the product or service category (see Figure 6.6). Such endorsers can take the form of trusted bodies such as medical or financial professionals, specialized resellers, and brands from complementary categories. The main thing about these endorsers is that consumers consider them to be highly knowledgeable and trustworthy.

Endorsed brands rely upon third parties that are relevant to their product or service category to provide credibility or authenticity. It is essential that the endorsing party is seen to be independent, credible and trustworthy, and that its opinions or choices regarding the product or service category are (universally) respected. Endorsement can come from various quarters such as consumer councils, government departments, NGOs, speciality magazines and professionals. The endorsement can also come from business partners – such as a dishwasher brand that recommends a washing tablet brand – from distributors – for instance through exclusive distribution – and from suppliers – for example, 'Intel inside'.

Relation	Qualities		
	Contextual	*Intrinsic*	*Associative*
Category specific	Pedigree brands	Quality brands	**Endorsed brands**
Category transcendent	Origin brands	Promise brands	Personality brands

Figure 6.6   *Endorsed brands*

Colgate's endorsement by US dentists helped the brand knock former leader Crest off its perch. Apparently, Colgate had such beneficial properties that the US dental association was willing to recommend the brand. Another example of such professional endorsement is Hill's petfood, which is recommended by vets for various pet ailments and has exclusive distribution through those same vets. Such specialist endorsement provides a brand with the credibility that it cannot build on its own.

Journalists can also be effective brand endorsers. They can be specialists such as automotive journalists and technology journalists, but also general journalists. When McDonald's entered China at the beginning of the 1990s, local newspapers endorsed the brand by writing about the nutritional qualities and the scientific composition of the food served, as well as the hygiene standards, unheard of in China at the time (Watson, 1997).

Consumer organizations are very credible brand endorsers, as their tests provide consumers with reliable, independent, objective information. However, the fact that a brand is considered for a test already places it within the consideration sets of consumers. Sales staff at retail outlets can function in the same manner, although their objectivity may be doubted somewhat by consumers.

The difference between endorsed brands and those that happen to find endorsement now and again is that the former consistently seek out relevant endorsers and persuade these influencers to voice their support for the brand. The white goods brand Miele is widely endorsed by sales staff at electronic shops, as well as by consumer organizations, which always include the brand in tests of white goods and almost without fail provide it with positive evaluations. This has a lot to do with the qualities of Miele's products, but also with its keen eye for the influencers of consumer perception.

Becoming an endorsed brand is difficult, because it requires the constant persuasion of very critical groups of endorsers. It is typically a route that is chosen by quality brands (see above) to surpass other brands in a category where product or service quality are very important, but where consumers have difficulties in determining that quality. This can be due to a difficulty in determining efficacy (as with petfood), durability (say, for white goods), or because consumers cannot oversee the entire competitive offer (as with Internet service providers).

Brand expression and endorsed brands

An endorsed brand wants to emphasize its own achievements, but by association with a significant party. This roundabout way provides the brand with added credibility. The brand's qualities are expressed through the following identity aspects: *values, purpose and ambitions*. These aspects are similar to those of quality brands, but are expressed through the values, purpose and ambitions of the endorser. Endorsed brands obviously derive their value from the fact that a company, organization or professional group is willing to recommend the brand to consumers, who themselves have no objective measures to assess the brand. Consumers thus rely on these endorsers to get it consistently right. A chewing gum brand may want to emphasize the tooth decay-reducing qualities of its products by having dentists endorsing the brand. The dentists convey the values (such as professionalism, health and hygiene), purpose (to prevent tooth decay) and ambitions (say, to promote oral health) of the chewing gum brand. If the endorser loses credibility, the brand will also suffer. In such a case, brand management can shift the brand towards a quality brand (for example, cleaner teeth), promise brand (for example, provides confidence) or a personality brand (celebrities use it).

Endorsed brands often rely on the personality of their endorser to rub off on the brand: the competence of professionals, the sophistication of distributors, the sincerity of consumer organizations, to name but a few.

Conventions and endorsed brands

Endorsed brands are mainly vulnerable to *security needs*. The basic premise of such brands is that there is some form of risk involved with the products and services within the category, such as health, well-being, social status or quality in general. Thus the endorsers that are sought out need to be credible and need to be consistent in their endorsement, not flit from one brand to the next.

The prevalent values and beliefs in a society can influence who is considered to be a credible endorser. Although professional health workers (such as doctors, dentists and vets) will be accepted as endorsers in most societies, their traditional counterparts (such as Indian Aryuvedic doctors) are not always acceptable. The same applies to selected distributors. In some societies, distribution through supermarkets will signify the accepted modernity of a brand, while in other societies this does not provide any such endorsement.

PERSONALITY BRANDS

Personality brands have developed reputations based on third parties that are not directly relevant to their particular product category, but are (widely) admired or respected for their professional or personal achievements in other fields (see Figure 6.7). The admiration for such spokespersons rubs off on the brand, providing it with borrowed equity.

Personality brands differ from endorsed brands in that the endorsement comes from a source that is not specific to the category. In other words the endorser has no specific qualifications, expertise or professional position relevant to be a spokesperson about a category. A personality brand is generally endorsed by a celebrity or by a specific user group.

Rolex's celebrity endorsement – ranging from Sir Norman Foster to Tony Bennett to Tiger Woods – provides the brand with the right mixture of superior quality and aspiration to make it one of the most sought-after watch brands in the world. Mandarin Oriental hotels follow the same route with their use of celebrities such as Martin Sheen and Joanna Lumley in their '(S)he's a fan' campaign. The intention of personality brands is to enlist spokespersons who are credible in the sense that consumers believe them to be fastidious about their choices, as well as being desirable people because they have achieved a status the rest of us can only dream of.

Another route is to find endorsement by a user group. Many premium beer brands have sought such endorsement by getting their brand into the hands and mouths of the trendy and hip in New York, London, Tokyo and Sydney. This type of endorsement does not necessarily have to come from real people. The chocolates brand Ferrero Rocher has used an endorsement by a fictitious ambassador and his guests to indicate good taste.

Relation	Qualities		
	Contextual	*Intrinsic*	*Associative*
Category specific	Pedigree brands	Quality brands	Endorsed brands
Category transcendent	Origin brands	Promise brands	**Personality brands**

Figure 6.7   *Personality brands*

A way of obtaining celebrity endorsement is through sponsorship. Compaq sponsors Formula One motor racing team Williams, and thus associates itself with the likes of Jenson Button and Ralph Schumacher. Compaq apparently feels that the excitement and mastery of motor racing and its perceived technological prowess will rub off on its own brand. Although celebrity endorsement can seemingly be bought, the parties involved must fit together well. Attempts to put together Chiquita bananas and Naomi Campbell cannot but fail. The difference between personality brands and those that are able to snare a celebrity for an advertising campaign is that the former consistently seek out relevant endorsers and persuade these influencers to voice their support for the brand.

Becoming a personality brand is typically a route that is chosen by quality brands (see above) to surpass other brands in a category where product or service quality are difficult to judge for consumers, but are also regarded as less important than the association that the brand brings.

Brand expression and personality brands

The personality brand's qualities are expressed through the values, purpose and ambitions of the *endorser*. A credit card company may find a football player to endorse its brand, which leverages the celebrity's values (such as mastery and competitiveness), purpose (for example, attacking player) and ambitions (say, be an international success). If the endorser loses credibility or is damaged, then that is reflected upon the brand. Celebrity endorsement is easier to replace than professional endorsement. Sometimes a brand will need to shift away from celebrities, as consumers can tire of them.

Conventions and personality brands

Personality brands are sensitive to *values and beliefs* as to who is a credible endorser of a particular brand in a particular category. In Japan, the 23-year-old son of Prime Minister Koizumi is accepted as endorser of a new low-alcohol malt beverage called Happoshu. Would it be acceptable in Britain if Euan Blair appeared in a television spot for Bacardi Breezer, or in the United States if President Bush's daughters took part in a commercial for Bud Lite? Apart from aspects of underage drinking (drinking age is also a cultural belief) such activities would probably do both statesmen more harm than good.

As most personality brands appeal to personal aspiration, they need to be aware of consumers' *self-esteem* needs. Do consumers wish to identify themselves through the brand with celebrities or specific user groups? Nike is an interesting case, as its reputation at first glance appears to be based on athletic endorsement, but a second glance reveals that it is the endorsement by celebrity sports stars, and the subsequent identification with them, that so appeals to consumers. However, sports stars differ from country to country, as does the role of sports in society. Tiger Woods even shows that one and the same celebrity endorser can provide a different meaning to a brand in different places. In the United States he is an embodiment of black emancipation and success, in Asia he embodies the rise of sports stars with an Asian heritage (just like Michael Chang did a few years earlier), while in Europe he is simply seen as great young athlete who challenges older incumbents.

Personality brands are also sensitive to conventions of media. Many personality brands tend to stick to cosmopolitan formats such as international news magazines and broadcasters, and glossy magazines. This is not only because brand management expects its target market to be the audience for such media, but also because it is acutely aware that such media provide the brand with additional status to those consumers who do not and never will buy the brand's products or services.

CONCLUSION

The brand reputation is more important to some brands than to others. Specifically, brands that rely on authenticity and credibility among consumers must pay added attention to this element. However, what constitutes a compelling brand reputation can differ markedly across societies. It is, therefore, imperative to understand which narratives strike a chord with consumers and what the factors are that determine the credibility of the narrative.

According to a Dutch saying, 'a good reputation comes on foot and leaves on horseback'. Building and maintaining a particular reputation across multiple societies is clearly a demanding task, and care needs to be taken to defend those aspects that are core to the reputation. At the same time, brand management must also be on the lookout for the erosion or inadequacy of the brand reputation's foundations, and decide when it's time to make a shift towards another (adjacent) reputation or brand typology.

The next chapter deals with the third element of the brand perception, brand affinity. This element determines why consumers form a relationship with a brand.

Case: Iams petfood

Iams is a premium petfood brand. The brand derives its name from the company's founder Paul Iams, who in 1946 decided that pets needed specially formulated food. To this day, the stated mission of the Iams company is 'to enhance the well-being of dogs and cats by providing world-class quality foods and pet care products'. The resulting dry food (kibbles) has a very high animal protein content, as this is most similar to what these animals would eat in the wild. The brand proved particularly successful among pet lovers in the United States, who were looking to provide their pets with long and healthy lives. Over the years Iams introduced a number of petfood innovations, such as Omega fatty acids for healthy skin and coat, specific fibres for a healthy intestinal tract, and vitamin E and beta carotene to help strengthen the animals' immune systems.

In Europe, where Iams was introduced as catfood only, the company encountered markets largely dominated by wet food (cans) in the northwest, and an emerging market still largely relying on home-made food (such as pasta, rice or table scraps) in the south. These feeding habits were based upon local beliefs as to what is healthy and enjoyable for a cat. This behaviour contradicted Iams' core notion that healthy petfood consists of kibbles with a high animal protein content. However, it soon became clear that the local beliefs and habits were pretty well entrenched in northwest Europe, although they differed between the countries. In the up-and-coming petfood markets of the south, mainly urban Italy and Spain, the gap between feeding table scraps and feeding premium kibbles was very large. Iams reluctantly introduced wet food in cans. It showed. The canned food can probably best be described as a rather amorphous moisturized paté version of the Iams kibbles, thereby challenging conventions of product experience which consisted of meaty paté and chunks in jelly. The rather tiny format of most of the cans challenged packaging conventions. Coupled with a relatively high price, the Iams wet food did not experience great sales successes.

As for the Iams kibbles, these are oval shaped and a dull uniform brown. At the time, European consumers were used to feeding their cats with multi-coloured and (sometimes elaborately) shaped kibbles. Many European consumers also put great stock in providing their cats with variety in their diet by feeding them kibbles in a variety of flavours. Again, this went against one of Iams' core notions, namely that cats do not need variety and chicken protein is the healthiest for them. An added complication was that, because of the high animal protein content of the food, Iams could not resort to simply adding flavours to its kibbles. The food had to be redesigned around a different protein base, such as lamb and fish. However Iams again relented, as it was clear that these notions were well established and that European consumers would not be convinced to change their cat feeding habits.

The regular Iams kibbles were packaged in orange paper bags adorned with a stylized grey silhouette of a cat. The specialty products' bags had various striking colours, such as purple and aquamarine. The packaging conventions at the time dictated that kibbles should be sold in cartons bearing photos of adorable cats. This challenge by Iams to packaging conventions did not sit well with European consumers. The rather stark pack design was not considered attractive, and the environmental advantages of using paper bags were largely lost on pet owners. After a number of years, Iams introduced a bag made of resilient plastic sporting a photo of a handsome cat.

Most of all, Iams was intent on getting its healthy petfood message across to European consumers. For this purpose, Iams enlisted influencers such as breeders, vets and pet shop owners to promote its brand rather than rely on traditional advertising. Most Iams users are actually introduced to the brand by these influencers. The endorsement of the brand by such evidently knowledgeable individuals persuaded many pet owners to choose Iams, despite its high price, and to stick with the brand for the duration of their pets' lives. By challenging the conventions of medium, Iams not only avoided head-on confrontations with competitors, but (more importantly) was able to add considerable credibility to its pet health claims. In addition, Iams chose to distribute its brand solely through the specialty channel – mainly pet stores and vets – in order to support its premium brand proposition. However, in Germany where petfood is commonly sold at garden centres, Iams chose to include this channel.

Following the purchase of the Iams company by Procter and Gamble in 1999, the brand was to be introduced into supermarkets in Europe, as had been successfully done in the United States. So far, Iams is still mainly distributed through speciality channels in Europe. This is partly due to the importance of these channels to the brand, and partly due to strong competitive reactions by the likes of Whiskas and Purina, who introduced their own premium cat food in supermarkets.

The case of Iams in Europe demonstrates that a brand may have to change its specialization from one society to the next. In this case, Iams changed from being a domain specialist – product innovation-driven – in the United States to being a reputation specialist – endorsed by vets, breeders and shopkeepers – in Europe. And even within Europe, the brand needed to be tweaked to fit with the individual societies.

7

The brand affinity

THE BRAND AFFINITY DEFINED

A brand's affinity is the reason consumers feel attracted to it, why they desire it, why they feel a kinship with it. Consumers' affinity for a brand can be based on various aspects, whereby some provide a stronger bond than others. Figure 7.1 shows four dimensions of brand affinity. The labels used to describe the dimensions are general ones, and need to be defined more specifically for individual brands. Brands can perform more strongly on certain dimensions than on others. Once a strong affinity has been established, brands will generally strive to reinforce that particular dimension. However, some affinities can be transitory. McDonald's often achieves a strong cosmopolitan affinity among consumers when it first enters a market (such as China and Russia), but this wanes as the brand becomes more firmly established in the local community, and is replaced by another, for instance a functional affinity (say, does what it promises). Affinity can thus also vary between societies due to local perceptions of the brand.

Brand affinity specialists

Brand affinity specialists bond with consumers, based on one or more of a range of affinity aspects. A brand affinity specialist needs to outperform its competition in terms of building relationships with consumers. This means that a brand affinity specialist needs to have a distinct appeal to consumers, be able to communicate with them effectively, and provide an experience that reinforces the relationship building process.

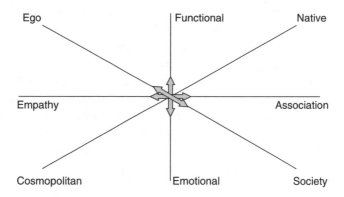

Figure 7.1   *Dimensions of brand affinity*

Affinity specialists are generally able to pluck the heartstrings of consumers. The way they do so differs markedly between brands, but the common result is unrivalled brand loyalty. Some affinity specialists are able to standardize their brands across societies by using themes that are common across various societies. For instance, Mercedes is a brand that many (successful) people around the world wish to be associated with. However, most affinity specialists need local brand management in order to be able to build a worthwhile rapport with consumers. Affinity specialists need to get close to consumers to be able to connect with them. This closeness requires affinity specialists to understand exactly which conventions can and cannot be challenged. This also means that the brand's organization must encourage local brand management initiatives.

Affinity specialists usually make use of brand personality traits as a means of brand expression. This is because it is easier for consumers to relate to a brand with clear and strong personality traits than to a brand that does not offer such affability. However, brand personalities are seldom real people or even fictitious characters.

Affinity specialists rarely express their brand through positioning. This is because affinity specialists rarely have specific product or service attributes, usage or benefits that are more powerful than, or add significantly to, their brand personality and identity.

FUNCTIONAL AFFINITY

Functional affinity can be based on such issues as being simple, sensible, practical, efficient and effective. ING Direct is a largely Web-based bank that offers 'Straightforward banking' in Australia, Canada, France, Italy, Spain and the United States. Although the bank's brand proposition differs somewhat from country to country, the emphasis is consistently on simplicity and getting a good deal. This simplicity clearly has its appeal, as ING Direct had 5 million customers by the end of 2002 (ING Group, 2003). This figure includes approximately 1.4 million customers at ING's German direct outfit called DiBa (ING Group, 2002).

To many consumers in Europe and the United States, Birkenstock is the epitome of sensibleness in footwear. Its shoes, clogs and sandals are ergonomically designed, but most are distinctly dowdy. The brand's affinity is clearly based upon functionality (foot health) over design.

Ikea is renowned throughout much of the world for being practical and efficient. The catalogue provides insight into the entire product range, the well laid-out showroom adds to this, there are trolleys for all customers, the flat packs are efficient, the furniture design is smart and simple, home assembly is easy, and the furniture is so affordable that there is little room for cognitive dissonance.

To build functional affinity a brand needs to focus on what consumers deem important in terms of functionalities of products and services, and make a virtue of its dedication to delivering those. Functional affinity specialists are often confused with value specialists (see Chapter 5). Although functional affinity specialists may also offer good value for money, their primary aim is to create a bond with consumers based on practicality, sensibility and astuteness. Low prices or value for money are only part of this bonding process, and functional affinity specialists will try to offer an honest price rather than the lowest possible one.

Brand expression and functional affinity

Brands with a functional affinity will express themselves as being competent, reliable, uncomplicated or practical. The attraction of such brand personalities often rests on being unfashionable, clear-cut and uncompromisingly sensible. The Birkenstock brand personality may be dull, but it is extremely practical.

A brand's functional affinity can be reinforced through the expression of its identity aspects. For example, a brand's express purpose may in fact be a desire to be the most practical, no-nonsense brand in its category. Functional affinity can be supported by some form of positioning, such as product or services benefits, a specific usage or a value for money positioning.

Conventions and functional affinity

Functional affinity brands generally need to be sensitive to various conventions prevalent among consumers in particular markets. When Ikea moved into the United States, it found that Americans had different furniture tastes (*aesthetic needs*) from northern and western Europeans, were more accustomed to customization of furniture (*service experience*) and were less frugal (*values*) than their European counterparts. This led the US consumers to be initially less enthusiastic about Ikea. When moving into Asia, Ikea needed to adapt its offering to smaller housing by offering more space-saving solutions (*product experience*) and to a low private car ownership by offering free home delivery (*service experience*).

EMOTIONAL AFFINITY

At the opposite end of the dimension from functional affinity is emotional affinity. Emotional affinity is based on positive emotional aspects such as fun, excitement, inspiration, romance, love, longing and passion. Clearly, nothing could be further from the practical no-nonsense world of the functional affinity brand.

Calvin Klein's appeal is rooted in a form of excitement founded on sexuality. Print and billboard ads for CK One perfume border on soft pornography. For example, one billboard shows a picture of a naked young couple in a passionate embrace, in which a bottle of CK One functions to barely conceal breasts.

Revlon is an inspirational brand that celebrates women of glamour and style. The brand appeals to women's self-image and sets out to enhance their self-confidence by having the glamour rub off on the women who use the brand.

In China, brands are springing up that cater to a longing for the days of the Cultural Revolution. Red Capital in Beijing has a Mao-style restaurant, provides a city tour by vintage Red Flag limousine, and sells the Chairman's Cologne. In Hong Kong, Shanghai Tang also caters to Cultural Revolution chic by offering Mao memorabilia such as wristwatches and cufflinks bearing the Great Helmsman's effigy.

To build emotional affinity a brand needs to seek out purposefully a particular emotion that strikes a chord with consumers, and devote itself to providing that particular emotional experience. The difficulty lies in claiming a particular emotion, living up to it, and not overdoing it.

Brand expression and emotional affinity

Brands that rely on emotional affinity will communicate such personality traits as excitement, fun, enthusiasm, friendliness, affection and passion. The attraction of such brand personalities is obvious, as they are designed to make us feel good in one way or the other. The cat food brand Felix has an actual brand personality of a cartoon character black and white cat which emanates cuteness and playful mischief.

Expressing values such as stimulation, daring and affection can strengthen a brand's emotional affinity. Benetton clearly expressed daring with its print campaigns featuring AIDS patients, mafia hits, death row prisoners, and the bloodstained clothes of a Bosnian soldier. The question was whether Benetton was taking its daring just a bit to far for most people's taste. The brand has recently started to emphasize more of its caring rather than its daring side in advertising.

Conventions and emotional affinity

Emotional affinity brands are sensitive to prevalent values among consumers. The Porsche Web site provides some fine insights into how the brand differs between societies based on local values. The information on local Porsche clubs for various countries provides a number of interesting observations. In Germany, the brand's homeland, club membership is encouraged for those with a love for Porsche and its technology. In Britain, the club aims at sports cars enthusiasts. In the United States, the club is all about the driving experience, camaraderie and passion for the brand. In France, the club is for those with a sporting passion for racetrack driving. In Latin America, the club unites the family to share the Porsche driving experience. The most telling, however, is the Singapore club. A few excerpts from the Singapore Porsche Club information Web page: 'Porsche has always been deemed as an exclusive brand, targeted at an elite market.... The ring of successful people with like-minded interests in the enjoyment of driving the best sports cars.... Events organized ranged from those that allow extreme tests of their own Porsches, exclusive launch events and also networking nights.' These examples almost run the full gamut of Schwartz's value dimensions (see Chapter 4) from various forms of pleasure and excitement (affective autonomy) through ambition and success (mastery) to family values and togetherness (embeddedness).

NATIVE AFFINITY

The native versus cosmopolitan affinity dimension is one that pits consumers' senses of local pride against their feelings of being world citizens. Native affinity is based on such sentiments as patriotism, chauvinism, regionalism, ethnic background or even an urban versus rural pride.

National airlines, so-called flag carriers, traditionally make use of prevalent patriotism to build a relationship with consumers in their home markets. Many Dutch consumers have a 'feeling for blue', the signal colour of KLM Royal Dutch Airlines. The demise of Swissair and Sabena in 2001 were substantial blows to Swiss and Belgian national pride respectively. Thais were shocked when Prime Minister Thaksin Shinawatra stated publicly that Thai Airways was lousy, as he described the airline's first- and business-class seating (Asiaweek, 2001).

Regional pride plays a major role for German beer brands. German beer drinkers tend to prefer their local brews to those of other regions and foreign brands. As a result, truly national beer brands do not exist in Germany.

In Malaysia, Proton is a car brand that ethnic Malays are proud to own, because it is largely produced and designed by Bumis (ethnic Malays). This is important in a society where traditionally much of the economy has been dominated by the Chinese minority.

Native affinity specialists need to be able to claim pride whether that is local, regional or national. Within a category, there is usually only one brand that is able to do so. National airlines are able to build patriotic ties with consumers, while secondary airlines seldom trade on these sentiments. The difficulty for native affinity specialists is to convince consumers to choose them even when a better proposition is being offered in terms of quality, value, convenience or appeal. The native affinity is often used as a buffer against (foreign) competition, and works to insulate a brand. The danger is that such a brand becomes negligent. Once this affinity barrier is broken down it becomes increasingly difficult for native affinity specialists to win back customers.

Brand expression and native affinity

Brands with native affinity express such personality traits as being genuine, proud, down to earth, natural and small town. The attraction of such personality traits is that they mirror the feelings that consumers have for the locality of the brand, whether those are positive feelings about plainness or pride. KLM is a proud airline, a pride mirrored for a long time by many Dutch consumers. Competition from low-cost airlines has eaten into this pride, as consumers increasingly felt that they were being overcharged for their loyalty.

Native affinity can also be expressed through the roots and heritage of a brand. For such brands this often means tapping into its city, region or country of origin. However, most native affinity specialists need not be explicit about it. Some brands can achieve native affinity in more than one country. For a long time consumers in various countries considered Philips to be a local electronics company. Obviously, Philips did not try to change their perception by communicating its Dutch origins.

Native brand affinity is based on a sense among consumers that an indigenous brand is closer and better suited to them than a foreign one. In some cases this is rooted in nationalism or regionalism. In other cases, local brands simply better reflect local beliefs, desires and tastes.

Conventions and native affinity

However, native affinity brands are sensitive to exactly the same factors as cosmopolitan affinity brands. Brand and patriotism are interwoven in such a manner that foreign brands are considered a threat to national identity. When Japanese brands first made a dent in the US car market, there were many who thought it was an unpatriotic act to buy one. In the wake of the terrorist attacks on 11 September 2001, US car manufacturers sought to rekindle the link between their brands and US patriotism. GM introduced 0 per cent financing on its Chevrolet, Pontiac, Oldsmobile, Buick, Cadillac, Saturn and GMC brands under the banner: 'Keep America rolling'.

This means having a good understanding of consumers' senses of belonging. What provides consumers with their identity? Do they feel firstly to be a citizen of a city (such as Hong Kong), a region (such as Quebec), a nation (such as France) or a supranational entity (such as Europe)? And how are these senses of identity changing? For instance, nationalism is a relatively new phenomenon in China, as it had been usurped by communism.

Another factor influencing native affinity brands is consumers' aesthetic needs. Recognizable local artwork can enhance consumers' affinity with a local brand. Cathay Pacific reengineered its entire style in 1994 by changing its rather generic green and white striped airline design and livery into a distinctly Asian design and colour scheme: the white brushstroke symbol against a dark green background (see Figure 7.2). This reflected the shift in customers that the airline had experienced, from

Figure 7.2   *Cathay Pacific's livery*

mostly European and American passengers to mainly Asian passengers. Together with the tag line 'The heart of Asia', Cathay Pacific was able to demonstrate its Asian-ness and fortify its customers' native affinity with the brand.

COSMOPOLITAN AFFINITY

Cosmopolitan affinity is based on brands being regarded as international, urbane, sophisticated and stylish. Typical examples of cosmopolitan brands are fashion brands such as Gucci, Louis Vuitton and Prada. Their allure stems from a perceived refinement, and appeals to consumers who consider themselves to possess discerning tastes. Other cosmopolitan brands have an affinity that is based on being perceived as a global or international brand. Heineken is renowned for being the first truly international beer brand. The implication for Heineken is that it is a *worldly* brand, actively exploring, sophisticated, open-minded and at ease wherever it goes.

Cosmopolitan affinity specialists need to make themselves desirable to consumers through a perceived superiority that stems from their demeanour. The difficulty is to consistently convince consumers of that superiority without being seen to exaggerate. One pillar that is often employed is the brands' actual presence in major urban centres around the globe, whereby 'international' suggests 'pre-eminence'. Another is the use of selective or exclusive distribution and media. Finally, premium pricing must convince consumers of the superiority of these brands.

Brand expression and cosmopolitan affinity

Brands with cosmopolitan affinity express personality traits such as sophistication, superiority, refinement, uniqueness, originality and modernism. Chanel is an elegant, feminine brand and as such appeals to women of discernment around the world. Cosmopolitan affinity can also be expressed by communicating the roots and heritage of a brand. For such brands this often means tapping into its city, region or country of origin, or leveraging the mystique of its founder. Giorgio Armani has become a figure representing glamour, sophistication and opulence.

Lewis Edison Waterman not only invented a much-improved fountain pen in 1883, but also clearly understood the need for style and elegance for such an instrument. Today, vintage Watermans are still sold, sometimes for hundreds of dollars. After the demise of the L E Waterman Company in the United States, the Waterman brand lived on in France and still produced bold and elegant designs such as the modernist Sérénité, the futurist Edson and the Combustion, which was developed in collaboration with Harley-Davidson. Waterman ownership returned to the United States when the company was purchased by the Gillette group in 1987.

Conventions and cosmopolitan affinity

Many cosmopolitan brands are sensitive to consumers' aesthetic needs. Absolut Vodka is one of the most well-known brands that secures its cosmopolitan affinity through aesthetics. As Schmitt and Simonson (1997) describe it, 'In the aesthetics strategy pursued by Absolut, the commonplace word that was the brand name and the product's distinctively shaped bottle became the centre of an artistically imaginative campaign.'

This campaign, featuring the Absolut bottle shape in various more or less artistic situations, worked extremely well with US consumers to whom this kind of artistic advertising appealed. In Asia, it looks as though Absolut still needs to find its form. Apart from the fact that vodka is not (yet) a favourite alcoholic beverage in the region, it also seems like the aesthetics of Absolut do not translate well. The three images in Figure 7.3 of the Absolut Cities of Asia campaign show the characteristic bottle shape imposed on all too recognizable Asian settings.

Cosmopolitan affinity is also often embedded in a sense of people's belonging. This can be a need for feeling like a modern citizen of the world, or a need to belong to those initiated to the finer things in life. In Moscow and Beijing, the arrival of McDonald's provided an opportunity for consumers to feel that they were a part of the modern world rather than living in an isolated society. Such a sense of cosmopolitanism surrounding a fast food chain strikes many in the West as odd. Most of us would be pretty hard-pressed to discover sophistication, style or refinement at McDonald's.

EGO-ORIENTED AFFINITY

The affinity dimension of ego versus society orientation pits consumers' selfishness against their altruism. Ego orientation is based on issues such as pleasure, indulgence, individualism and egotism. The reason consumers feel a bond with such brands is because they allow them to do their own thing, to release their inhibitions or simply to have a good time.

ABSOLUT COUNTRY OF SWEDEN VODKA & LOGO, ABSOLUT, ABSOLUT BOTTLE DESIGN AND
ABSOLUT CALLIGRAPHY ARE TRADEMARKS OWNED BY V&S VIN & SPRIT AB © 2003 V&S VIN &
SPRIT AB

Figure 7.3 *Absolut Vodka's Cities of Asia campaign*

Club Med stands for a holiday filled with fun, excitement and relaxation. If you go to a Club Med village you can learn to dive, you can participate in activities and games, you can eat as much as you like, and generally have a good time. Häagen-Dazs allows consumers to indulge in creamy ice cream with rich flavours. Häagen-Dazs encourages consumers to not care about their health or weight, but simply to enjoy the sumptuousness of the ice cream. Celestial Seasonings is a herbal tea brand that has an affinity based on its orientation towards consumer well-being and health. On its Website (www.celestialseasonings.com), the brand states as its mission 'to create and sell healthful, naturally oriented products that nurture people's bodies and uplift their souls'.

Ego orientation specialists must be able to sense consumers' prevailing moods and connect to these. In the 1980s in Europe and the United States the prevailing mood was that personal affluence and subsequent pleasure were no longer seen as bad things. This was a climate in which Häagen-Dazs could flourish, with its appeal to personal indulgence. The 1990s were characterized by consumers seeking well-being and health. This was a perfect breeding ground for a brand such as ArginMax, a nutritional supplement to enhance male and female sexual health.

Brand expression and ego-oriented affinity

Brands that build a relationship with consumers through ego orientation express personality traits such as being uninhibited, bohemian and ingenious. The attraction of these personality traits is that consumers feel justified in being egotistical, narcissistic or imprudent. Consumer orientation is reinforced by expressed values such as novelty, pleasure seeking, hedonism, contentment and health. The Magnum Ego ice cream was introduced in 1998 with clearly self-centred values aimed at younger consumers. This was followed in 1999 by the introduction of Magnum Double, which was aimed at indulgence.

Conventions and ego-oriented affinity

Ego-oriented brands are susceptible to consumers' experiential desires, part of their *cognitive needs*. The brand experiences need to be new, uplifting, inspiring, soothing or improving each time round. Another influencing factor on ego-oriented affinity brands is a need for *self-esteem*. Beauty brand L'Oreal is famous for its hair and skincare products aimed at glorifying female beauty. The brand's tag line says it all: 'Because I'm worth it'. In a similar manner, Häagen-Dazs encourages its consumers to leave their concerns behind and indulge in its ice cream. However, this need for treating oneself is not felt in the same manner around the world. In the UK, the brand appeals to indulgence and pure pleasure, while in France it gushes about the elaboration of the ice cream's scents and the development of perfect tastes. In Hong Kong, the appeal of the brand is based more on its super-premium positioning, a form of self-esteem derived from buying the correct brand. Hong Kong is one of two Asian countries where members of the Häagen-Dazs Club, an affinity program, get priority seating at Häagen-Dazs Cafés (www.haagen.dazs.com)!

Many design brands (such as Alessi) are able to foster ego-oriented affinity, as consumers consider their products to be for their personal enjoyment. Design brands obviously need to be sensitive to consumers' *aesthetic needs*. Such needs vary considerably across societies, as well as the importance assigned to design and styles.

SOCIETY-ORIENTED AFFINITY

At the opposite end of the scale are society-oriented brands, which build their consumer relationships on public issues. The issues involved are those such as animal welfare, the environment, social justice, fair trade, education and workers' rights. Brands with a specific society orientation can count on the sympathy of like-minded consumers. There are the charity and NGO brands that are focused on one or more societal issues such as Amnesty International, Greenpeace, WWF, Oxfam and Warchild. Such brands are often able to monopolize a specific issue in the minds of consumers, and thus attract the bulk of donations in this realm.

Commercial brands can also own such societal issues alongside the non-commercial ones in a kind of symbiosis. Take for example the way in which the Body Shop and Greenpeace work alongside each other on environmental issues. For the former, the societal issues have a much wider scope, which is due to the company's activities. For the Body Shop, it is impossible to single out the environmental issue, as the organization is involved in research and development, production, trade and distribution.

Ben and Jerry's have a dedication to the creation and demonstration of a new corporate concept of linked prosperity, consisting of three interrelated parts: first, to make, distribute and sell the finest quality all-natural ice cream and related products; second, to operate the company on a sound financial basis of profitable growth; and third, to operate the company in a way that actively recognizes the central role that business plays in the structure of society.

The outdoor wear brand Patagonia donates 10 per cent of its annual profits or 1 per cent of sales, whichever is greater, to grassroots environmental groups. The company has also been promoting its efforts to use 100 per cent organically grown goods in its products, absorbing the financial drawbacks of working with smaller, more expensive growers.

Many brands that have come under public scrutiny have tried to develop a societal orientation. Shell and BP have done so, but for now their efforts seem to be aimed mainly at convincing NGOs to stop picking on them. For instance, Shell publishes the *Shell Report: People, planet and profits*, which documents the actions the company has taken in 2001 to meet economic, environmental and social responsibilities. How many consumers read this report, and how many feel that their relationship with Shell is based on its responsible corporate citizenship?

A society orientation specialist must choose between being values-led and being cause-led. The former means that the brand extols certain values which it abides by and which imbue all its activities. The latter means that the brand chooses one or more particular causes to donate resources to. A values-led brand must determine which principles it wants to stand for that offer value to consumers and that are distinct enough to be owned. Then it needs to gear the entire organization to deliver on these principles, whether through policy, communications, operations or philanthropy. A cause-led brand must choose a cause that fits well with the organization's values and activities. Consumers will generally expect a cause-led brand only to lead on those specific issues. However, the brand is generally also expected to be conscientious in other areas. This narrower focus means that the brand needs to gear the entire organization to its cause, but does not need to bother too much with other issues. For instance, the Body Shop is not expected to take a stance on education or drug abuse.

Brand expression and society-oriented affinity

Brands that consumers relate to for their society orientation often show personality traits such as sincerity, consideration, honesty and ardency. The attraction to consumers is that they can feel that they make a considered moral choice for a brand that they trust to uphold certain values. Although Ben and Jerry's produce ice cream that is not dissimilar to Häagen-Dazs, consumers are not attracted to the former by selfishness or hedonism.

A society orientation is reinforced by expressed values such as social justice, human rights, equality, responsibility and environmentalism. Witness such brands as Patagonia, the Body Shop, Ben and Jerry's, not to mention cause brands such as Doctors without Borders, Greenpeace, Amnesty International and the Halo Trust.

Conventions and society-oriented affinity

Society orientation, whereby brands take a stance on societal and environmental issues that form the focal point for their business, allows consumers to bond with a brand based on their *transcendence needs* and their *values*. This means that the social, environmental and business values of a brand need to match those of consumers, as well as the manner in which these are expressed. Commonly held values differ considerably between societies, as does the manner in which consumers' transcendence needs are expressed. In western Europe, Greenpeace is considered as a respectable member of society, because of prevalent values regarding the conservation of the environment. In the United States Greenpeace is more often regarded as a bunch of tree huggers, disconnected from economic reality. This is partly based on the mastery type values in the United States regarding success and ambition. In much of the rest of the world, Greenpeace is considered an antagonist to vested business interests such as farming, fishing, logging, and oil and gas exploitation. This is largely because of the materialistic values that are common in many developing and recently developed countries. For instance, in Nigeria almost two-thirds of respondents in the World Values Survey think that protecting the environment and fighting pollution are less urgent than is often suggested (Ingelhart, Basañez and Moreno, 1998).

EMPATHY AFFINITY

The empathy versus association dimension contrasts consumers' desires for personalization against their longing to be united under a banner. Empathy brands are able to understand and cater to specific consumer requirements. This entails getting close to consumers, constantly obtaining feedback about the products and services offered, and customizing the offer to (groups of) consumers. International empathy brands are rare because of the need for consumer closeness and customization, which require substantial local management attention as well as production or assembly.

Dell is an example of a brand that is able to successfully understand consumer requirements and to offer individualized products. The success of the Dell model is not only due to its management of inventory, its online channels, its state of the art technology and its affordable products. Other computer brands are also good at this. Dell's success is largely because it recognizes that consumers have increasingly differing requirements for computers. The Dell organization is totally geared to meeting these needs through its ordering and customization process, delivery process and after-sales service.

MTV caters to young people's need for music and related youth information around the world. MTV determines for each market what the charts and topics are, and customizes its offer to the youth segment in each society. This success has not come easily in every part of the world. Until the mid-1990s MTV was considered markedly less relevant by youths than Channel [V] in large parts of Asia. By customizing its content to its various markets, MTV has been able to establish itself in the region (see the case study at the end of this chapter).

Egg is an online financial services provider in the UK set up by insurance company Prudential. It recognizes that everyone's financial needs are different, and thus tailors its services to customer requirements and offers solutions that meet customers' circumstances. Egg's goal is 'To give you the freedom and flexibility to manage your money and go about your life the way you want' (www.egg.co.uk). By 2002 Egg had acquired some 2 million customers in the UK. Its current advertising strapline is 'What's in it for me?' Egg launched in France in November 2002, spearheading its introduction with an Egg Visa credit card that offers 1 per cent cash return on total purchases with the card within a year. Within a month Egg had signed up 28,000 new cardholders (www.fr.egg.com).

Empathy specialists need to have intimate consumer knowledge in order to understand how products and services should be tailored to consumer needs. This kind of knowledge can come from a clear understanding of a category and consumers' frustrations, from consumer research and from customer systems (for example sales information, complaints and account management). The key is that this information is systematically applied to the brand proposition to provide a customized customer experience.

Brand expression and empathy affinity

Brands that build their relationships with consumers based on empathy employ such personality traits as caring, thoughtfulness, friendliness and independence. The attraction for consumers is that they have the feeling that the brands with such personality traits are really interested in and care about them. Despite its cool and hip image, MTV consistently needs to demonstrate that it is genuinely interested in young people. Empathy brands may employ positioning by emphasizing certain features of their products and services that underpin the affinity. Consumer orientation can be strengthened through features and benefits that help achieve the self-relevance of the brand, such as added vitamins. Expressing such values as compassion, modesty and consideration can reinforce affinity based on empathy. Gateway computers state their values as being caring, respect, teamwork, common sense, (positive) aggressiveness, honesty, efficiency and fun. Its slogan is, 'You've got a friend in the business'.

Empathy brands bond with consumers based on their knowledge of and insight into consumers' problems and requirements. Not surprisingly, empathy brands are often to be found in service industries such as banking, hotels and airlines. The main point with empathy brands is that they are close to consumers, and try to understand how they behave and what their frustrations are in order to tailor their products and services accordingly. The aim of empathy brands is to achieve customer loyalty, and to induce cross-selling of products and services.

Conventions and empathy affinity

Consumers only feel that a brand is empathetic if it truly shows that it values them. Therefore, an empathy brand needs to be sensitive to consumers' esteem needs. In Belgium, customers of Fortis Bank were unpleasantly surprised to find that the bank had decided to relocate many branch office managers with whom customers had built up personal relationships. The branch office managers had provided many of their customers with personal service, even for the simplest of transactions. This also has to do with values. In a relatively stratified society like Belgium, the brand's empathy is expressed through showing deference to customers. In a more equitable society like the Netherlands, the empathy is expressed through advice pertaining to the customers' specific financial situations. Fortis's ambitions in this respect are summed by their motto, 'Solid partners, flexible solutions'.

ASSOCIATION AFFINITY

There are brands that people wish to be seen with, that they wish to identify with, that they wish to let everyone know they own, and that they want to be part of. These are association brands. Harley-Davidson is the epitome of an association brand. Not only does the brand provide owners with a unique form of rugged self-expression, it also provides them with membership of the Harley Owners Group (HOG) if they so choose. This is reinforced by Harley meets which take place from Myrtle Beach in South Carolina to Faaker See in Austria to Port Lincoln in Australia. Apple is another association brand that thrives on consumer enthusiasm and in some cases passion. A core segment of Apple buyers are almost religious about the computers.

Fashion, apparel and automotive brands are conspicuous and therefore provide self-expression to consumers. Being seen wearing FUBU clothes signals urban coolness from New York to Kuala Lumpur. Carrying a Louis Vuitton handbag signals discernment from Paris to Tokyo. The new Mini sets hearts racing in Europe, Japan and the United States, and consumers vie with one another to own one of these delightful cars.

Association specialists must have an intimate knowledge of consumers' affiliation needs and desires for belonging. This kind of knowledge can come from a clear understanding of a category and consumers' desires, and from consumer research. These needs and desires must be operationalized and projected back at consumers. Much of this takes place through advertising, customer events and selective distribution.

Brand expression and association affinity

Brands that rely on consumer association tend to express the brand through personality traits such as being exciting, ambitious, cool, off-beat and aspirational. The attraction for consumers is that they want to be part of or be seen with the brand. Red Bull makes sure that it does not dispel any of the mythology that has been built around the brand – such as being made from bulls' testes – as this adds to the mystique of the brand. In addition, Red Bull organizes extreme sports and game events that provide consumers with the opportunity to be part of the brand, for instance, soap box races in various European countries, the Crashed Ice event in Austria (skating on an ice slope), and the Moonwalker indoors motor trials in the UK.

Affinity based upon association can be strengthened by a brand's stated ambitions and by expressing values such as daring, success and aspiration. Diesel's Donald Diesel character and its Web environment are designed to communicate campy coolness. As the Diesel corporate press pack puts it, 'When Renzo Rosso founded the company in 1978, he wanted it to be a leader, a company which took chances and carved out a niche for itself in its field. He surrounded himself with creative, talented people – innovators who, like him, rejected the slavish trend-following typical of the fashion industry.' Diesel's idiosyncratic style is driven home through its faux derelict clothing, its ironic style of advertising, its hip flagship stores in major cities around the world and Diesel's eclectic Pelican Hotel in Miami Beach, Florida. The hotel has individually designed rooms sporting names such as Jesus Christ Megastar, Psychedelic(ate) Girl and (the most popular room) Best Whorehouse, and styles to match. Apparently, it's a favourite among fashion and movie celebrities.

Conventions and association affinity

Association brands need to be sensitive to a number of consumer needs, namely *self-actualization, self-esteem* and *affiliation* needs, as well as to their value systems. To start with the latter, a willingness to associate oneself with a brand can be based on shared values. Mercedes-Benz's values are those of prestige and achievement. Those who purchase a Mercedes wish to be associated with these values, as they reflect their own ambitions and success. The more dominant certain shared values are in a society, the more consumers will want to be associated with a particular brand. Even within Mercedes' home market, Germany, differences in values exist between the former East and West Germany. Alexander Makat of Fritzsch and Makat, an eastern advertising agency, describes the eastern ethos as 'Prussian puritan', its values including order, discipline and modesty. This is one of the reasons successful Ossies, unlike their western countrymen, shun Mercedes and rather choose a more 'demure' Audi or BMW (Guardian, 2000). The very materialist and mastery-type values held in most parts of East and South-east Asia also explain the coveting of the Mercedes brand, along with other prestige marks, among those in business and government.

Association brands often provide consumers with a sense of *self-esteem*. When purchasing or using such brands consumers feel that they have made the right choice, that they are sophisticated, discerning consumers. This is not only true for highly visible brands with badge value, such as fashion, mobile phones and automotive brands, it also occurs with less ostentatious products and services, such as alcoholic beverages, financial services, underwear, mineral water and cosmetics. For example, few of the people who buy Björn Borg underwear do so because they think other people will notice. In a similar way, banking with Insinger de Beaufort will provide certain people with a feeling of self-worth without being ostentatious about it.

Association brands also cater to consumers' social needs. In other words, consumers want to feel part of something, such as a movement, an in-crowd or a particular class of people. For example, Manchester United supporters the world over feel a strong affiliation with the English football club, based on the success of its team. 'We reckon we have a worldwide fan base of 20 million and we believe we can double that figure in the foreseeable future', says Manchester United Chief Executive Peter Kenyon. The supporters want to be a part of that. In Singapore and Malaysia, the club has even opened (part owned) merchandise mega-stores and Manchester United Red Cafés. A little of this enthusiasm seems to stem from the British colonial heritage in these two countries. That does not, however, explain the popularity of the club in places such as Thailand and China which do not have a British colonial history. Manchester United's premiership triumphs over the past decade have made it such a favourite in the region. 'Every one loves a winner' may be an American maxim, but it certainly also applies in Asia. It helps that a player like David Beckham is considered *kawai* (cute) by Japanese female fans (Economist, 2002c).

Association brands can also meet consumers' self-actualization needs, their feelings of fulfilling their potential. One key to self-actualization is a search for exclusive experiences, which can involve overcoming personal challenges. These experiences can take the form of purchasing elite brands, staying at boutique hotels, visiting unique art exhibits, getting a glimpse of rare birds, or cycling around the world. Self-actualization can also take the form of overcoming obstacles or outdoing oneself, and an association brand can be part of that. Nike's motto of 'Just do it' is perfectly suited to those who put great stock in physical exercise as a way to self-improvement. This has almost become a religious undertaking in the United States, where almost all presidents since Jimmy Carter have been expected to be seen jogging regularly. Political leaders in other continents seldom feel this overarching need to display their physical prowess. There are exceptions, such as Vladimir Putin who likes to be considered a skilled *judoka*, despite once being floored by a 10-year-old Japanese schoolgirl (CNN, 2000).

CONCLUSION

This third element of the brand perception shows the significance of building relationships with consumers, or – to put it in other words – ensuring that consumers feel a bond with or a liking for a brand. This brand affinity is often the most difficult to effectuate, as can be attested by all those who have tried and failed. Sometimes the affinity grows organically through experience, as is often the case with functional affinity. Yet in other instances, brand affinity is gained through carefully understanding consumers' deeper needs, desires and values, as in the case of association brands.

The next chapter deals with the results of the activities aimed at forming the brand perception. Chapter 8 deals with brand recognition, a term that includes a whole lot more than simple awareness measures. Brand recognition is rather the way in which consumers relate a brand to other brands, including competitors, partners, components and so on.

Case: MTV in Asia

MTV entered Asia in 1991 on Star TV's satellite feed. Star TV had been established by Richard Li – son of Hong Kong Tycoon Li Kashing – as the first pan-Asian satellite television provider. When Star TV was purchased by Rupert Murdoch's News Corporation two years later, a disagreement with the new owners about the amount of local programming saw MTV withdraw from the region. Star TV almost immediately launched Channel [V], which differentiated its programming to suit local Asian markets. Channel [V] placed more emphasis on local artists than MTV had, and introduced local VJs (video jockeys), who quickly proved popular among the youths in their local constituencies. For instance, US-born David Wu (aka the Wu Man) became amazingly popular in Greater China in the mid-1990s.

The success of Channel [V] demonstrated to MTV the value that Asian consumers placed on local (music) content. MTV returned to Asia in 1995, this time adapting its offer to local circumstances. MTV Networks Asia no longer functioned as a single company, but structured itself into three separate divisions, MTV Asia (covering Indonesia, the Philippines and Singapore), MTV India and MTV Mandarin (covering Hong Kong, mainland China and Taiwan). In addition, MTV brokered slots with terrestrial broadcasters who reach more households than satellite broadcasts do (Ellis, 2001).

It is in fact amazing that MTV slipped up so badly in Asia in the beginning of the decade, as the brand's own explanation for its continued 'hipness' is: 'connecting with the audience and holding the audience first and foremost in everything we do by listening to them, reflecting them and responding to them' (SAM, undated). The relaunched MTV was certainly more successful than its previous incarnation. This was attained not only through local content, but also by organizing events such as road shows and dance parties in India, and by organizing music award shows on Chinese television. With most of these activities, MTV goes head to head with Channel [V] (Ellis, 2001). In many respects, both channels are fairly similar nowadays. However, MTV is generally considered more global (or foreign) and more 'cool and hip' than Channel [V] by Asian consumers.

The real challenge for MTV was to retain a similar brand perception across the region, while at the same time localizing its programming. Core to the MTV brand expression is its independent, irreverent brand personality, most clearly demonstrated by its quirky promotional spots. This personality speaks to young consumers, because it tells them in no uncertain terms, 'This is not television that your parents will understand necessarily. It's yours' (SAM, undated). This personality results in a perception of the MTV brand that is clearly driven by an empathy-based brand affinity. To achieve this, MTV needed to link into young Asians' esteem needs.

In a region where youth culture has long been discouraged, if not downright resisted, by paternalistic governments, this global MTV brand took young people seriously and provided them with a rallying point and a voice. Some even argue that MTV has done more to encourage local indigenous talent and local youth icons than those claiming to safeguard and nurture local culture (that is, governments) (APM, 2002). In addition, in order to be perceived as an empathy brand, MTV needed to understand and cater to Asian youths' personal values, and at the same time challenge existing social values. The shared personal values of young Asians consisted mainly of seeking pleasure and release from social strictures. The social values that MTV helped them challenge probably differed somewhat across countries, but may be summed up as respect for tradition, obedience and diffidence towards one's elders. By embodying these qualities, MTV was able to successfully maintain a similar brand perception across Asia. Only if MTV is able to keep its finger firmly on the pulse of and connect to young Asians will it be able to preserve its (more or less) uniform brand perception across the region, while continually further adapting its content locally.

MTV's persistent coolness allowed it to venture successfully into merchandising and licensing agreements around the region. MTV extended its brand to clothing, notebooks, backpacks and even pagers. The size of the MTV logos printed on such merchandise is larger in the Philippines than in Singapore, as branding needs to be more subtle in the city-state. Licensing earned the brand some 5 per cent of its total revenue, and is projected to grow by 20 per cent each year. By contrast Channel [V]'s merchandise generally consists of promotional giveaways and apparel sold for limited periods in conjunction with particular shows. Channel [V] was unable to make licensing and merchandising work in the same way as MTV, which is probably because of incompatible brand perceptions in various markets where it is not deemed as exciting or cool as MTV.

By 1998, MTV had passed Channel [V] in numbers of viewers in most Asian countries and had managed to double its revenues the previous year. However, both channels were still losing quite a lot of money and healthy profits were not yet in sight (Economist, 1998).

8

The brand recognition

BRAND RECOGNITION DEFINED

Brand recognition is more than mere brand awareness. Brand awareness is the function of communications only, while brand recognition is a result of the brand perception. What the brand means to consumers impacts on how the brand is considered in relation to other brands. Brand recognition has to do with how a brand is distinguished from and related to other brands. These other brands can be competitors, but also brands belonging to the same organization or to other non-competitive organizations (for example partners, endorsers and suppliers). Two brand recognition principles are discussed in this chapter, *brand discrimination* and *brand connections*. Brand discrimination deals with a brand's perceived distinctiveness from its competition, while brand connections examine the brand's perceived role in relation to 'friendly' brands.

The relationship of a brand to other brands often differs between countries. This is because there are often different competitive sets in a market, and the importance assigned to related brands can differ significantly. An example of the latter is Procter and Gamble, a brand name which hardly features on the corporation's individual brands in Europe and the United States, but is more prominent in Asia. In this region, television advertising for the company's brands often includes corporate signage at the end. The Procter and Gamble name functions as a so-called shadow endorser (Aaker and Joachimsthaler, 2000).

BRAND DISCRIMINATION

There are two important factors to consider when relating a brand to its competitors, how aware are consumers of the brand, and how distinct from competitors the brand is perceived to be. The combination of awareness and distinctness results in *brand discrimination*. Figure 8.1 shows six types of brand discrimination based on the combination of these two factors. Only four of these can be considered strategic brand options: niche, landmark, navigation point and sanctuary. The other two types are situations in which a brand may find itself, rather than a state of affairs achieved by design. For this reason, the four strategic positions are discussed first.

The importance of examining brand discrimination lies in the fact that consumers very seldom contemplate a brand in isolation. The result is that the perception they have of the brand – in terms of domain, reputation and affinity – is always judged within the context of the brand perceptions of competing brands. The various types of brand discrimination and their implications for the brand are discussed below.

Niche brands

Niche brands are known to (very) few consumers, but those people who are aware of these brands consider them to be (very) distinct from competitors. To the uninitiated, such niche brands may be indistinguishable from their competition. However, niche brands often have a fiercely loyal following who will swear that their brand significantly differs from others in the category. Hill's pet nutrition is little known among

Differentiation	Brand awareness	
	Low	*High*
High	Niche	Landmark
Medium	Indistinct	Navigation point
Low	Labyrinth	Sanctuary

Figure 8.1 *Types of brand discrimination*

consumers, unlike competitors such as Whiskas or Friskies, but has very loyal consumers who consider the food to be among the best possible for their pets. Asia Home Gourmet is a brand of condiments that is equally unknown and well liked by a small group of consumers for the quality of its spice pastes made from fresh herbs and spices. The Morgan Motor Company manufactures handmade cars for enthusiasts with a particular fondness for traditional British sports cars. The cars are still crafted around an ashwood frame. There is a two-year waiting list for delivery, a £250 non-refundable deposit for standard models, and prices are not guaranteed upfront!

Niche brands need to be able to inspire a relatively small following to devotion and the willingness to pay a (sometimes hefty) premium for the brand. This can only be achieved if consumers are convinced that the products and services offered by the brand are of extraordinary quality and uniquely suited to themselves. At first glance, surf gear brands Billabong, Rip Curl and Quiksilver all offer very similar products, and even their Web sites look remarkably alike, in both design and content. However, all three have ardently loyal customer groups who are clearly able to distinguish between the brands.

Niche brands often provide consumers with new and exclusive experiences. Designer hotels cater to this by offering consumers a different experience than they would have had at a hotel belonging to a chain. Banyan Tree Hotels and Resorts provides guests with a sensual and romantic experience. Almost each villa is secluded with its own pool, open terraces with fabulous views and a seductive atmosphere (Temporal, 2000).

A niche brand can have a perfectly good place in the market, just as long as it is well differentiated, the segment it services is large enough or growing at a sufficient pace to ensure future growth, and competition is moderate. If any of these three criteria is not met, brand management must find another avenue for growth. For instance, the entry of foreign competition into a market may destabilize a cosy market and require action. Differentiation may prove difficult, if local consumers are more interested in the foreign market entrant than in the local brand. This leads brand management to seek new market segments, which may be achieved by generating greater brand awareness and simultaneously widening the appeal of the brand. This may be difficult to achieve against a well-funded foreign rival, and may also dilute the brand's distinctiveness. In the best case, the brand will be able to achieve navigation point status; in the worst case it will become an indistinct brand (see below). A niche brand needs to be handled with great care, and should leave its niche only if forced to, or when the prospects of wider or new segments are too good to ignore.

Landmark brands

Landmark brands are widely known and are considered to be very distinct from the competition. Consumers can hardly fail to notice landmark brands. In some cases brands become landmarks by default, because there is no clearly discernible competition. This is sometimes the case in young industries and in the case of protected ones, such as public utilities. Microsoft is an example of a brand that, by being an early entrant to an industry and by being ferociously competitive, became a landmark brand. Almost everyone on the planet has heard of Microsoft, and most people would be hard pressed to name a direct competitor.

Landmark brands are often the target of both competitive attacks and consumer dissatisfaction, because of their apparent monopolistic tendencies. However, consumers are also loath to abandon landmark brands because of uncertainty about the quality of competitive offers. This means that landmark brands generally lose ground to competition only slowly. As competition catches up, landmark brands are forced to relinquish their once lofty positions. This has happened to incumbent national telecommunications operators which have seen their positions slip, as deregulation opened up their markets to competition. It may also happen to Microsoft. Various businesses and a number of governments, such as those of China and Germany, have already opted for open source software such as Linux.

Landmark brands need to be able to claim an entire category, either through market regulation or by successfully claiming to be the gold standard of the category. The latter is achieved by gaining market acceptance more rapidly than the competition. For instance, Matsushita's VHS beat Sony's Betamax and Philips's V2000 by being quicker to market, more agile (longer recordings), and getting movie companies to release more movies on its format.

Being a landmark brand is the best possible situation for a brand to be in. The brand will have a practical monopoly due to its dominant share of mind among consumers. In general a landmark brand has by far the largest share of a market, and needs to deal with niche competitors at most. Market deregulation has affected such luxury positions held by many national or regional telecommunications and utility companies, and they have been forced to react. Many have reacted by trying to increase their awareness through advertising, which seems rather unnecessary in view of their (top of mind) positions. The more logical route would have been to try to enhance their differentiation from the new competitors. Many incumbent brands have failed to do so, because they did not feel the need to demonstrate their advantages over these upstarts. Incumbent telecommunications companies were generally fairly reactive to innovations introduced by the competition, and subsequently lost market share. A case in point is the highly competitive and fast-developing mobile phone market in most countries.

Navigation point brands

Navigation points are brands that are well known and that most consumers can distinguish fairly well from competitor brands. At a minimum, consumers will be able to place the brand and its competitors on a single dimension, and thus can plot a course through the category. In the mass car market, consumers generally know many brands and also have some idea of what they stand for. Mercedes is a reference brand in the mass luxury car market. It defines elaborate status for senior executives and entrepreneurs. In a similar manner, Volvo defines understated status and safety for the same segment.

Navigation point brands need to be able both to gain high awareness and to differentiate themselves. This is a difficult task that entails both high media spend and clearly defined brand propositions. The latter means that such brands need to display a clear consumer understanding, in terms of what their brand stands for and whether this perception requires reinforcement or adaptation.

A brand that has achieved navigation point status is in constant danger of sliding towards an indistinct brand status. Therefore, such brands spend heavily on advertising to maintain their awareness lead over competition. This is also a situation whereby a high top-of-mind awareness provides brands with perceived quality advantages.

Sanctuary brands

Sanctuary brands are widely known, but consumers are generally unable to determine what makes them particularly distinct. Retail banks in most developed countries all appear to offer the same products and services. Therefore, consumers simply use their familiarity with the brands to choose their banks. This means that they generally choose between the top three to five banks in the country. These few top banks provide consumers with implicit assurances about the safety of their deposits, the rates on their money and the service they can expect. Hence, these banks become a sanctuary for consumers in a category that they are unable to oversee.

A sanctuary brand needs to be able to outstrip competition in terms of awareness, which is mostly a case of achieving presence through advertising and distribution. The more fragmented a category, the more likely that the brand with the biggest budget will come out on top. The Gallo wine brand is a sanctuary brand in the mass wine market. Consumers, who are generally unable to determine the differences between vineyards and their wines, opt for the safe choice of a well-known brand. Gallo's advertising expenditure clearly outstrips the competition's spending.

Being a sanctuary brand is an enviable position, as few competitors are in the same situation. Either the category is dominated by a few players that are interchangeable in consumers' minds, or the market consists of a labyrinth of brands with only a few sanctuary brands. The sanctuary brands are almost natural gravitation points for consumers who feel uncertain about the quality or reliability of less well-known competitors. In most cases, brand management only needs to keep an eye on the other sanctuary brands in the category and not fall out of step with them. However, such complacencies may be disturbed by disruptive developments. Evans and Wurster (2000) describe how the *Encyclopaedia Britannica*, after a successful 200 years, could not compete with the personal computer (PC). It was not that digital encyclopaedias were such strong competitors for the *Britannica*, but rather that parents – anxious to 'do something' for their schoolgoing children – would rather shell out for a PC than for an encyclopaedia.

Indistinct brands

An indistinct brand is generally stuck in a situation where it does not have the ability to differentiate itself enough, and at the same time lacks the means to increase its awareness. The latter is often made more difficult by being in a crowded marketplace, with a few competitors having achieved navigation point status, making spending on increased awareness a waste of resources. In many cases, the only route open to indistinct brands is to attempt to become a niche brand, which means that the brand needs to become highly focused. It must then ensure that the segment it wishes to retain is large enough or growing at a sufficient pace, and competition in its new niche is at the very least moderate. For instance in the mass automobile market in western Europe, there is a large number of brands that are fairly indistinct, such as Mitsubishi, Nissan and Rover. A more specialized position may be a logical choice for such brands.

Labyrinth brands

A labyrinth brand has few opportunities to differentiate itself, as it shares almost all its perceived characteristics equally with its competitors. Its opportunities for differentiation consist mainly of generic claims, such as country or region of origin (say, Rioja wine), types of ingredient (such as Robusta coffee beans), proximity (for instance, regional banks) and the like. By increasing awareness, such brands may become sanctuary brands. However, the market can only sustain a limited number of sanctuary brands. Therefore such windows of opportunity are scarce, and limited to markets that are highly fragmented.

A (rather drastic) development route lies in turning the brand into a niche brand by focusing on a relevant appeal to consumers' sensibilities. An example is coffee brands that have embraced fair trade principles by offering coffee growers higher than market prices. Such an approach will only be successful if a brand can latch onto a highly involving issue for consumers, and when the brand's assertions are not easily replicated.

Case: Hallmark Cards

Until the middle of the 1990s, greeting cards in the Netherlands were manu-factured and distributed by a host of companies whose products were largely unbranded. Cards were distributed through a range of outlets such as book-stores, tobacconists, supermarkets, department stores and specialty stores. The card brands were largely indistinguishable to consumers, and they were pretty much indifferent about the brands of cards they purchased, except for a niche player like Art Unlimited. Card availability and design were the all-important selection criteria. In short, the category was a brand labyrinth.

When Hallmark Cards purchased Uitgeverij Spanjersberg, the largest Dutch greeting cards manufacturer, it found a situation that was fundamentally differ-ent from the market in the United States. In its home market Hallmark already had the stature among consumers to be able to use the slogan 'When you care enough to send the very best'. Hallmark quickly realized that the lack of awareness of the brand, coupled with a perceived parity with other brands, were severely limiting factors in the Dutch greetings card market. Rather than designing new ranges or adding new outlets for cards, Hallmark started build-ing brand awareness in the Netherlands. This was done with billboards, and later with print and television campaigns. The slogan used for all three campaigns was 'The card that touches you', a clearly emotional proposition for the brand. In addition, and possibly more importantly, Hallmark branded all its cards, as well as the spinners and wall stands that contained its cards in the shops.

Hallmark's brand awareness quickly started to grow, and consumers started to develop a certain preference for the brand. Within a few years, these activities had turned Hallmark into a sanctuary brand within the greeting cards category. Hallmark had become a safe choice for consumers, who tend to be very concerned about the impression that the card they send makes on the recipient. By sending a Hallmark card they signal that they care enough to send a fairly expensive card.

BRAND CONNECTIONS

Consumers look at a brand not only in relation to its competitors, but certainly also in relation to non-competitive brands. These brands can belong to the same organization, but also to organizations that are somehow related, such as business partners, distributors and suppliers. These brand connections can be extremely important to consumers, as they provide assurances that the brand alone cannot.

The brand connections are a result of the combination of the brand hierarchy and brand role. The brand hierarchy here tells us how consumers view the brand's relationship in terms of a chain of command: which brand stands above and which brand stands below our brand? The brand role determines which brand consumers consider most important when making a purchase, and which one merely supports the purchase decision. The litmus test for a driver role is the consumer's answer to the question, 'What brand did you buy (or use)?' (Aaker and Joachimsthaler, 2000). The combination of the brand hierarchy with the brand role leads to eight types of brand connection, which are shown in Figure 8.2. Each type of connection is discussed in more detail below.

Role	Hierarchy			
	Master	Stand-alone	Sub-brand	Component
Driver	Corporate/ umbrella/ banner brand	Product/ service brand	Co-driver brand	Usurper brand
Supporter	Endorsement brand	Cobrand	Extension brand	Benefit brand

Figure 8.2   *Types of brand connection*

Corporate, umbrella and banner brands

Corporate, umbrella or banner brands are master brands providing a structure for sub-brands and labels. The corporate, umbrella and banner brands drive consumers' purchase decisions and transfer brand value to new product or service sub-brands. An example is Philips, which drives the purchase of all the corporation's consumer electronics sub-brands. A corporate, umbrella or banner brand generally provides an overarching structure for product or service sub-brands. This structure provides the sub-brands with qualities that they would be hard pressed to assert as individual brands. These qualities generally consist of brand values that are designed to garner trust among consumers. An example is Citibank, which provides 'dependability' to its credit cards in the United States and 'distinction' to its credit cards in Hong Kong. Sometimes a corporate, umbrella or banner brand will be carried by a physical brand personality (such as Marlboro man) enhancing the accessibility of the brand and facilitating the expression of the brand values.

Endorsement brands

Endorsement brands use their master brand position to reinforce another related brand. This is the case when a brand is endorsed by a group or a company to which it belongs. An endorsement brand provides a foundation for product or service sub-brands. No transfer of brand values is achieved, but the endorsement brand vouches for the qualities of the sub-brand. An example is 'Rothschild, a member of ABN AMRO Group'. This makes it clear to consumers that Rothschild is part of a professional financial services group, and at the same time enables it to exhibit different qualities and values to customers to ABN AMRO Bank.

Product and service brands

Pure product and service brands do not relate to any master brand, and also do not function as an overlying one themselves. Although such pure product and service brands obviously belong to an organization, the two are separate in the minds of consumers. The reasons for this can be that the organization has a weakly developed corporate brand (such as Henkel or Unilever), or that the product or service brand is so dissimilar from the corporate brand that it is best to keep a distance between the two. When British Airways founded Go it wanted to steer a wide berth from its own discount brand. Coca-Cola also keeps its non-cola brands, such as Fanta, at arms' length to ensure that there is no consumer confusion between the flagship Coke brand and its other carbonated soft drinks.

Co-brands

A co-brand is a brand from a different organization, or a distinctly different business within the same organization, that supports the co-branded partner. For example, Philips co-brands a line of portable audio products with Nike. Philips are hoping that this will allow it to reach out to a younger generation by turning their portable CD players into an athletic wear accessory. In this case, Philips badly needs Nike's support to provide it with credibility with this consumer segment.

In some cases, neither brand actually drives the purchase. An example is Visa, in conjunction with HSBC. In this case a customer will choose to take a card offered by his or her bank (HSBC) and then choose the card brand (Visa). Which is the driver brand here?

Co-driver brands

Co-driver brands are almost as strong as their master brand when it comes to the purchase decision. Examples are the IBM Thinkpad notebook computer and the Philips Senseo coffee machine. A co-driver brand is considered by consumers to be on a par with, or even more important than, the corporate, umbrella or banner brand. This is a higher risk approach than a simple endorsement, because the master brand is putting its credibility on the line. However, the dominance of the master brand over the co-driver can vary. For instance the master brand is more prominent in the case of IBM Thinkpad than in the case of Wall's Magnum. It is even conceivable for a co-driver to become so strong that it changes into a stand-alone brand and eventually a master brand.

Extension brands

Extension brands are basically a variation on the master brand, and as such the master brand drives the purchase. Although the extension is often a purely functional addition to a portfolio – such as washing powder, liquid, tablets and sachets – the extension brand is expected to embody the master brand's values. Thus, a new Sony extension product may be positioned as having specific features or a specific usage, but the product itself must exude certain key Sony qualities regarding design, innovation, advanced technology and compactness. If it does not, it may hinder or even damage the master brand. Sometimes an extension brand manages to become a co-driver brand, as in the case of Sony Walkman.

Benefit brands

A benefit brand is a branded ingredient that provides the main brand with added trust and credibility. A benefit brand functions as a security element to the main brand, so that consumers are sure of what they are buying. A benefit brand can provide functional, emotional or self-expressive benefits to the main brand. Some of the most well-known benefit brands are Intel for PCs (functional), Coca-Cola at McDonald's (emotional) and Pininfarina for Peugeot (self-expressive). The benefit brand must provide credibility that the main brand lacks in certain areas, and must have a good 'fit' with the main brand's proposition. For example, McDonald's lacks credibility in the area of soft drinks. No one is interested in drinking McDonald's cola. At the same time Coca-Cola is a perfect match, because of its US roots and international heritage.

Usurper brands

Usurper brands are similar to benefit brands, but in this case the branded ingredient drives the purchase. An example is Goretex, which is frequently considered to be a stronger brand than the outdoor wear brands that incorporate it in their coats and shoes. A usurper brand generally starts off as a benefit brand, and gradually takes over the driver role from the main brand. Even strong brands can be usurped, as was the case with Hello Kitty (a Japanese mouthless cat figure), which proved to be far more popular than the McDonald's Happy Meal it accompanied in a number of Asian markets. This is because the brand personality of Hello Kitty was far stronger than that of McDonald's. Customers pay a premium only for the usurper brand, not for the main brand, which may be fine in the short run but will be detrimental to the main brand in the long run.

It is essential to understand whether the usurper brand is filling the void of a weak brand, or has specific brand perception elements which may overpower the customer's perception of the main brand. In the case of a usurper with a very strong brand expression element, it is probably best to end the relationship. For a while Intel held an almost perfect stranglehold over most PC manufacturers, because consumers were loath to buy a computer that did not have 'Intel inside'. As AMD's processors started to close the performance gap with Intel – partly because of some stumbling by Intel – manufacturers became less reluctant to put AMD Athlon processors in their machines.

CONCLUSION

Clearly brands cannot be understood in splendid isolation, but must also be seen in relation to other (hostile and friendly) brands. Only then does it become clear whether the intended brand experience is somehow better than the competition, and compatible with partner brands. How brands relate to one another will often differ between countries, because of the local presence and roles of the brands. It can be advantageous to move a brand into a different relationship to the other brands, in order to provide security, differentiate, or support or be supported by other brands.

Case: Soundbuzz

Soundbuzz was set up in November 1999 by a group of professionals with music, Internet and finance backgrounds, with the objective of creating a pan-Asian digital music store at www.soundbuzz.com. After some limited marketing activities at the launch of the site in May 2000, it quickly became clear that sustaining the level of marketing to create a consumer brand was going to be difficult. This was reinforced by the fact that the proposition of an online music retailer yet had to be proven globally, and had been highlighted negatively by file swapping services such as Napster.

Within a year, Soundbuzz had been refashioned and reprogrammed into a music 'aggregator and platform provider'. Soundbuzz was now in the business of providing music amassed from 60 plus (major) record labels, on a delivery platform for encrypted music developed jointly with Microsoft, through a technology back-end hosted in Singapore – which provided excellent bandwidth and connectivity – to customers (or partners) across the Asia-Pacific. These customers include Indiatimes in India, ninemsn in Australia, msn in several markets in the region, as well as Hewlett-Packard. The major advantage for Soundbuzz's customers is that they can provide an online music store, with their own look and feel, without having to negotiate with record labels, without having to develop their own digital rights management systems and without worrying about operational matters.

In addition to the online music business Soundbuzz also helped Nokia develop its Club Nokia across the Asia-Pacific. Soundbuzz provides content (such as music and ringtones) and its management to Club Nokia. The joint service was launched towards the last quarter of 2001 and since then the service has expanded into 10 markets in the region.

In some areas however both the online and wireless markets were problematic in terms of business potential, and in particular Indonesia, where Internet and mobile phone penetration are still relatively low. However, the deregulation of the media industry and the proliferation of terrestrial channels provided the opportunity for Soundbuzz's trained music television production team. That provided the third pillar of the business: music television production and syndication.

As the business grew, Soundbuzz balanced online, wireless and media depending on the state of the individual markets and the opportunity. In all three cases, the content source – and major beneficiary – remained the music industry. The customer base however grew to include Internet portals, computer hardware manufacturers, mobile phone operators and manufacturers, and television stations (see Figure 8.3).

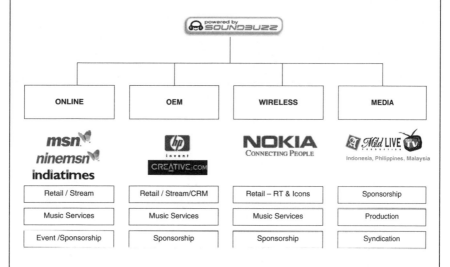

Courtesy of Soundbuzz

Figure 8.3   *Soundbuzz's customer base*

Although Soundbuzz started off with the intention of being a consumer brand, it has clearly become an industry and trade brand. Soundbuzz positions itself as the only choice and innovator in digital distribution in Asia, and as being a player who understands the legal and technological issues associated with the music industry. The 'powered by soundbuzz' logo appears on all customer sites: digital download sites, promotion sites, ringtone sites and in television programming.

In the space of a few years Soundbuzz has gone from a stand-alone service brand to a benefit brand. Currently, the benefit brand position is most important for Soundbuzz's customers rather than consumers. The selection, security and trust that Soundbuzz can bring to online music retailing are unmatched in Asia. Their partnership with Soundbuzz ensures customers that they have the latest music on offer – which helps drive traffic to their sites – that all content is legal, and that they can have a digital music store that does not distract them from their core businesses.

PART III

GLOBAL BRAND STRATEGY ISSUES

9

Taking a brand global

APPLYING THE MODEL

The global brand proposition model, which was discussed in the introduction, is specifically designed to analyse brands in their local and global contexts, to determine the manifold influences on brands in different markets, to help resolve local versus global brand proposition tensions, and to develop strategic options for the brand which offer both competitive advantage and value to stakeholders.

The following chapters deal with a number of typical global brand strategy issues. These matters will be examined using the global brand proposition model as an analysis framework that can be applied across markets, societies and cultures. The subject matter of these four chapters is rather general, and in practice brand managers will need to use their own skills, business acumen and creativity to determine the fitting propositions for their brands. This chapter describes how to take a brand that is established in a particular local or regional market into foreign realms.

THE ISSUE

Even strong brands are at some time faced with limits to their expansion in the market or markets where they operate. These limits can consist of a slowing growth rate for the entire category, saturation of the brand's target segments, price erosion because of intensified competition, price pressures from retailers or suppliers, an end to the brand's main products' lifecycles, reduced margins because additional marketing and sales efforts are required, overcapacity as a result of optimistic market predictions, and so on. For some brands these kinds of pressure come early in their life, as they will only be able to survive if they can enlarge their geographic markets. These are generally niche brands, which by definition serve small local markets, or technology or pharmaceutical brands that need high rates of investment to keep up the pace of innovation without pricing themselves out of the market. For other brands these pressures only reveal themselves when their key products or services become outdated in their home markets, and they seek markets where such products or services are still sought after. Especially in smaller developed markets, brands face saturated markets where growth will likely occur only at the expense of competition. The logical step, therefore, is to enter new markets abroad.

However, those brands that have become global household names, the Coca-Colas and McDonald's of this world, have often taken decades to achieve that position and have exerted great efforts in the process. Many more brands have been unsuccessful in their foreign adventures and have raked up considerable losses. The geographical extension of a brand is clearly a demanding task and needs to be undertaken with due care.

INTERNAL ANALYSIS

The three elements of the internal analysis – organization, brand expression and marketing – are discussed separately below. In the case of taking a brand global, quite a lot of the analysis will deal with how these elements differ from those in the home market.

The organization

Business strategy

The first thing to ascertain when taking a brand into foreign markets is whether the business strategy is ready to go global. Often, a business strategy is rooted in the organization's home market and is not applicable to foreign markets. Rangan (1999) identifies three basic criteria that any organization needs to meet before contemplating going global:

▌ The organization needs to possess a valuable intangible asset (such as technology, patents or a brand proposition).

■ There needs to be sufficient and steady demand in the new markets for the kind of services or products offered.

■ The organization needs to be able to replicate the consumer experience abroad.

Chevalier (1999) cautions that barriers to entry may complicate market entry, such as legal barriers, the total size of the market, sunk costs needed for market entry, network externalities that may affect the uptake of a product or service, and advantages that accrue to incumbents in the marketplace.

The organization's managers need to consider whether the inspirational elements of the business strategy – the vision, mission and ambition – still apply when crossing borders, and ask themselves questions such as:

■ Are the anticipated technological, social, political, economic and regulatory developments the same and as relevant outside the original country or region?

■ How do the players in the foreign market differ from those in the home market?

■ Are there different stakeholder groups to consider in these foreign markets, such as local distributors, local partners, local communities, governments and environmental pressure groups?

■ What are the push and pull factors that are driving the business strategy into foreign markets?

■ What are the expectations of and objectives for such a move?

■ How does the business model differ in the foreign market?

■ What are the skills, technologies and talents that are needed to make this move a success, and how do they differ from the home market?

■ What are the resources that are needed to make it a success, and how do they differ from the home market?

■ Are management and staff motivated to make this move a success?

Internal conventions

Similarly, management needs to think about how to transplant the relevant internal conventions, such as symbols, culture, rituals and routines, and control systems to foreign shores. It is necessary to determine which of these will reinforce the brand in its new country, and whether these aspects can be transferred with or without adaptation. There also needs to be a good idea how the transfer of internal conventions can best take place. Should management be hired locally and given an induction programme in the brand's home country, or should expatriate management be put in place that can prepare future local management? The approach may differ from country to country, depending on such issues as the availability of local talent, the need for speed to market, the perceived distance between the cultures of the home country and the host country, and local legal requirements.

Internal brand legacy

The internal legacy of the brand is often transferred to foreign shores, but its relevance may differ. Henry Ford's presence may still loom over the brand in Detroit and the rest of the US organization, but how relevant a figure is he to company staff in China? In a similar way, brand milestones will be different in other countries. The most important milestone will often be the introduction of the brand into the country. The role of the brand to the local organization is also likely to differ from that in the brand's home market. The brand may be the lead brand for the organization in a new country, while it is one of a portfolio of brands in its home market.

The brand expression

It is important to determine whether the home market brand expression can be or should be transplanted to a host market. This follows from the organizational analysis, as described above. If the business strategy, the internal conventions or the internal brand legacy are different from that in the brand's home country, there may be good reason to alter the brand expression accordingly. For example, in its home market a brand may be faced with a saturated market, and the business strategy is focused upon attaining customer loyalty, while in its host market the brand is new and the business strategy is geared towards market penetration. The subsequent brand expressions may concentrate on the brand's personality in the home country (to build relationships with consumers) and on the brand's positioning in the host country (to demonstrate advantages over the competition).

At the same time, management also needs to assess whether the competencies and resources available to the organization in the host country are compatible with transferring the home country brand expression. It may not be possible for local brand managers to implement a sophisticated brand personality, simply because they lack the skills or the tools to do so. Such a situation is particularly common when a local distributor is responsible for brand management. Local distributors generally handle multiple brands, and therefore lack the time, knowledge and incentive to build a brand long-term. Brand management must ask themselves the following questions:

■ What is the required brand experience that the brand expression is supposed to achieve in the host country?

■ Does management in the host country understand the brand the same way management does in the home country?

■ What is the role of the brand for the organization in the host country?

■ Does it matter whether the brand expression differs between the home and the host country?

■ Do the stages of brand development in the host country warrant a differing brand expression (for the time being)?

Marketing

Can the home country marketing mix be transferred to the host country? This is influenced partly by the brand expression and partly by local circumstances. This paragraph focuses on the influence of the brand expression on the marketing mix, while the influence of external factors is discussed in the paragraph dedicated to the external analysis. If the brand expression in the host country differs from that in the brand's home country, the marketing mix is also likely to differ. However, this does not follow automatically. A differing brand expression can still be supported by a similar marketing mix. And conversely, even when the brand expression is transferred unchanged to the host country the marketing mix may differ.

Price

All other things being equal, the price is the marketing mix element that is most likely to vary between a brand's home and its host country. The main thing to determine, when taking a brand to a foreign country, is the relationship between the price of products and services and the local brand expression. This entails that prices are set relative to local prices for similar goods and services, with a mark-up or mark-down that is based on the brand's expression. A brand that offers qualities that are unmatched in a foreign market may mark up its prices to reflect such superiority. A brand that offers only additional choice to consumers needs to set its prices accordingly, in line with the market.

People

The next element that is likely to differ between the home and host markets is the people supporting the brand. Obviously, staff in a host country will be different from those in a brand's home country in terms of culture, education, experience and so on. However, the main issue here is whether the service that they provide to support the brand differs by design. A brand with strong values may not feel the need to emphasize these in its home country, as everyone there already knows this fact and staff are steeped in the brand's principles. In a host country this brand identity aspect (its values) may need to be played up by staff. This is not only an external exercise to convey the values to consumers, but also one to make sure that staff keep these values at the top of their minds in their work.

Products and services

In a similar manner, the products or services offered can differ even while the brand expression does not. Sometimes the products or services are designed differently, because they better convey the brand expression that way. A brand of iced tea may have an established premium position in its home market. This allows the brand to be sold in multiple packaging formats such as PET and cans. But, in order to attain the same stature elsewhere, the brand might be sold only in glass bottles, as these better convey its premium placing. Many automotive brands sell different car models and designs in different parts of the world. The main Volkswagen model in Brazil is the Gol, while in China it is the Santana.

Distribution

As discussed in Chapter 3, brand distribution often varies because of the need to adapt to local distribution structures. However, brand distribution may also differ in order to better express the brand. The luxury brand Louis Vuitton is sold through exclusive distribution in most parts of the world to emphasize its exclusivity. However, in Hong Kong its bags are also sold from stands in shopping centres such as Times Square. Apparently this does not damage the brand locally, and it gets it into the hands of many more aspiring millionaires. US cosmetics brand ~H2O+ ('an oasis of water-based skin care') requires its distributors in foreign countries to build flagship stores to properly reflect the brand's elegance. So far, distributors in Asia and the Middle East have complied.

Communications

Marketing communications, and advertising in particular, are the things that many global brands would most dearly like to standardize across their markets. This is because most organizations consider communications mainly as a cost burden, if not a downright waste of money. However, even purely from the perspective of the brand expression the marketing communications will still differ between the home and the host country.

Apart from the media structure, as discussed in Chapter 3, there can be reasons to choose different media channels and use differing messages for such communications.

easyJet's value for money positioning is clearly the same in all countries where it operates, and so is most of its marketing mix. However, the marketing communications differ both in channel choice and messages. For example, easyJet advertised in local newspapers and on the sides of trucks plying the M1 and M6 motorways to draw attention to its new routes from London Luton to the north of the UK. In the Netherlands, the brand relies heavily on billboard advertising and (more recently) television advertising. In the UK, where easyJet battles mainly with British Airways, it happily latched onto the news that Prime Minister Tony Blair had selected the airline for his family's holiday in southern France. The news proved to be false, as the Blairs were actually flying Ryanair. In the Netherlands easyJet competes with KLM, and it takes every opportunity to poke fun at KLM's symbols: the colour blue and its white swans. In a recent television ad, swans are seen boarding an easyJet plane.

Marketing implementation

Can the marketing implementation be transferred from the brand's home country to the host country? That is, should operations be duplicated when a brand moves abroad? Apart from the fact that many global brands start out as imports, and therefore cannot duplicate production or logistics until sufficient volume has been achieved, there is the question whether duplication is wise from the brand expression perspective. For example, Wal-Mart is famous in the United States for its customer service and its employee evangelism. When Wal-Mart tried to duplicate this in Germany, customers were unimpressed by its meeters/greeters at the doors. Worse still for the company was that the German staff hid in the toilets to avoid the morning Wal-Mart cheer (Economist, 2001). Marketing management need to ask themselves the following questions:

- How does the brand expression translate into the actual marketing mix in the host market?
- Does local adaptation of the brand expression require an adaptation of the marketing mix?
- Does standardization of the brand expression lead to a standardization of the marketing mix, or is an adaptation of the marketing mix required?
- Should the marketing implementation be transplanted to the host country, or should the organization adapt its operations and customer interface to ensure that it functions according to the brand expression?

EXTERNAL ANALYSIS

The previous section dealt with the internal factors that influence a brand when it travels to a foreign country. Once it arrives there, the brand is faced with a number of factors that are external to its organization. This section discusses these external factors and how they influence the brand in its host country. The three elements of the external analysis are discussed below: the local conventions, the brand perception and the brand recognition.

Conventions

When entering a market with a brand, it is necessary to understand what moves and motivates consumers and what will influence their brand perception. Apart from structural factors (category conventions), the factors affecting a brand either can be learnt (cultural conventions) or are motivational (needs conventions). The impact of the three types of convention varies according to the type of brand, as discussed in the previous chapters. The matter to contemplate during market entry is whether to abide by or to challenge prevalent conventions as a way of creating value for consumers and their local communities.

A convention is considered to be 'solid' when consumers are unwilling to accept an alternative. Then, there is little alternative but to adapt the particular aspect of the brand to this convention. A convention is considered to be 'flexible' when the convention is undergoing development or erosion in consumers' minds. Then, there is an opportunity to challenge such a convention, and to obtain differentiation from competitors and offer distinct value to consumers. Figure 9.1 shows the issues that need to be examined in order to test the solidity of a convention.

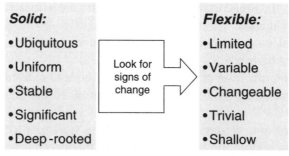

Figure 9.1   *Testing the solidity of a convention*

The solidity of conventions

Judging the *solidity* of a convention is dependent upon:

■ *Ubiquity.* How widely is something practised by competitors or consumers?

■ *Uniformity.* Does every competitor or consumer behave in exactly the same way or think exactly the same about this matter?

■ *Stability.* Has the convention changed much over time? Has it begun to show changes recently?

■ *Significance.* Does the convention have a particular relevance to competitors or consumers? Do they feel that they could do without it?

■ *Depth.* Is the convention rooted in the fabric of the category or in the society? How valuable do competitors and consumers consider it to be to them?

Category conventions

First of all, however, it is necessary to determine what the prevalent conventions are in the host country. The category conventions are a good starting point for the analysis of the influence of the external conventions on a brand. This is because:

■ These conventions are openly observable and thus the easiest to collect and analyse.

■ They give a clear understanding of the brandscape as witnessed by consumers.

■ Knowledge of competition provides perspectives for sustainable differentiation and competitive advantages.

■ Category conventions may be related to consumer needs or local culture, which aids our understanding of the influence of needs and cultural conventions on the brands in the category.

The category conventions can be uncovered using a number of sources of information, such as purchase of competitive products, mystery shopping, advertising analysis (content and form), media research publications (available to most advertising and media agencies and from specialized research agencies), retail and promotional information (available from specialized research agencies) and interviews with category experts (such as consultants and retailers).

The complexity of the competitive environment and the category conventions will depend on how homogeneous the market is and how dissimilar the competitive brands are. In large countries such as India, China and Brazil, markets are often more regional than national. For instance, the Chinese beer market consists of a multitude of local brands, a few national brands and a rather large number of foreign brands, which in their turn are not all represented nationwide. The only way of making sense of such a market is by breaking it up into relevant regions and reviewing the brands in each region to understand their roles, the value they offer consumers, their expressions and so on. However, even small markets may be culturally or structurally diverse, and need differing approaches for regional markets or ethnic segments. For instance, in a country like Malaysia with three distinct ethnic populations (Malays, Chinese and Tamil), the popularity of brands varies according to ethnicity. A review of competitive brands is mainly aimed at obtaining expressions of these brands from various sources, such as advertising, promotional materials, packaging, press clippings, consumer research and so on. The objective is to understand competitive:

- product(s) and/or service(s) offered;
- visual identities;
- information provided;
- presentation of and assertions about the brands;
- types of media used;
- types of distribution used;
- consistency, uniformity, and ubiquity of brand expressions.

Needs conventions

The next set of conventions that has a direct bearing on the brand's category is the needs conventions. Needs conventions are not always openly observable, and need to be teased out through various forms of (participative) research among consumers. The examination of the category conventions may provide some indications of prevalent needs, for instance in the form of product design, advertising messages and distribution channel usage, but consumer needs may already have moved on while the category conventions have remained unchanged. In particular, category conventions that have required substantial investment will not be got rid of easily. An example is the bank branch office distribution system, which is being overtaken by electronic and Internet distribution systems. Although the former still meets a need among a certain segment of consumers (such as small retailers and the elderly), it is clear that in many countries the Internet better meets the needs of speed, convenience and modernity.

Apart from primary research, needs conventions may be uncovered using a number of sources of information, such as syndicated consumer studies (such as lifestyle studies) and interviews with category experts (such as consultants and researchers). For some countries, these sources will be harder to find than in others. For example, in Germany market researchers are generally loath to assume the role of experts, while in Italy they generally feel more at ease with that role. Particularly in developing markets there is often a dearth of information sources, which means that researchers needs to rely more heavily on their own observations and consumer research. Such (participative) research often involves:

▌ Observation of consumers as they shop for and use products and services. Unilever does a lot of in-home observation of cooking methods, whereby researchers record on video how housewives prepare their meals. This method has the advantage that it clearly shows the housewives' needs regarding cooking products and their ingredients. The information is particularly relevant to research and development and to marketing management.

▌ Participation in consumers' daily lives. This is a more intrusive method, but it can be applied when the use of products or services permeates consumers' lives. For example, mobile phones are accessories that many teenagers feel they cannot live without. By participating in their daily routines, researchers can uncover the role that the phones play in their lives and the use that is made of them. SMS was never designed for consumer use, let alone teenagers. It was designed for the phone company service engineers. However, SMS met an unforeseen need among teenagers for staying in touch, a typical social need.

▌ Qualitative research (such as group discussion and in-depth interviews) can help uncover more manifest needs among consumers. Especially when entering a host market, it is important to listen to what consumers have to say and the language they use to express themselves. In Belgium, consumers express totally different needs regarding bottled and tap water than across the border in the Netherlands. In Belgium, bottled water is considered a basic necessity because people distrust tap water (*security need*), while in the Netherlands bottled water is considered a bit of a luxury and often purchased for when people entertain guests (*esteem need*).

Cultural conventions

Cultural conventions are the most intricate collection of rules. Cultural factors that are seemingly outside of its product or service category can affect a brand. The research conducted to uncover the category and needs conventions may provide clues to the influence of cultural conventions. Particular needs conventions can be derived from underlying cultural factors. For example, the aesthetic needs for simplicity and plainness in

Sweden (apparent in Swedish design) can probably be traced back to the Lutheran values of humility and moderation. However, it is a mistake to assume cultural influences without checking them. For example, Unox sausages (a Unilever brand) were successfully introduced in Hong Kong. At first sight it would seem that the product was totally alien to Cantonese cuisine and therefore not suited to the local culture. However, local housewives quickly incorporated the sausage in their fried rice, as it was very convenient and tasty.

There is all manner of qualitative and quantitative information about cultures. There are anthropological studies that can be accessed through universities and libraries, and there are various comparative values studies in the form of source books. However, this type of information is generally rather general –for example, focusing on social and personal values – and is therefore difficult to apply to brands. This information should be used mainly by way of cultural introduction. To get a handle on cultural conventions that can affect a brand, it is best to participate in a society, for instance spending time with consumers as they interact with the brand. Watson (1997), while doing anthropological fieldwork in Hong Kong's New Territories, describes how aghast he was when his Chinese host family took him to McDonald's rather than for a traditional dim sum meal. During subsequent visits he discovered how deeply the fast food chain had affected the lives of his host family. Qualitative research can also help uncover cultural factors, but it is less powerful than participation. However, also with cultural issues, it is important to listen to what consumers have to say and the language they use to express themselves.

Brand perception

Uncovering conventions that may function as lenses and filters is one thing, applying them to your brand is another. It can never be predicted with certainty which external factors will influence a brand in a particular locality, but there is sufficient evidence of how particular types of brand are vulnerable to particular kinds of convention, as discussed in Chapters 5 to 7. For each of the brand perception elements, the best thing to do is to carefully map out their aspects and the conventions that may affect them. To illustrate this process, this section will use a hypothetical US fast food brand called ABC which entered China in the early 1990s.

Brand domain

Mapping out the brand domain involves unravelling its four aspects – products and services, media, distribution and solutions – into their constituent attributes, confronting these with relevant conventions, and determining how these affect the domain. Figure 9.2 provides a map of the brand domain of ABC in China.

This example shows that carefully listing the aspects that the organization inputs into the domain, and then systematically listing and assessing

	Aspects	Conventions	Assessment	Results
Products & services	Service system Queue before counter Find own table Clear up own table Service with a smile Products Basic: burgers, fries & coke Extended: breakfast rolls Pack: Styrofoam Price: relatively high	Service experience Plate service Shown to table Waiter clears up Staff demeanour: serious Product experience/beliefs Rice basis for every meal Breakfast: fritters and noodles Pack: Styrofoam and cardboard Price: low	Service experience Flexible Flexible Solid Solid Products experience/beliefs Very solid Very solid No difference Flexible	Service system Queue before counter Find own table Introduce clear-away service Serious demeanour Products Describe products as snacks Drop breakfast product Styrofoam packs Retain high price
Media	Above the line TV Print Below the line PR Promotions gifts	Message delivery No advertising Representation Newspaper editorials No promotions	Message delivery Flexible Representation Solid Flexible	Above the line TV Print Below the line PR to target print media Promotional gifts
Distribution	Distribution system Car-oriented (eg drive-in) Outlets Colourful and inviting	Distribution Public-transport oriented Representation Austere	Distribution Very solid Representation Very flexible	Distribution system City centre locations Outlets Colourful and inviting
Solutions	Problem Monetary restraints (affordable) Time pressure (quick meals) Family duty (place for kids) Routines Eat out of doors Celebrate occasions	Needs Physiological (nourishment) Social (place to meet friends) Cognitive (affordable) Esteem (show status) Transcendence (little emperors) Customs Regularly eat out of doors Social events out of doors	Needs Flexible Solid Flexible Solid Very solid Customs No difference No difference	Problem Location restraint (hang-out) New experience (modern) Place to be seen (status) Family duty (place for little emperors) Routines Eat out of doors Celebrate occasions

Figure 9.2 *The brand domain of ABC Fast Food in China*

relevant conventions, leads to a fine-tuning of the domain. This example also shows that the brand domain can be perceived radically differently in the brand's host country from how it is perceived in the home country. In the United States, the emphasis for the ABC brand is on its efficient service system and its affordable products. In China, the emphasis is on the solutions it provides by offering a new and modern experience, by offering a place to hang out with friends, by being a place where one likes to be seen, and providing the opportunity to spoil the little emperors or empresses (a phenomenon of the country's urban one-child policy).

Brand reputation

The brand reputation can be mapped out in a similar manner. Figure 9.3 provides the reputation map of the ABC brand in China. The map shows how various reputation aspects can be described and assessed for their relevance to local consumers. Again, it is clear that such a brand perception element can vary considerably between a home and host country, as a result of external pressures. For example, the ABC brand lacks all credible endorsement in the United States, but finds that it is beneficial to obtain endorsement in China from those supposedly in the know, such as the press and user groups. The press may run stories on the educational benefits of ABC's truly modern dining experience and the restaurant's strict hygiene standards. The newly wealthy classes may be enticed to frequent the restaurants by encouraging business meetings in a separate part of the restaurant.

Brand affinity

Finally, mapping the brand's affinity provides insight into the aspects that consumers may apply to their relationship with a brand, and what factors influence their decisions regarding such a relationship. Figure 9.4 shows the affinity map of the ABC brand in China. ABC's brand affinity in the United States is fairly weak and contains rather unexceptional aspects. In China, however, the brand finds substantial affinity, mainly based on it being perceived as modern, sophisticated and aspirational.

The whole process of mapping the three brand perception elements and their underlying aspects allows brand management to get a better grip on what shapes consumers' perceptions of the brand. Once it has this understanding, the brand can be tailored to provide better value to consumers. Such a mapping exercise can also be conducted for other stakeholder groups in a host country, such as local shareholders, governments, employees and communities, in order to better understand what shapes their value demands of the brand.

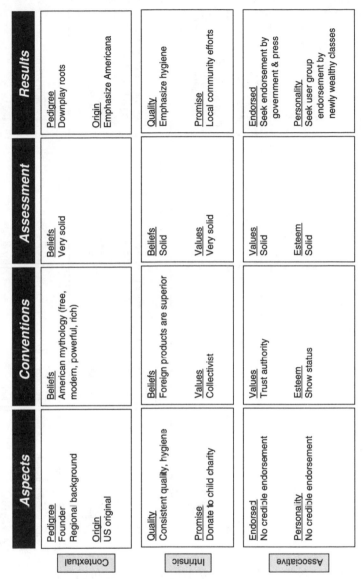

Figure 9.3   *The brand reputation of ABC Fast Food in China*

Brand recognition

Brand discrimination

Establishing a particular brand perception in a host country is possibly the most intricate part of the branding process, but it comes to nothing if consumers do not know the brand and do not consider it to be distinct

Aspects	Conventions	Assessment	Results
Functional Place to eat when in a hurry No frills	Service experience Used to fast Chinese food Used to austere settings	Service experience Flexible	Functional Ignore
Emotional Childhood memories	Transcendence needs For little emperors	Transcendence needs Very solid	Emotional Play area and dedicated staff for kids
Native US original Grassroots organization	Beliefs American mythology	Beliefs Solid	Native Ignore
Cosmopolitan No traits	Needs Aesthetic (modern) Affiliation (world citizen)	Needs Solid	Cosmopolitan Americana symbolism Modern setting (eg aircon)
Ego Indulgence	Needs Cognitive (new experiences) Self-esteem (I'm worth it)	Needs Solid Solid	Ego Emphasize modern and educational experience
Society No traits	Values Collectivist	Values Solid	Society Local community efforts
Empathy Fast, efficient, friendly	Values Hierarchic	Needs Solid	Empathy Deference to customers
Association No traits	Needs Affiliation (rich classes)	Values Solid	Association Emphasize brand status

Figure 9.4   *The brand affinity of ABC Fast Food in China*

from competitive brands. Brand awareness and differentiation must never be the sole objective of branding, but they are significant outcomes of that process. Brand management must decide whether the same type of brand discrimination must be transferred from the home country to the host country. Brands undergo particular stages of development when they enter a country. Figure 9.5 shows how our hypothetical fast food brand ABC has fared over the years in China.

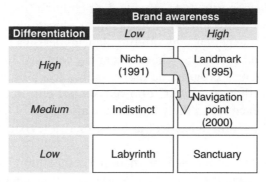

Figure 9.5 *The brand discrimination for ABC Fast Food in China*

Having established a number of restaurants in a few of the large urban centres in the east and south of the country, ABC was a niche brand for most Chinese consumers in the early 1990s. To most of them the brand was unknown, but those consumers who were in the know considered the brand to be very distinct from the largely local fast food competition. ABC's main branding activities were aimed at enticing affluent urban consumers to visit their restaurants. These activities consisted of establishing the required brand perception through PR activities aimed at local and national government and the local media (for instance, kitchen tours for journalists to demonstrate hygiene standards), training staff to provide the required brand experience in the restaurants (for example, understanding and preparing the 'exotic' food, operational efficiency, correct service demeanour), and some advertising (billboards and flyers) and promotional activities (such as a popular comic figure with the ABChildren's Menu). The brand's inherent novelty was sufficient to draw in the crowds. The main challenge was to ensure that the experience led consumers to repeat their visits.

During the 1990s, as the brand expanded both within the major urban centres and to secondary cities, the brand became a household name among Chinese consumers. The brand had progressed towards landmark status. The brand had become very well known among the country's urban population, who considered it to be one of a kind. ABC's branding activities during this period were mainly aimed at broadening its consumer base, both by encouraging less affluent consumers in the major cities to occasionally visit the restaurants, and by attracting affluent consumers in the secondary cities. On the one hand, this meant trying to duplicate what had been successful in the major cities to the secondary cities. On the other hand, it meant reducing the brand's rather selective appeal in the major urban centres. ABC realized that main attraction for less well-off consumers was the opportunity to provide their children (the little emperors and empresses) with a modern, and therefore educational, experience. ABC enhanced this experience by offering dancing lessons to children at their restaurants and by hosting children's essay contests. In addition, it focused its community programme on providing teaching materials to local schools. Furthermore, ABC allowed school children to use the restaurants as a place to do their homework after school. Advertising activities widened to include local and regional television and radio stations.

However, by 2000, national and international competition had started to catch up with ABC, and the brand could not maintain its landmark status. It started to slip towards a navigation point position. By now the brand was very well known to Chinese consumers, and most of them considered it as their reference point in the fast food category. This is a position where the brand is likely to remain for the foreseeable future. Branding activities are now mainly aimed at encouraging consumers in the major cities to remain loyal to the brand, broadening the appeal of the brand in secondary cities, and expanding restaurants to tertiary cities inland. Apart from trying to replicate the successful formulae to these places, ABC has introduced localized products, such as Red Bean Milkshakes and Mapu Tofu Burgers. For the first time it used national television and radio stations, and it has launched a Chinese Web site with restaurant information, games, contests and promotions to capitalize on growing Internet usage in the country.

This example shows that it is important to understand a brand's discriminatory abilities and how these can evolve during various stages of market development. The paths that brands follows differ: some brands retain a niche position while others move quickly through the spectrum of awareness and differentiation.

Brand connections

ABC also has relationships with non-competitive brands. There are the brand's own sub-brands, such as the ABurger and the ABCoolshake, and there are brands owned by other organizations that have a connection to ABC. The relationships with these brands are important, because they reflect on the ABC brand perception. The ABC brand functions as an umbrella brand for its extension brands, offering assurances to consumers about the quality and tastiness of these products. In China, this proved particularly important because consumers at first considered the food rather exotic. The link with the ABC brand guaranteed that they would receive products in line with the brand promise: American, quality ingredients, hygienic and modern. The decade-long development of the ABC brand has lessened the need among consumers for this particular brand promise, as the brand started to become a local institution and the Americana aspects were slowly played down. What remained was an expectation by consumers that ABC products would offer consistent quality and taste.

ABC meals are accompanied by a Coca-Cola drink, which functions as an ingredient brand to the ABC meals. The relationship with Coca-Cola is a natural one to Chinese consumers, because both brands are symbols of Americana in their own right. In addition, the Coca-Cola brand ensures Chinese consumers that they are getting the 'Real Thing', and this reinforces the perception of ABC as the original fast food brand. Not all relationships with other brands have turned out to be beneficial, though. Using the popular cartoon character Dragon Ball Z as a promotional item in the ABChildren's Menus turned out to be a disaster. Dragon Ball Z was so much more powerful than ABC that it functioned as a usurper that relegated the ABC brand to a mere distributor of the item. Although the promotion drew in the crowds and helped sell a record number of ABChildren's Menus, it weakened the main ABC brand to a certain extent.

CONCLUSION

Introducing a brand to a foreign society is no mean achievement; doing it in multiple societies (simultaneously) makes the process that much more difficult. A structure needs to be in place to determine how best to introduce the brand locally, while at the same time making sure that it does not diverge too much from the global standard. The global brand proposition model can provide that structure, as it is fully comparable across countries. Not only can internal issues such as business strategy and marketing implementation be matched up between countries, the conventions analysis and the brand perception sub-models also allow for direct comparisons between countries. It becomes instantly clear where the brand diverges internally and externally, and what factors are responsible for these differences. The model also allows brand management to look at successful brand developments in one country and assess whether these can be applied elsewhere, or whether they are specific to local circumstances. Finally, the model provides a feedback loop which helps in evaluating the success or failure of particular developments and in fine-tuning the brand to specific societies.

Brands that have been present in various societies for a long period of time have often diverged considerably for relevant, but sometimes (now)

irrelevant, reasons. Global competitors with standardized brand propositions can make use of economies of scale and scope, and put considerable
pressure on the divergent brand. In order to pre-empt or remedy such a
situation, many global brands are being harmonized across countries. The
next chapter takes a look at how the global brand proposition model can
be applied to brand harmonization.

10

Harmonizing a global brand

THE ISSUE

A global or international brand can differ between markets. These differences have often grown over time and have a rationale of local market adaptations, competitive activities and market dynamics. This can lead to a situation whereby the same brand is organized and supported in a different manner in each market and plays a differing role for consumers. However, when the brand faces stern competition from brands that successfully leverage a single brand proposition across markets, it lacks the economies of scale to fight back and defend its value to consumers. To remedy such a situation or pre-empt one, brands are harmonized across markets. Brand harmonization is a synchronization of the brand proposition across countries or other geographic markets. Brand harmonization can also include a synchronization of the brand across company divisions.

This is an extremely delicate operation, as it threatens to upset both local brand management's and local consumers' sensitivities, if not handled well. The key to successful brand harmonization is to determine which aspects of the brand proposition are or should be core to the brand across markets, and can be standardized without upsetting local management and consumers – or better still, while inspiring them! It is equally important to determine which aspects of the brand proposition should be left to the discretion of local brand management, and how they should deal with these aspects to deliver maximum consumer value locally.

In some cases, it is sensible to restrict brand harmonization to a number of key markets. Not only does this have the greatest effect where it counts most, but the key markets also function as a proving ground for secondary markets. If it works well in the important places, there is less reason to oppose harmonization elsewhere.

INTERNAL ANALYSIS

The three elements of the internal analysis – organization, brand expression and marketing – are discussed separately below. In the case of global brand harmonization, the analysis focuses on how these elements differ and converge across countries.

The organization

Business strategy

The business strategy is the driver of brand harmonization, and is based on inspirational elements that favour a standardization of the brand. Management must have a vision of converging consumer requirements across countries and continents, it must have a mission to deal with single issues worldwide, and have the ambition to be one of the major players in a category. Only if consumer requirements are or become similar does brand harmonization stand a chance. Furthermore, the core of the brand needs to be reduced to its essentials for harmonization to succeed; otherwise it will be too difficult to manage the brand centrally. Finally, the brand needs to have (the potential for) scale before any harmonization efforts are undertaken, otherwise the brand will be unable to compete with the brands that do have sufficient scale.

Brand harmonization is based upon a strategic rationale of economies of scale, gained through a concentration of production, distribution, support, advertising, promotions and development. These economies allow the brand to be more profitable, which in its turn provides a brand with the resources to leverage its equity into new markets and segments, into extensions, into strategic alliances, into mergers, into takeovers, and so on. There are a number of mistaken strategic notions about brand harmonization:

▌ Scale as strategy, which holds that the bigger the market share, the higher the profits. The pursuit of scale can lead to a situation whereby market share is bought at the expense of cash flow and margin.

- Economies as strategy, which holds that the organization with the lowest unit costs makes the highest profit. The pursuit of economies, however, may lead an organization to neglect necessary development investments.
- Global as strategy, which holds that only fully harmonized global brands will be able to compete for the hearts and minds of consumers. This is based upon the assumption that harmonized global brands are so powerful that they are able to outspend and thus crush competition.
- Standardization as strategy, which holds that consumers want to experience the same brands in exactly the same manner no matter where they are on the globe. This is based on a doubly mistaken premise: first, that consumers around the world are becoming unavoidably more and more similar, and second, that when consumers travel to foreign countries they expect to find the exact same brands there as at home.

An organization also needs the competencies, resources and motivation to harmonize a brand. The competencies needed for such an exercise are difficult to define, but they do encompass some of the following shared skills, technologies and talents:

- *Cultural sensitivity and diplomacy.* Global brand management must be able and willing to understand local brand management issues and drivers in order to be able to define what is core and what is peripheral to the global brand, and what aspects are left to the discretion of local management. In addition, global brand management must be able to persuade and enthuse local management; otherwise the harmonization process is ill fated.
- *Systems understanding.* Global brand management must appreciate the systems that underlie local brand management. How are local managers rewarded, how are they held accountable for the brand, what is their current position in the local organizations, what is their average tenure with the brand, for what other brands are they responsible as well? Such issues can affect how willing local managers are to participate in the harmonization exercise. In some cases the brand management systems may have to be altered before brand harmonization can take place.
- *Local talent.* Local brand managers must possess skills, such as language skills (say, speaking English) to be able to communicate effectively with global brand managers and local brand managers in other countries, open-mindedness that allows them to see the global brand's big picture, a tolerance for the unavoidable stress and aggravation of the harmonization process, and negotiation skills to be able to stand up for the local brand.

▌ *Common forum.* Global and local brand managers of a set of countries must be able to exchange views mutually in order to better define the global brand's core aspects, to learn from each other and understand the communalities and differences between the local brand aspects. Such a forum might be an electronic one (an e-mail group or via an intranet) or a physical one (such as regional and global brand meetings).

The resources required before starting brand harmonization are a number of centralized or regional functions such as research and development, production facilities, logistics and marketing communications. These need to be in place in order to make full use of the economies of scale that accompany harmonization. For instance, a salty snack brand will only be able to reap economies of scale if the harmonization of its brand allows it a form of centralized production with subsequent logistics, and (perhaps) standardized advertising.

The organizational motivation for harmonization is important, as responsibilities for the brand are removed from the local level and moved to central or regional brand management. Those responsible for a brand at a local level may feel that their authority is being usurped by head office. Such sentiments can be disastrous for implementing brand harmonization. Local brand managers need to be involved in the harmonization process and understand its value to themselves.

Internal conventions

It is very important to determine what the internal conventions are regarding the brand, to understand who has which responsibilities for the brand before brand harmonization, what the sensitivities are about harmonization, what the complacencies are and what the corporate culture is like. In highly decentralized organizations, where most decisions about brands are taken locally, it is often wise to start the brand harmonization process by defining a global brand proposition as a point of reference or a benchmark for local brand management. In this manner local brand management can get used to referring to the global brand proposition when it takes certain branding decisions locally, and to explaining its reasons for deviating from the benchmark. If this is coupled with an active global brand management, which provides benefits to the brand on a regular basis, the brand can be gradually harmonized. However, competitive pressures often push the process and thus create tensions between the global and the local organizations. Often, a common framework will speed matters along and allow all participants to discuss the brand in the same terms, on the basis of the same analysis, and based on the same strategic objectives.

Internal brand legacy

In many cases, a brand that has been managed mainly locally will have a differing internal legacy from country to country. Not only will very different people have been responsible for the development of the brand, but the brand will likely play a different role for each local organization. The brand's role depends on what other brands the local organization carries, and the importance to the local organization of the brand in relation to these other brands, the local developments (for example, extensions) that the brand has undergone, and the manner in which the brand has traditionally been expressed locally. Brand harmonization may have the paradoxical effect that the importance of the brand to the local organization is increased, while the local responsibility for the brand decreases. This is a result of the increased attention paid to the brand globally, and the subsequent restrictions put on local brand management.

The brand expression

A brand that is managed locally will usually have a brand expression that differs from the expressions in other countries. Without central coordination, local brand management will act using its best judgement as to how the brand can best provide value locally. Once brand expressions start to diverge between countries, and in many cases this happens from the moment the brand is introduced in a country, it becomes increasingly difficult to restructure the brand expression from the centre. Usually, the best way forward in such a situation is not command and control style brand management. First of all, it is useful to determine what the communalities are between the brand expressions in the various (key) countries, and whether these communalities define a core expression for the brand. The fact that there are communalities does not in itself mean that these common aspects form the core of the brand. Only if the common aspects of the brand expression are in agreement with the organizational analysis, particularly the business strategy, can they form the core of the harmonized brand expression. Otherwise a new core global brand expression must be devised that can provide the required brand experience to consumers in the various countries.

The core of the brand expression needs to provide value not only to consumers (the subject of the next paragraph), but also internally. Local brand managers must feel that they too benefit from the brand harmonization. One way of defining a new core for a brand is introducing a new product or service that staff can rally around. Sometimes such products and services can be leveraged from lead markets where they have proved successful. In other cases, a breakthrough product or service may be released simultaneously around the globe. Lays, a PepsiCo brand, conducted a rebranding of its salty snack brand Smiths. Simultaneously Lays introduced a number of its US products, such as Doritos, Dippas and Cheetos, thereby underscoring the global scope of the Lays brand and gradually replacing Smiths' local identities in the Benelux countries.

A breakthrough product or service can have a very strong effect in harmonizing the brand expression, especially if the product or service becomes the main or lead product or service for the entire organization. The introduction of the Sony Walkman 1979 helped define the Sony brand worldwide, as the consumer electronics brand that had pocketability at its core. Although this may not have been an intentional brand harmonization, the revolution that the Walkman brought to the way people listened to music spearheaded the brand's standardization around the globe.

Lacking lead or breakthrough products, a brand harmonization exercise still requires something new or novel. Otherwise, the brand is simply the same old thing under a new name, and provides no value to internal or external stakeholders. Vodafone acquired numerous local mobile phone companies and their brands around the world. This disparate group of brands was rebranded to Vodafone, and brand harmonization took place around the core of the Vodafone brand promise, 'Welcome to the world's largest mobile community'. This promise is new for the customers of the local brands that have been morphed into the Vodafone master brand, and raises their expectations regarding the quality and costs of international roaming. In addition, it raises expectations about new services. Vodafone tries to meet these expectations by introducing services such as Vodafone live!, offering picture messaging, news, advanced ringtones, information, e-mail, chat, location-based services, games and shopping.

Local brand management may be given a free hand in decisions about non-core brand expression aspects, as long as these do not disagree with the core aspects. For instance, a bank may have a core positioning of 24/7 accessibility through phone, Internet and mobile banking worldwide. Local brand management may have a free hand in enhancing this positioning with brand identity aspects such as reliability and trust, or with brand personality traits such as competence or sophistication, depending on their local circumstances.

Marketing

The marketing mix is generally considered the prime sphere of influence of local brand or marketing management, and resists harmonization.

Global brand management does not have the access or the local knowledge to tailor the marketing mix elements. However, the harmonized brand expression does help shape these marketing mix elements.

Price

Price and pricing structures are generally the most persistent element in the marketing mix. This is due to issues such as local historical pricing, local competition and local purchasing power. As discussed in Chapter 3, even a highly standardized product such as a Big Mac shows a whole range of prices around the world (Economist, 2002a). However, the brand expression does provide clear indications of whether a price is to be set at, below or above average prices in the category. For example, mobile phone operator O2 may have differing prices and pricing structures in its local markets, but they are all set at competitive rates compared with its competition. Similarly, prices for an Apple iMac may range from some 1,350 euros in London to 1,550 euros in Rome (Haskell and Wolf, 2000), but the pricing remain well above that for most Windows-compatible computers.

People

The people who support the brand are difficult to harmonize. Especially if they have sustained the local brand for a long time, there will be a tendency to behave as if the brand harmonization never took place. It is, therefore, imperative that staff are prepared for the brand harmonization. This can be done through induction courses, but is probably better achieved by means of integrated internal communications. If there is a lead or breakthrough product or service, communications can centre on that and act as a conduit for behavioural harmonization. If such a silver bullet is not available, a conscious effort must be made to align all internal communications (such as intranet, news briefs and management) and external communications (such as advertising, promotions, the sales force and via the Internet) to provide an understanding of the core brand expression. Obviously, behaviour and demeanour will still have to fit with the local cultural context. This is discussed in the next section.

Distribution

Distribution channels are also difficult to harmonize. Channel choice is often based on historical relationship with the brand's local organization, and channel choice can be restricted by local circumstances (such as wholesale monopolies, retail structures and infrastructure). An insurance company that wishes to harmonize its channels into direct writing (for instance by mail, telephone or Internet) may find that it is difficult to get rid of established intermediaries (so-called channel conflict), and that communicating directly with consumers is hampered by poor telecommunications and postal systems. It is generally wise not to abandon established channels for the sake of brand harmonization, unless the fruits of that challenge can be demonstrated upfront.

Products and services

Products and services are the heart of almost all brands, exceptions being luxury brands, or what Kapferer (1997) calls *griffes,* and lifestyle brands. Therefore, brand harmonization inevitably means that core products and services are standardized across countries, but not necessarily all the brand's products and services. A lead or breakthrough product or service can function as a rallying point for synchronization. In the absence of such a flashpoint, products or services must be chosen that best represent the harmonized core brand expression. This is not particularly difficult if the brand offers few products (as with Coca-Cola), but it is increasingly difficult if the brand offers many products and has many localized versions of its products. For example, Danone is known best for its plain yoghurt in France, but for its children's deserts in the Netherlands and its flavoured yoghurts in the United States (albeit under the Dannon name).

Communications

Marketing communications, and advertising in particular, are the things that many global brands most dearly want to standardize across countries. This is because most organizations consider communications mainly as a cost burden rather than an investment. Marketing communications follow from the core brand expression, the brand's core products and services, pricing, support and distribution. Therefore, standardization of marketing communications can only be realized when the other marketing mix elements are in place. Otherwise consumers will be confronted with a single message that does not conform to their brand experiences.

Whether marketing communications can or should be standardized across countries depends on such issues as on historical media relationship of the brand's local organization, local media circumstances (media structures, infrastructure and so on), and penetrations and usage of media channels. A beer brand looking to launch an integrated media campaign globally may find that its local brand management is loath to work with the global advertising agency, that media owners are not always flexible regarding when and where advertising is placed, that retailers do not agree to the intended promotions, and that Internet or mobile phone penetration and usage differ from that in the home market.

Marketing implementation

Marketing implementation is crucial when it comes to brand harmoniza-tion. How is the core brand expression going to be conveyed at customer touch points? The so-called 'localization' (that is, translation) of software is a form of implementation that directly impacts on the core product and, in extension, the core brand expression. Sloppy translations of the soft-ware and user manuals annoy users and detract from the products' func-tionalities. No matter how well harmonized the brand is, such issues can become stumbling blocks that convince consumers that the brand does not care much about consumers in a particular country.

The same problem arises with localization of Web sites. Poor Web site translations can provide comic relief. In 1996 Panasonic licensed the cartoon character Woody Woodpecker to serve as a user guide on the company's new Web site. Just a week before the launch of the site, an American staffer alerted his Japanese colleagues that the advertising slogan might need a bit of revising for English-speaking markets. The slogan? 'Touch Woody – the Internet pecker' (CFO, 2001).

Localization of Web sites does not stop with translation, though. E-commerce sites need to be able to handle local currencies, units, distri-bution and payment systems. A particular issue that needs attention during brand harmonization is whether to have multiple local Web sites or one global site. In many cases, Web sites have been created by the local organ-izations that all have a different look and feel to them, as well as different content and tone of voice. This situation is often exacerbated by a global Web site that provides corporate information only. Harmonizing local Web sites and keeping them aligned can be very time-consuming or even impossible. Moving everything to the corporate Web site may alienate local brand management and consumers. There are companies such as Brandsoft (www.brandsoft.com) that provide solutions for such Web site brand implementation problems.

Lead or breakthrough products are susceptible to out of stock or over-stock situations. Precisely because the demand for the products is global it is hard to predict how it will develop, and in which countries and regions the demand will be greatest. Upon its launch in the United States in October 2000, Sony's PlayStation 2 was plagued by availability problems. After Sony created a hype for the product, demand far outstripped what-ever it was able to provide, because of a shortage of certain components. It was even rumoured that the shortage was due to Saddam Hussein purchas-ing PlayStations to build weapons with. Whatever the reason, consumers, retailers and game developers were seriously irked by the situation.

EXTERNAL ANALYSIS

The previous paragraph dealt with the internal factors that influence brand harmonization. However, brand harmonization is not solely an internal matter, although many organizations tend to treat the process as such. It must also provide value to consumers. In the short term, this may entail providing additional benefits that the brand could not do locally, such as reduced international roaming charges for mobile phones on the brand's global network. In the long term, the brand harmonization may offer consumers access to technology or expertise that the local brand could not offer alone, such as third-generation mobile phone services. This section discusses the external factors, and how they influence brand harmonization. The three elements of the external analysis are discussed below: local conventions, the brand perception and brand recognition.

Conventions

Brand harmonization should not be a quest for the brand's lowest common denominator. Therefore, global and local brand management must not shy away from conflict, internally or externally. But there must be a clear understanding of the various conventions that affect the brand locally. Some conventions may be similar across countries, while others are typical for a market, a culture or a stage of socio-economic development. Even when conventions are similar in various countries, their solidity may not be. In some of the countries a challenge to conventions may provide value to consumers, while in others the same challenge is acceptable without clear positive or negative effects on the brand, and in yet other countries the challenge may be unacceptable. Judging the *solidity* of a convention is dependent upon:

▪ *Ubiquity.* How widely is something practised by competitors or consumers?
▪ *Uniformity.* Does every competitor or consumer behave in exactly the same way or think exactly the same about this matter?
▪ *Stability.* Has the convention changed much over time? Has it begun to show changes recently?
▪ *Significance.* Does the convention have a particular relevance to competitors or consumers? Do they feel that they could do without it?
▪ *Depth.* Is the convention rooted in the fabric of the category or in the society? How valuable do competitors and consumers consider it to be to them?

Category conventions

First of all, it is necessary to determine the prevalent conventions in the various countries where the brand is active. The category conventions are a good starting point for the analysis of the influence of the external conventions on a brand. This is because:

■ these conventions are openly observable and thus the easiest to collect and analyse;

■ we get a clear understanding of the brandscape as witnessed by consumers;

■ knowledge of competition provides perspectives for sustainable differentiation and competitive advantages;

■ category conventions may be related to consumer needs or local culture, which aids our understanding of the influence of needs and cultural conventions on the brands in the category.

As the brand is already established in each of the countries involved in the harmonization exercise, there is usually plenty of information and data available to determine local category conventions. Sources may be industry reports, primary consumer research reports, competitive analysis reports, purchased competitive products and staff hired from competition. Also, because the brand has been in the market for a (long) time, it may itself have contributed to creating category conventions.

The main problem for global brand management is to determine the communalities and differences between the category conventions in the various countries, and to determine their solidity in each country. For a start, it is important to use the same language to discuss such issues between local and global brand management. Next, it is vital to determine what causes the category conventions to be solid or flexible in the various countries. Is it because the main players in the country have set standards to which they stick, or is it because consumers feel a deep attachment to a particular convention? Finally, it may be sensible to set some norms for the assessment of the flexibility of the category conventions, as this helps when making comparisons between countries. How many of the main competitors in a country abide by a particular convention? What percentage of the main consumer segment value a particular convention so much that they want it to remain unchanged? The final appraisal of the category conventions that can or must be challenged by the brand harmonization remains the responsibility of global brand management.

Needs conventions

The examination of the needs conventions differs from that of the category conventions, because they are more difficult to observe and determine. There will likely be various reports on consumer lifestyle and consumer needs in each of the countries involved in the brand harmonization effort. However, unless research designs have been standardized, it may prove very difficult to compare these things between countries. Primary research is usually needed to uncover relevant needs conventions. Such (participative) research may involve:

▮ Observation of consumers as they shop for and use the brand. This shows whether consumers interact differently with the brand in different countries, which may be a manifestation of differing needs. In addition, observation may demonstrate whether the brand is meeting needs, or these have changed without the brand following suit. For instance, an insurance company may require its customers to file claims in person in some countries. The personal interaction may meet certain assurance needs in a country, but when the brand's reputation already meets those needs, customers may be ready for a less time-consuming method of interaction.

▮ Participation in consumers' daily lives. This is a more intrusive method, but it can be useful when the use of the brand pervades consumers' lives. For example, an instant coffee brand may find that in some countries it helps meet social needs among employees who gather for a cup, while in other countries the brand is mainly seen as a convenient alternative to brewing coffee at home.

▮ Qualitative research can help uncover manifest needs among consumers. It is important to listen to what consumers have to say, and the language they use to express themselves. A bank may find that its customers in India talk mainly about wanting high interest rates, while in Thailand they show more interest in Internet services, such as online share trading and money transfers.

Cultural conventions

Cultural conventions are not only the most difficult to uncover and interpret, but also the most difficult to compare. This is where local brand management's knowledge and skills come in. Not only must local brand managers be able to explain the cultural factors that influence a brand, they also need to be able to assess their solidity, and be able to relate them to other cultural contexts. Only then are they able fully to inform and convince global brand management to take account of specific cultural traits.

At the same time, global brand managers must also have informed themselves sufficiently about the local culture to be able to understand the context of local brand management. An example of how not to go about brand harmonization is the case of Coca-Cola, which purchased India's Thums Up cola brand in 1993 in order to replace it with the Coca-Cola brand, by making use of the existing bottle plants and distribution network. Coca-Cola did not understand that young Indian consumers were not impressed with Coca-Cola. They had already pledged their allegiance to Pepsi, which had entered the market in 1991. Coke also rankled the bottlers. Consumers and bottlers loyal to Thums Up believed that Coke was trying to kill the brand, which caused further problems. This rigorous approach did nothing for Coca-Cola and provided a chance for growth for Pepsi in India. Reintroducing Thums Up has not been fully successful, as a bad feeling about Coca-Cola's moves lingers.

Brand perception

Harmonization must create value for consumers

Brand harmonization must be aimed at increasing consumers' perceptions of the value of the brand. If consumers do not see harmonization bringing benefits or inspiration to the brand, they are likely to turn away from it. Therefore, the primary concern of brand management cannot be economies or efficiencies of scale, but must be the added value that the harmonization brings to consumers. This means that brand management must consider what the core elements of the brand expression will achieve in terms of brand perception among consumers in the countries participating in the harmonization exercise.

The brand harmonization process usually starts by defining a concept of global brand perception. This is an exercise conducted by global brand management, and should reflect their views on and aspirations for the brand. The global brand perception can be considered a gold standard to which local brand managers should aspire. However, they should not use such a benchmark uncritically and follow it unquestioningly. It is often sensible to test the global brand perception and the options with a panel of experienced local brand managers to see how it fits with their own ideas about the brand and how it may be amended. An additional advantage is that it provides the opportunity for them to buy into the global brand proposition.

Brand perception convergence and divergence

The next step is to identify the communalities shared and the differences between the brand perceptions in the brand's (key) markets. The aim is to determine which brand perception elements are driving the brand locally, and how these affect the continuity and vitality of the brand. The greater the communalities between these core brand perception elements, the easier the harmonization exercise becomes. If there are great differences between markets in the brand perception, the global brand perception can be used as a point of reference to see how the brand could grow more similar across markets. As mentioned above, the real test for brand harmonization is that it provides consumers with better value than the former local brand proposition. This means that the global brand perception that evolves from the harmonization process must aim higher than all of the local brand perceptions. The harmonization process must include new impetus for the brand. Offering new value to consumers will make the harmonization exercise a lot easier. It also provides local brand management with a clear reason to cooperate, and provides consumers with a reason to remain loyal to the brand.

The following issues must be taken into consideration when developing a harmonized brand proposition:

▐ The brand domain is the most basic area for brand harmonization, as it is concerned with products and services (and their assorted attributes and benefits), the media channels and distribution channels used, and the solutions offered to consumers. However, harmonization in these areas can be very difficult because of differing legislation, tastes, needs, customs, spending power, development of distribution systems and so on. For service brands, the harmonization of the brand domain is particularly difficult because services have traditionally been localized to suit conventions prevalent in local markets. Harmonization of a brand domain requires a thorough understanding of the category, needs and cultural conventions that need to be obeyed, and those that can be challenged.

▐ The brand reputation can be easy to harmonize if the brand's local reputations are not too disparate from one market to the other. The reasons for such variations generally lie in the development stages of markets and the subsequent need for information among consumers. Heineken often enters a market as an origin brand (Dutch, European or even international). As the market evolves, Heineken becomes a quality brand (premium beer), and finally it tends to become a promise brand (enjoyment). Whether Heineken becomes a promise brand is also dependent upon the beer drinking traditions of a market. In China it is likely to do so, but in France it is doubtful.

▐ The brand affinity is probably the most difficult element to harmonize because consumers' feelings for a brand are not easily influenced, and any overt attempts to do so may be met with cynicism. When Philips moved from its technology-dominated stance to 'Let's make things better', it was met with enthusiasm in various parts of the world but not in its home market of the Netherlands. Here the slogan was considered another weak attempt at putting a human face on a staid techno-bureaucratic institution.

ABC Beer

To illustrate the difficulties of harmonizing disparate brand perceptions, this section will use the example of a hypothetical ABC Beer brand. ABC Beer is a Belgian brand that was initially exported to European and North American markets. During the last two decades, the brand has purchased (stakes in) beer brewers and signed licences for production and distribution of the brand around the world. Currently, the brand is available in over 100 countries.

Because of the various ways in which the international expansion was achieved, through importers, licensees, joint ventures and wholly owned subsidiaries, brand management has always been a decentralized activity. Local managers have formulated different brand expressions and have supported the brand in many different ways to suit their local circumstances. In some countries, most notably the United States, this approach has been very successful. However, in other places the brand has never managed to get beyond embryonic development stages. ABC Beer global management are concerned that increasingly global competition will be able to put pressure on the brand by outspending on crucial marketing communications and distribution development. If ABC were to lose its position in one or more of its key markets, that could spell the end of its international venture. Management conclude that to defend ABC Beer's turf where it has been successful and to improve the situation in less successful markets, the brand must pool its marketing resources. They conclude that brand harmonization is the only option.

Global brand expression

Brand managers set about devising a core global brand expression that focuses on the brand's values of youthfulness, fun, rebelliousness and irreverence, which have stood the brand in such good stead in the all-important US market. But even there, the brand has lost some of its sparkle and has difficulty battling newcomers who offer a different beer experience: long neck bottle, pale beer and a novel drinking ritual. It is, therefore, clear that harmonization in itself will not suffice. Beer drinkers must be offered a new experience.

Therefore ABC develops a new lead product, an almost transparent beer in a disposable, yet stylish 0.2 litre PET bottle. The beer's transparency signifies a brand that is in touch with the Internet-connected generation's values of openness and clarity. The bottle is designed to appeal to modern aesthetics, sleek, smart, and with clean lines and individuality. Obviously, the bottle is transparent to emphasize the product's clearness. The brand is to be introduced first of all at venues for active young adults. Primary channel choice is trendy clubs, raves, extreme sports events and alternative music venues and events. Advertising will be minimal, as ABC expect word of mouth to be more effective to gain awareness and relevance among the young, urban, well-educated and well-heeled lead consumer segments in each country. Mass-marketing efforts will be the next stage to accomplish the brand harmonization cum rejuvenation.

Key countries

Global brand management decide to focus first on a number of key countries, based on their present and potential importance to the brand. These countries are the United States, Brazil, Russia and China. Of these countries, the brand has only been very successful in the United States. Brazil has long been a significant export market, and the recent acquisition of a minority stake in one of the country's major brewers provides an excellent opportunity to do better. Russia is a relatively new market, where ABC has bought a controlling stake in a minor brewer. In China, ABC has a joint venture with a major brewer in the south of the country which has never really been successful. ABC blames this on the lack of attention that its local partner pays to the brand. New expatriate brand management must change that.

Brand domain

Figure 10.1 shows the map for ABC Beer's brand domain across the four key countries. The listing of the domain aspects and their influencing conventions shows that a full harmonization of the brand domain is not possible, and that the aspects that can be most easily harmonized (media and distribution) are not the most important aspects in the entire exercise. The product and the solutions offered by the brand both encounter conventions that hinder full harmonization. For instance, the clear beer itself is a challenge to conventions of product experience that are likely to hold (some) value to consumers in Brazil, Russia and the United States, but not in China where traditional pilsner (lager) beer is a reference drink for the entire alcoholic category.

In addition, the 0.2 litre PET bottle does not fit well with the way beer is consumed in Brazil and China, namely shared by (large) groups. Larger bottle sizes need to be developed for these two countries. Also, the solutions offered by the brand to problems of self-expression and new

	Aspects	Conventions	Assessment	Results
Product	Clear beer 0.2 litre FET bottle	Brazil Beer not reference drink 0.3 cans & 0.3–1.0 glass bottles China Pilsner 0.3 cans & 0.7 glass bottles Russia Beer not reference drink 0.5 cans & 0.5 glass bottles United States Lite beer 0.3 Cans & 0.3 glass/PET bottles	Brazil Product: flexible Bottle: somewhat solid China Product: solid Bottle: somewhat flexible Russia: Product: flexible Bottle: solid United States Product: somewhat flexible Bottle: flexible	Brazil Clear beer Bottle: 0.2–0.7 PET China Clear beer (less emphasis) Bottle: 0.2–0.7 PET Russia Clear beer Bottle: 0.2 PET United States Clear beer Bottle: 0.2 PET
Media	Below the line PR Events Bar promotions Web site	Brazil: above & below the line China: above & below the line Russia: below the line United States: above & below the line	Brazil: little difference China: little difference Russia: little difference United States: little difference	Below the line PR Events Bar promotions Web site
Distribution	Outlets: Clubs & bars Extreme sports events Alternative music venues	Brazil: clubs, bars, cornershops China: clubs, bars, cornershops Russia: clubs, bars, kiosks United States: clubs, bars, supermarkets	Brazil: somewhat flexible China: somewhat flexible Russia: flexible United States: very flexible	Outlets: Clubs & bars Extreme sports events in United States (Alternative) music venues
Solutions	Problem Self-expression New experience Individual serving Routines Night out Weekend outings	Brazil: embeddedness & pleasure values China: embeddedness & achievement values Russia: modernism needs & pleasure values United States: self-expressive needs, individualist & auton omy values	Brazil: solid China: solid Russia: flexible United States: no difference	Problem Brazil: family/friends outings China: drink with colleagues Russia: modern experience United States: self-expression Routines Night out Weekend outings

Figure 10.1   *ABC Beer's brand domain across four key countries*

experience may provide value to Russian and US consumers, but do little for Brazilian and Chinese consumers who do not drink a brand of beer to stand out, but rather to be accepted within specific groups. Thus, the brand domain does not appear to be the area that will provide the key to brand harmonization.

Brand reputation

Figure 10.2 shows the same kind of map for the ABC Beer brand reputation. It is immediately clear that both the contextual and the intrinsic aspects of the brand do not provide much of a hook for the brand harmonization. The associative aspects, however, show that an endorsement of the brand by a young and hip user group in each country is acceptable and can be of value to the consumers there. In the case of Brazil and the United States, this links into inherent beliefs about the value of youth and feeling young. In China and Russia, such an endorsement would be a challenge to existing social values being eroded by social change. The success of the challenge will depend on whether it strikes a chord with emerging social values among (segments of) consumers in these two countries. The aspect of endorsement by young and hip user groups is core to the brand expression, and therefore a definite candidate for the brand harmonization to centre on.

Brand affinity

Finally, Figure 10.3 details the map for ABC Beer's brand affinity aspects. The brand affinity area is difficult in itself, because it deals with the bond that consumers feel with a brand. ABC Beer is trying to be very bold in this area by attempting to become the beer that consumers wish to be associated with (the beer to be seen drinking). The issue becomes more complicated because the affiliation needs among consumers differ so much across the four countries. It seems that ABC Beer will need to tone down its aspirations in the affinity area and settle for an affinity that differs between the countries, that is based on an ego orientation of fun and pleasure in Brazil and the United States, and on self-expression benefits in China and Russia.

Two-stage harmonization exercise

Having decided to focus the harmonization efforts on the brand reputation's endorsement aspects (young and hip consumers), global and local brand management must jointly figure out how best to obtain a consistent backing by this fickle and ever-changing group of consumers. This involves gaining an improved knowledge and understanding of this group's desires and activities in each of the countries. It entails conducting an additional loop through the organizational, brand expression and marketing areas specifically to suit the brand to this consumer segment. In this case, the brand harmonization process becomes a two-stage exercise, whereby harmonization among mainstream consumers has to wait until harmonization is achieved and acceptance has been created among a group of lead consumers.

	Aspects	Conventions	Assessment	Results
Contextual	Pedigree none Origin Belgian / European	Brazil: none China: none Russia: Import superior United States: Belgian beer superior	Brazil: none China: none Russia: solid United States: somewhat flexible	Brazil: no mention China: no mention Russia: import United States: no mention
Intrinsic	Quality Premium Promise Pleasure	Brazil: pleasure China: status Russia: status, modern United States: fun	Brazil: solid China: solid Russia: solid United States: solid	Brazil: pleasure China: status Russia: status, modern United States: fun
Associative	Endorsed No credible endorsement Personality Young & hip user group	Brazil: young at heart China: respect for elders Russia: respect for authority United States: youth worship	Brazil: solid China: somewhat flexible Russia: somewhat flexible United States: solid	Brazil: young & hip China: young & hip Russia: young & hip United States: young & hip

Figure 10.2   *ABC Beer's brand reputation across four key countries*

One of the issues that global brand management may need to face during the second loop of internal analysis is that of the brand's social responsibility. Two issues warrant more attention. The first is the issue of the young and hip lead consumer segment. Brand management must decide how to define this segment by age, as the brand cannot be seen to target teenagers or promote alcohol use among young adults. The second

Aspects	Conventions	Assessment	Results
Functional Quench thirst Emotional Excitement, fun	Brazil: pleasure China: status Russia: modern United States: excitement	Brazil: solid China: solid Russia: solid United States: solid	Brazil: fun China: premium Russia: new United States: excitement
Native Belgian / European Cosmopolitan International Stylish	Brazil: aesthetic needs China: affiliation needs Russia: affiliation needs United States: European beer mythology	Brazil: flexible China: solid Russia: solid United States: flexible	Brazil: stylish China: international Russia: international United States: stylish
Ego Personal pleasure & self-expression Society No traits	Brazil: collectivist values China: collectivist values Russia: cognitive needs (new experience) United States: individualist values	Brazil: solid China: somewhat flexible Russia: solid United States: solid	Brazil: personal pleasure in friends/family setting China: self-expression Russia: self-expression United States: personal pleasure
Empathy No traits Association Beer to be seen drinking (see young & hip user group)	Brazil: affiliation: friends & family China: affiliation: rich class Russia: affiliation: things modern United States: affiliation with youth	Brazil: solid China: solid Russia: solid United States: solid	Brazil: friends / family China: wealthy classes Russia: modern classes United States: young people

Figure 10.3   *ABC Beer's brand affinity across four key countries*

issue is the environmental impact of the use of PET bottles rather than glass. Measures may need to be taken to reduce this impact through introducing a recycling system for bars and clubs. Also, the brand perception analysis shows that the challenge that the PET bottles constitute to conventions of representation is not likely to be (equally) successful in each country. The combination of these issues may warrant a rethink of the packaging.

Finally, the brand perception analysis also shows that the enthusiasm for the challenge that the Clear Beer offers to conventions of product experience is not equally great in the four countries. This may just be an issue among the general beer-drinking population and not among the young and hip lead segment. Once the brand is adopted by the lead segment, acceptance among general beer-drinking consumers is likely to grow.

Brand recognition

Not only can the perception of a brand differ between countries, so can the brand recognition. This has to do with the time that the brand has been present in a country, the position that local brand management has awarded it (for example, niche versus mass market), the investments made in the brand locally, the positions of other competitive and non-competitive brands in a country, and so on. Because brand harmonization is ultimately aimed at strengthening the brand by making it function in a similar manner in various geographic markets, brand recognition is an area not to be dismissed.

Brand discrimination

Figure 10.4 shows how ABC Beer's brand discrimination differs between the four countries at the outset of the harmonization process. The brand is relatively new to Russia and has not found its way outside of the major urban centres yet. Consequently, the brand is not well known yet, and those that do know it consider it to be a very special brand.

The brand was introduced almost at the same time to Brazil and China. The introduction activities were similar in both countries. In both these countries, the brand has been unable to set itself apart from foreign and domestic brands. However, being one of the first foreign brands in China, ABC Beer was able to become a brand that functions as a reference point in the category for consumers. In Brazil, ABC Beer was a latecomer and has always faced an uphill battle against established brands.

In the United States, ABC Beer has been present for such a long time that most consumers have heard of the brand. This renown helps the brand to ward off newcomers and imitators, as consumers will generally plump for the beer brands they know and therefore trust. However, this position does not provide it with any defence against the new trendy beers and alcopops that are flooding the US market.

The intention of the brand harmonization process is to remedy some of these situations by offering the brand a way to distinguish itself more from

	Brand awareness	
Differentiation	*Low*	*High*
High	Niche (Russia)	Landmark
Medium	Indistinct (Brazil)	Navigation point (China)
Low	Labyrinth	Sanctuary (USA)

Figure 10.4   *ABC Beer's brand discrimination across four key countries*

competitors. In Brazil, increased brand differentiation will move the brand into a more lucrative niche position. This needs to be accomplished on the one hand by a selective choice of distribution channels for the new Clear Beer, which demonstrate the link with young and hip consumers (for example, specific clubs and bars). On the other hand, the brand needs to increase its differentiation by catering to consumers' needs for new experiences (for example, by organizing and sponsoring specific events). In the United States, the brand needs to move into a position resembling navigation point status. The emphasis will be mainly on offering new experiences to consumers (again, for example by organizing and sponsoring specific events).

At the end of the harmonization exercise, this leaves the brand with two different discrimination positions instead of four. The advantages are that global brand management is better able to support local management, as the issues facing the brand locally become more similar and may be dealt with in a more uniform manner. This helps the brand deal better with local and global competition.

Brand connections

The ABC beer brand has few connections to other, non-competitive brands. There is the ABC master brand and its pilsner (lager) extension brand, ABC Premium, available in all four countries. The role of ABC Premium is to underscore the brand's tradition, and therefore provide the brand with the required continuity and trust. The Premium extension therefore caters to consumers' security needs. The role of the Clear Beer extension is to provide the brand with vitality. The Clear Beer extension thus caters to consumers' needs for new experiences and variety.

CONCLUSION

Competition drives brand harmonization efforts. The brand's global management wants either to pre-empt global and local competition, by concentrating the brand and taking advantage of the resulting economies to beat competitive brands, or to defend against other global brands, by cutting away at the expenditure on the brand, to withstand the pressures on margins and revenues caused by the global competition. A brand harmonization analysis takes into account the communalities of a brand across markets, but with a focus on the aspects of the brand proposition that provide the brand with continuity and vitality. It is not an exercise in finding the lowest common denominator, but rather one in identifying the core elements that provide consumers with value. The consumer understanding must therefore focus upon obtaining an appreciation of how similar the brand is across markets, and whether these similarities actually represent part of the core of the brand or are marginal to the brand.

The brand harmonization may be driven by an organization's need for economies of scale. More important, however, can be the efficiencies of scope that they bring about. These efficiencies allow organizations to manage their brand more effectively and take better advantage of opportunities that come the brand's way. One of the most important efficiencies of scope is the capability to introduce global brand extensions. These extensions are new products and services that are offered to consumers under the same brand name. Being able to do so in the same (or similar) way across the globe allows an organization to pool its research and development resources, as well as leverage its combined branding and marketing skills. Global brand extensions are the subject of the next chapter.

11

Extending a global brand

THE ISSUE

For many brands, the most obvious way to grow is through introducing new products and services. These new products and services are commonly known as brand extensions. Extensions can be either 'close', that is, within the same category, or 'remote', that is, into another category. Remote extensions are also known as 'brand stretching', an elastic band as a metaphor for the brand's ability to move beyond its traditional domain. This metaphor is not all that accurate, because not all brands stretch their extensions into adjacent product or service categories. Some brands are actually able to skip and jump into seemingly unrelated categories.

However, it is necessary that in the minds of consumers there is some kind of 'match' between the brand and the extension product or service, otherwise the brand extension may do more harm than good to the brand. This perceived 'match' between the brand and the new product or service need not necessarily be based on the brand's current portfolio of products and services. In some cases it can be based upon matters such as the brand's values or principles, on its heritage, on its symbolism or on its type of relationship with consumers. What constitutes a good 'match' may differ between countries and cultures. Han and Schmitt (1997) found that US consumers generally look for a 'fit' between the brand extension and the existing products. For East Asian consumers, company reputation is also important, especially under conditions of low 'fit' of the extension with existing products. A company with a strong reputation is able to extend into categories that are not close to its core business. Han and

Schmitt provide the example of the Japanese cosmetics company Shiseido, which successfully introduced diapers in Japan, but failed with the same product in the United States.

It is clearly necessary to have a thorough understanding of the brand and how it may be broadened to include new products and services. Conducting such an exercise across multiple countries is greatly facilitated by the use of a universal framework that allows an analysis of internal factors as well as influences from the brand environment.

INTERNAL ANALYSIS

In a brand extension exercise, the internal analysis is aimed at understanding and defining the strategic reasoning behind the extension, the ability and willingness of the organization to champion the extension, the influence that the extension has on the brand expression, and the necessary modifications to the marketing mix and implementation activities.

The organization

Business strategy

Brand extensions are often born out of a vision of change and the opportunity that change provides. This change may be technological, legal, social, economic or motivational, and may apply to the brand's category only or may have a much wider scope. An example of an extension based on a vision of change is NTT DoCoMo's i-mode mobile phone service, which offers continuous online Internet access and assorted information and entertainment services. DoCoMo recognized that the convergence of speech and data services offered an opportunity to provide consumers with a valuable innovation. In Japan, i-mode has been very successful, with 35 million subscribers by October 2002 (www.nttdocomo.com). In Europe, where KPN introduced the service in Belgium, Germany and the Netherlands, the uptake has been relatively slow, but KPN firmly expects to have 1 million i-mode subscribers in these three countries in 2003 (Het Financieele Dagblad, 2002c). This is probably due to a number of factors, namely the rather high Internet penetration via PCs, the lack of handsets for the service because of longer than expected delivery times, and competition from services such as Vodafone Live! that offer multi-media messaging services (MMS).

As another example, the introduction of Bacardi Breezer was based on a vision that correctly identified motivational change: young adults were looking for an alternative to beer on their nights out. Apparently, Generation Y has developed a sweeter tooth than Generation X and is more demanding in terms of variety.

It is imperative to understand the strategic rationale behind the brand extension. The reasons for extending a brand rather than creating a new brand include (Kapferer, 1997):

▌ To offer new experiences to consumers, thus keeping the brand up to date. Such continuous innovation or improvement demonstrates a brand's will to respond to changes in consumer taste, habits and expectations.

▌ To limit the costs of brand development and advertising. The rise in global brands means that it becomes increasingly difficult to support multiple product or service brand advertising. Concentrating advertising and development costs on one brand provides an organization with sufficient share of voice for its brand while supporting multiple products or services at the same time.

▌ To defend the brand against incursion by competition and as a way to stay abreast of category-threatening innovations. The former is particularly relevant in categories where products or services are easily imitated. For instance, a paper products brand may want to branch out from toilet paper to tissue to paper towels in order to limit exposure to retailers' private labels. The latter occurs in categories where the technology is superseded by developments that often come from outside the category. Brand management should be watchful for such occurrences, and should extend the brand into the most promising new technologies at an early stage. A recent example is the demise of Polaroid, which once owned the instant photography category. The brand became caught between 30-minute development outlets and digital imaging technology. An early move into the latter might have saved it.

▌ To use and reinforce the accumulated image capital of the brand. Each brand has developed some kind of meaning in consumers' minds, and this meaning can be leveraged into other categories, although there is a difference from brand to brand in how well this can be done and how close or far the category lies from the existing products or services. At best the extension not only provides a brand with additional revenue and profits, but also with added credibility. Kapferer (1997) gives the example of Salomon, which extended from ski boots and bindings into skis themselves, thereby reinforcing its reputation as a skiing brand.

▌ By being attached to a product, a brand is dependent upon the product lifecycle and is thus doomed to obsolescence. By transcending the actual product, the brand can stay young and pretty while the products disappear. This is practised by all washing powder brands, as well as by some automotive brands that stick to a model name, but (more or less) change the entire car (for example the Volkswagen Golf, Renault Laguna, Ford Mondeo).

▌ Finally, brand extensions limit the risks involved with new product or service introductions. It is a well-documented fact that brand extensions stand a much better chance of succeeding in the marketplace than newly minted brands. Retailers are more willing to allocate shelf space to a well-known brand than to a new brand. In addition, consumers generally show a higher rate of trial, conversion and repeat purchase for a brand extension than for a new brand.

There are also wrong reasons to choose to extend a brand, such as:

▌ Production as strategy, whereby the simple fact that a product can be produced means that its should be. Kapferer (1997) gives the example of Campbell, which branched out from soup into spaghetti sauce simply because both products contain tomato sauce as a basic ingredient.

▌ Technology as strategy, whereby the fact that something is technically feasible is enough to decide to extend the brand. Many brands rushed onto the Internet simply because they felt it was the thing to do. Many newspapers have extended their brand online without asking themselves how much value consumers attach to these online versions and what their subsequent willingness to pay for the service would be.

▌ Brand as strategy, whereby the fact that an organization has an established brand is enough reason to extend it. Virgin entered the cola market because it has such a strong and extendable brand. However, how much value does Virgin's rebellious reputation provide consumers when it comes to cola? Is Virgin able to challenge incumbents' complacencies and thus redefine the cola business, as it did with airlines? For some very strong brands, extending the brand may actually risk losing the brand's legitimacy among consumers. For instance, Heineken does not venture into extensions that could affect its position as a premium flagship beer brand. The risks of harming the brand outweigh the advantages that extensions may provide. In fact, at the beginning of 2003, Heineken discontinued its Cold Filtered lager in the UK because it was harming the brand's premium status (Het Financieele Dagblad, 2003).

▌ Efficiencies of scope as strategy, whereby the existence of production facilities, distribution channels and brand communications is enough reason to extend the brand. Reuters's decision to target the consumer market just because it has all the capabilities to do so is probably such a folly (Write News, 2002). How many consumers are going to be willing to pay for up-to-the-minute news from Reuters when such information is freely available from a multitude of sources on the Internet and on television, supplemented by a daily ration of news from newspapers?

▌ Rumour around the brand as strategy, whereby the extension is used as a way of showing consumers that the brand is active and up to date. Although this may be one of the objectives of a brand extension it cannot be a business strategy objective. In a way, the introduction of New Coke was such a mistake. Coca-Cola brand management was so intent on demonstrating to consumers that it was keeping pace with the times that it forgot why consumers bought Coca-Cola in the first place.

An organization also needs the competencies, resources and motivation to extend a brand. The competencies needed for a global brand extension include such shared skills, technologies and talents as:

▌ A clear understanding of the developments that shape a category, either the brand's current category or the one it is to enter. Some categories are shaped globally, for instance through technological developments, while others are shaped locally. Global brand management must therefore be alert not to mistake developments in the brand's home country for global ones. Certainly societal and motivational developments are never exactly the same in different countries.

▌ A structured approach to innovation that allows original ideas to be put forward and evaluated. A common mistake is to delegate all responsibility for developing innovations to a research and development department, and all responsibility for assessment to the marketing department. A structured multi-disciplinary approach is generally more fruitful and quicker. Also, innovation must be considered outside of the traditional technological realm, but as a concern for renewal throughout the organization. Finally, innovation should not be driven solely by head office, but should include people from around the organization.

▌ Global brand management must be able and willing to understand local brand management issues and drivers in order to be able to assess the likely success of an extension under local conditions. In addition, global brand management must be able to persuade and enthuse local management; otherwise the brand extension is doomed to fail.

The resources required for a brand extension can vary widely between organizations. This is partly due to technological differences between categories, but is also because extensions do not always require an organization to own development and production facilities. In some cases, extensions can be introduced using the resources of other organizations. This is most apparent in the cases of licensing and merchandising. Licensing and merchandising do carry a great risk of brand erosion, where consumers are confused or disappointed by the products or services offered under the brand name. Especially in high-tech categories it has become common to jointly develop innovations in order to reduce costs, share knowledge and increase the speed to market of innovations. Consortia are formed to develop and promote innovative products and services, such as Symbian (mobile phone software), World Wide Web Consortium (interoperable technologies) and United Linux (Linux development).

The organizational motivation for the brand extension is important, as local brand management may feel that it is being forced to introduce something that it does not fully support. Local brand managers need to be involved in the brand extension process, even if this only means being kept informed about progress, and need to be convinced of the value of the introduction. They will be responsible for taking the new product or service and turning it into a success locally by convincing local management, staff, wholesalers, retailers and consumers that the brand extension is worth their while. In some cases it is sensible to introduce the brand extension in a number of key markets first in order to gauge reactions and assess and learn from the launch process, before moving to other countries with the product or service. This can also serve to gain buy-in from sceptical local brand managers by demonstrating the success of the launch in other countries.

Internal conventions

It is important to determine the internal conventions regarding the brand, to understand who has which responsibilities for the brand globally and locally, what the sensitivities are about brand extensions, what the complacencies are and what the corporate culture is like. When Mercedes-Benz decided to develop the compact A-Class car, the management and the A-Class development team had a lot of convincing to do inside the company, as the model was such a departure from the brand's traditional saloons.

In a highly decentralized organization, it may be difficult to get local brand management to participate in the brand extension process when there is traditional distrust or competition between local and global brand management. Also, differing power and organizational structures between global and local, and local and local, may affect the extension process. Global brand management must also appreciate the systems that underlie local brand management. How are local managers rewarded, how are they held accountable for the brand, what is their current position in the local organizations, what is their average tenure with the brand, for what other brands are they responsible as well? Such issues can affect how willing local managers are to participate in an extension exercise.

Internal brand legacy

In many cases, a brand that has been managed mainly locally will have a differing internal legacy from country to country. Not only have very different people been responsible for the development of the brand, but the brand will likely also play a different role for each local organization. The brand's role depends on what other brands the local organization carries, and the importance to the local organization of the brand compared with these other brands, the local developments that the brand has undergone, and the manner in which the brand has traditionally been expressed locally. The question is whether the brand extension will fit with this internal legacy, or change the role of the brand for the local organization. Certainly in a situation where (global) brand extensions have not been common, a global extension may put a strain on the local organization.

The brand expression

Although the final litmus test for a brand extension is whether there is a match with the brand perception and whether the extension provides value to consumers, it is essential to determine first whether there is a match with the brand expression. Famously failed brand extensions, such as Bic perfume and Smith and Wesson mountain bikes, probably would already have failed at this stage if anyone had bothered to examine the matches with their respective brand expressions. However, the link between the brand expression and the brand extension is not one-sided. It is not just a matter of determining whether the extension fits the expression, but also whether the extension enhances the expression. A brand extension will invariably affect its brand's expression, simply because a product or service is added to the brand. This may affect the brand positioning, for instance by adding new benefit or offering a different usage. An extension may affect the brand identity, for example by introducing new values or changing the visual identity of the brand. An extension may change the brand personality, for instance by adding more competence or more excitement to the personality.

Some brands rely mainly on extensions to provide vitality and continuity to the brand expression. Conversely, with other brands their own vitality and continuity rubs off on the extension. This is not necessarily a function of the strength or weakness of a brand. In categories such as detergents, mobile phones or automobiles, regularly introducing new products is a necessity to retain consumers' consideration. In categories such as strong alcoholic drinks or entertainment, new products and services are mostly a way of creating additional experiences of the same brand.

Correctly understanding the relationship between the brand expression and the brand extension is key to conducting a successful brand extension exercise across multiple countries. The complexity of the exercise will depend on whether one is dealing with a mono-brand or a portfolio brand, the degree of brand harmonization, a product or service that is pertinent in all countries or only a few countries, and whether one is up against global competition or multivarious local competitors.

An extension that is part of a wider brand portfolio will often be easier to introduce, but will also be likely to have less individual impact on the brand expression. However, global brands tend to have varying numbers and types of sub-brands across countries. Amstel Beer has a variety of sub-brand extensions, including Amstel Light, Amstel Gold, Amstel 1870, Amstel Bock, Amstel Malt and Amstel Bright. In some countries, Amstel is only available as regular pilsner (lager). In other countries Amstel offers various of its sub-brands, including some that are only available locally, such as Amstel Special in Hungary and Amstel Reserva in Spain. In the United States, Amstel Light is the number one imported beer and the brand's lead product.

The degree of harmonization of a brand across countries has an impact on the ease or difficulty of (simultaneously) introducing a brand extension in multiple countries. The issue is actually not how much of the brand is harmonized, but whether the key brand expression aspects that drive the relationship with the extension are similar across the countries. Unless there are sufficient common aspects it may prove difficult to introduce the new product or service successfully.

Sometimes, the extension's product or service is simply not relevant in all countries where the brand is available. Several global automotive brands sell particular models in only some of their markets, such as the Ford Mondeo, which is not available in the United States, and the Mercedes A-Class, which is similarly absent from US roads. In such cases, the extension simply is not expected to meet consumers' tastes or needs. When lead, or at least significant, products and services from a brand's portfolio are absent the impact on the brand expression is evident.

If a global brand faces mainly or only global competition, the task of extending the brand may be difficult, because of the strength of competitive reactions. It is also rather straightforward because it is easier to understand and assess the competitors' brand expressions, and their products or services that the extension is up against. It is quite easy for Cisco to keep an eye on the few competitors it faces around the world, while it is a hell of a job to keep track of the multitude of global and local competitors faced by Lipton tea.

Marketing

Developing a brand extension is not possible without devising an accompanying marketing mix. The product or service has been developed and so it requires accompanying pricing, distribution and media channel selection, communications and support. For a global brand extension, it is all but impossible to maintain exactly the same marketing mix across multiple countries, and sometimes even between regions of a country.

Products and services

The most consistent element of the marketing mix for a global brand extension is likely to be the product or service. Certainly when products are imported, instead of manufactured locally, there will be reasons not to tamper too much with them, but even standard products usually need some tweaking to meet local requirements. Beer is sold in different types, sizes and styles of containers in various countries. Cars are sold with different tyres, headlights and accessories in different countries. Software requires localization of language, measures and manuals.

Communications

As mentioned before in this book, marketing communications, and advertising in particular, are the things that many global brands would most dearly like to standardize across their markets. This certainly applies to global brand extensions. As so much of the preparations for the extension have been undertaken globally, it seems almost inevitable that communications should be standardized across countries. But is this reasoning sound? For brand extensions that are unlikely to have much sensitivity for local circumstances this may be true. Microsoft's global 'One degree of separation' advertising campaign for its enterprise software and .NET technology is essentially the same the world over. For brand extensions that need to manoeuvre between the Scylla and Charybdis of local concerns this is seldom the best route to follow. McDonald's only produces local advertising, especially because most of its brand extensions are essentially local.

Distribution

Usually, brand extensions will be distributed through the brand's established channels. This is generally easiest to organize, and as most extensions are 'close' ones, these channels will suit the extension. However, when the brand extends into a new category it may be necessary to seek new channels. Brand management is then faced with a choice of using traditional channels or exploring entirely new ways of getting the product or service into consumers' hands. When Mars ventured into the ice cream category, it was obvious that it could not rely on vending machines, filling stations, supermarket checkout counters and the like as outlets for the extension. The product required refrigeration not only during transport, but also at the points of sale. This placed restrictions on the types and numbers of outlets that were suitable for the new ice cream product. Therefore the entire manufacture and distribution of the ice cream was subcontracted to ice cream companies, such as Dreyers in the United States.

Even when entirely new distribution channels are selected for a brand extension, it is generally not possible to standardize these across countries, simply because of local distribution structures. In addition, distribution channels may also need to differ between countries to best express the brand.

People

The people who support the brand extension locally will generally be the same as those who support the main brand, and possibly other previous extensions. Certainly in the case of close extensions this allows for consistency in the way customers are serviced. However, this does depend on the complexity of the extension. For example, a savings bank that introduces a mortgage product as a brand extension will commonly hire additional staff with specific skills to provide the advisory skills required for such a product. When the brand extends into a new category, staff will generally require different backgrounds and skills to be able to service its customers. When Virgin set up its Virgin Atlantic airline, it needed to hire all new air and ground crew, as well as all support staff.

Staff in various countries will differ from each other in terms of culture, education, experience and so on. However, the main issue is whether the service that they provide to support the extension must differ by design from country to country. If the support provided to the main brand or existing extensions already differs between countries, there may be good organizational reasons to adapt the customer service accordingly. However, if the extension must function as a lead product or service that is to revitalize the brand, standardizing key elements of customer service may be essential. A global bank that introduces a service extension aimed at high net worth individuals around the globe will want to ensure that its service to these jet-setting clients is comparable wherever they may wish to contact or even visit their bank.

Price

The price for a brand extension will almost always differ between countries, depending on local purchasing power and competition. However, the extension's relative price settings should be similar across countries in order to ensure a price that is consistent with the brand expression. With a very close extension (line extension), the price is generally related to the prices of the brand's existing products or services. A new variety of an Oral-B manual toothbrush may fetch a premium over the existing ones, depending on the benefits it brings to consumers. With increased 'remoteness' of the extension the price link between the original products or services and the new one weakens. The price of Oral-B toothpaste is still related to the 'premiumness' of its toothbrushes, but for the price of its electric toothbrush (co-branded with Braun) the relationship weakens.

Marketing implementation

The implementation issues for brand extensions centre mainly on availability and on customer service issues. The former has to do with production and logistics: will there be sufficient quantities to meet demand, and will these be in the shops on time? In order to meet higher than expected demand Audi had to rev up production of its sporty TT model from a scheduled 40,000 to 50,000 in 1999. Production lines needed to be retooled and production extended from five to six days a week (Automotive Intelligence, 1999). In this case, the tightness of supply actually added to the attraction of the car, whereas increased supply in latter years has made the Audi TT less appealing to potential customers. It is somewhat doubtful whether the recent introduction of the Audi TT in China will also meet with such high demand. The starting price of RMB 550,000 (approximately US $66,500) is equivalent to some 60 times the average urban wage in China.

For service brand extensions, design of the customer service often does not suffice. Staff need to be prepared to fully understand the service and appreciate its intentions in order to be able to deliver on it. The previously cited example of Virgin Atlantic Airways shows how ground and air crews needed to be imbued with the brand's dedication to consistently providing better service than its competition. In the Sky Trax Global Airline ranking, Virgin Atlantic was ranked among the 10 best airlines worldwide in 2002 and was ranked as the second best transatlantic carrier (behind British Airways) (www.airlinequality.com).

EXTERNAL ANALYSIS

The external analysis is, in many respects, the most important for the success of a global brand extension. In the end, it is the perception that consumers have of the brand extension that determines the value that they attach to the new product or service. As this book argues, that perception is shaped by the activities of the brand's organization, and the filters and lenses that consumers apply when observing and experiencing the brand. We start the external analysis with an examination of those filters and lenses: the local conventions. This is followed by a discussion of the brand perception and the brand recognition, as these apply to brand extensions across multiple countries.

Conventions

Most global brand extensions are aimed at introducing a new product or service that will provide similar benefits to the main brand across all countries. As the consumer perception of the brand is crucial to the success of the extension, it is important to understand the factors that affect that perception. The factors internal to the brand's organization have been discussed in the previous paragraph. There must also be a clear understanding of the various conventions that affect the brand locally. Some conventions may be similar across countries, while others are typical for a market, a culture or a stage of socio-economic development. Even when conventions are similar in various countries, their solidity may not be. In some countries a challenge to conventions may provide value to consumers, while in others the same challenge is acceptable without clear positive or negative effects on the brand, and in yet other countries the challenge may be unacceptable. Judging the *solidity* of a convention is dependent upon:

▌ *Ubiquity.* How widely is something practised by competitors or consumers?
▌ *Uniformity.* Does every competitor or consumer behave in exactly in the same way or think exactly the same about this matter?
▌ *Stability.* Has the convention changed much over time? Has it begun to show changes recently?

▌ *Significance.* Does the convention have a particular relevance to competitors or consumers? Do they feel that they could do without it?

▌ *Depth.* Is the convention rooted in the fabric of the category or in the society? How valuable do competitors and consumers consider it to be to them?

Category conventions

As mentioned before in this book, the category conventions are a good starting point for the analysis of the influence of the external conventions on a brand. As the main brand is already established in each of the countries involved in the extension exercise, there is usually plenty of information and data available to determine local category conventions. Sources may be industry reports, primary consumer research reports, competitive analysis reports, purchased competitive products and staff hired from the competition. Also, because the brand has been in the market for a (long) time, it may itself have contributed to creating category conventions. The main issue for global brand management is to determine the communalities and differences between the category conventions in the various countries, and to determine their solidity in each country.

Needs conventions

The examination of the needs conventions differs from that of the category conventions, because they are more difficult to observe and determine. There will likely be various reports on consumer lifestyles and consumer needs in each of the countries. However, unless research designs have been standardized, it may prove very difficult to compare these between countries. Primary research is usually needed to uncover relevant needs conventions. Such (participative) research may involve:

▌ Observation of consumers as they shop for and use the brand. This shows whether consumers interact differently with the brand in different countries, which may be a manifestation of differing needs. In addition, observation may demonstrate whether the brand is meeting needs, or they have changed without the brand following suit.

▌ Participation in consumers' daily lives. This is a more intrusive method, but it can be useful when the use of the brand pervades consumers' lives.

▌ Qualitative research can help uncover manifest needs among consumers. It is important to listen to what consumers have to say, and the language they use to express themselves.

Cultural conventions

Cultural conventions are not only the most difficult to uncover and interpret, but also the most difficult to compare. This is where local brand management's knowledge and skills come in. Not only must local brand management be able to explain the cultural factors that influence a brand, they also need to be able to assess their solidity, and be able to relate them to other cultural contexts. Only then are they able to fully inform and convince global brand management to take account of specific cultural traits. At the same time, global brand management must also have informed themselves sufficiently about the local culture to be able to understand the context of local brand management.

Brand perception

The brand perception is actually the starting point for any extension exercise. Only by understanding how consumers view a brand can brand management decide what the possibilities are for extensions. This does not mean that the brand is supposed to be seen as given, as a static entity. Rather, an understanding of the brand perception allows brand management to assess how well the extension fits the main brand and how the extension will influence the main brand. This means that brand management must clearly keep in mind the strategic rationale for the extension. There are two broad reasons for extending a brand. The first motive is to invigorate or strengthen the brand by adding products or services that help enhance the entire brand. The second reason is to give the extension leverage from the perceived value of the brand.

The brand perception determines the scope of the extension: how close or remote the extension can be. This depends on the brand perception typology. Generally speaking, domain specialists are more likely to be restricted to close extensions. This has to do with consumers' perceptions of such brands being expert and innovative in their chosen fields. Most domain specialists conduct extension for reasons of keeping their brands current. For reputation specialists, the closeness or remoteness of their extensions depends on whether their repute is based on category-specific traits or on traits that transcend their categories. Pedigree, quality and endorsed brands are likely to introduce close extensions, while origin, promise and personality brands are in a better position to contemplate remote extensions.

Generally speaking, reputation brands generally extend for reasons of leverage. Their established standing among consumers allows them to exploit the power of the main brand for the purpose of additional sales.

However, if extensions are only used to milk the brand and do not themselves help enhance the brand, it is a matter of time before a reputation specialist loses its standing and its ability to leverage its inherent value. Affinity specialists are ideally suited to brand extensions, because their relationships with consumers are based on wider notions than their products, services or credentials. Whether their extensions are close or remote depends on how much the consumer bonding is based on the brands' perceived capabilities. Brands that base their relationships on functional, ego-orientated, empathy and native affinity usually introduce close extensions, because such affinity is the result of being the perceived leader in a category. Brands that base their relationships on emotional, society-oriented, association and cosmopolitan affinity are generally better able to introduce remote extensions, because such affinity is the result of their attitudes and behaviour.

When extending a brand across multiple countries, it is imperative to know whether the brand perception typology is the same in these countries, whether they are based on exactly the same traits, and what conventions affect the brand perception locally. In most countries where it is available, *Elle* is considered a leading fashion and cosmetics magazine. Most of its extensions are into related magazines (such as *Elle Decor, Decoration, Interior* and *Wonen*) and online. In Asia, and particularly Japan, Elle is considered to be much more than a fashion and cosmetics magazine. The Elle brand in Asia stands for women, fashion, youth and international sophistication. The associative allure of the brand was so strong to Japanese women in the 1980s that they started asking the magazine if they could buy the special gift items that it gave out to entice new subscribers. By 2002, Elle was the fourth largest licensed brand in Japan, selling around US $500 million worth of merchandise a year. In the rest of Asia, it sells another US $450 million of merchandise annually. Products include Elle clothing, Elle bed sheets, Elle tableware and even Elle baby accessories (Far Eastern Economic Review, 2002a).

ABC Bank

In order to determine the impact of the brand perception and the influence on the external conventions on the extension process, it is a good idea to map out the three brand perception elements: domain, reputation and affinity. To illustrate the process, this section employs the hypothetical ABC Bank and its extension into capital-guaranteed mutual funds in four countries where the potential demand for such a product is considered highest by the organization: Belgium, India, Taiwan and Uruguay. One of the problems facing global brand management is that the brand differs markedly between these countries.

Belgium. The Belgian outfit is a rather traditional consumer and small-business banking operation with 200 branch offices, mainly located in the Flemish part of the country. The bank offers a full range of banking services to its customers, such as current and savings accounts, loans, mortgages and personal financial planning. In recent years, the bank has successfully moved most of its transactional business online. As a result, local management has decided to close and relocate branch offices, and restrict personal services mainly to business clients. The bank traditionally has an excellent reputation among consumers and small-business owners for its reliability and pleasant service. The worldwide economic downturn has encouraged Belgian consumers to seek more financial security. This has resulted in increased savings and increased purchases of bonds, a traditional staple for Belgian investors.

India. ABC Bank set up in India some five years ago to take advantage of the growing urban middle classes. The bank has full branch offices in five major urban centres and satellite offices offering only transactional services in 10 secondary cities. The major thrust of the bank is to offer current and savings accounts, credit cards and online banking topped up with asset management services (such as unit trusts, offshore investments and retirement insurance plans). The bank is one of several foreign banks vying for the Indian middle class, including HSBC, Citibank, Standard Chartered and ANZ Grindleys. ABC Bank India is considered rather stylish thanks to its swank offices, its rather ostentatious advertising and its handsome front office staff. The recent revelation by the Unit Trust of India (UTI) that the value of its investments were considerably lower than had previously been reported led to an exodus of investors and a subsequent freezing of all the UTI transactions in order to avoid its meltdown.

Taiwan. ABC Bank Taiwan entered the country 10 years ago to take advantage of the local stock market boom. The bank built up a consumer brokerage outfit with a string of offices in the major cities of the island: Taipei, Taichung, Tainan and Kaoshiung. More recently, the brokerage has gone online in reaction to initiatives by local and global competition. The brand is seen as a specialist stockbroker, especially popular among small investors such as taxi drivers and housewives. The Asian financial crisis and the worldwide slump that followed it have hit small investors hard, and trading volumes have declined sharply.

Uruguay. In Uruguay, the bank was originally established as a merchant bank, and it only became a consumer bank during the past two decades. The bank offers a full range of consumer banking services and has 20 branch offices mainly situated in the country's capital city Montevideo and the beach resort Punta Del Este. ABC Bank is known primarily for its personal and considerate service. The recent crisis in neighbouring

Argentina has led to a run on all banks in Uruguay, and banking operations were temporarily suspended. The Uruguayan peso depreciated by
more than 50 per cent against the US dollar. In contrast to Argentina,
deposits and loans in US dollars have not been converted to pesos. Peso
and dollar deposits and accounts are still being paid normally.

Given the circumstances in these four countries, ABC Bank foresee a
strong demand for safe investments with a better yield than savings
accounts. Global brand management are asked to prepare plans for an
extension into capital-guaranteed mutual funds. Such funds are fairly
sophisticated products combining bonds, stocks, stock index futures and
option contracts. Investors are guaranteed to retain their original investment even if stock markets slump. The ABC Capital-Guaranteed Fund
will be sold to investors via the Internet only, in order to reduce costs.

Appraising the extension

Figure 11.1 maps out the brand, the match with the extension, the prevalent conventions, their assessment and the results.

This simple map quickly shows the issues surrounding the extension of
a brand in multiple countries. It is clear that the brand perception differs as
a result of the history and behaviour of the bank, ranging from a kind of
national institution in Belgium to an efficient money machine in Taiwan.
The fit of the extension with the main brand is not equally good in all the
countries, because of the current perception. Also, the impact of the extension on the brand differs as a result of the perception. In Belgium, the
extension is seen as an impetus to a respected, yet unexciting brand. In
India, the extension matches well with the main brand, but it does not
offer the brand any new momentum. In Taiwan, the match between the
extension and the brand is poor, because the latter is considered to be a
specialist. The extension itself is also too cautious an innovation to invigorate the brand. In Uruguay, the empathetic brand and the considerate
extension make an excellent match. The extension also underlines the
empathy of the brand for its customers.

Looking at the conventions in the four countries, we observe a set of
category, needs and cultural conventions. The Belgians are very fond of
their bonds (kasbons) and savings accounts for their security and accessibility. This has been reinforced by the recent worldwide slump in stock
markets. Distribution of banking products has traditionally been via large
numbers of branch offices in Belgium, and Belgian consumers have traditionally been keen on personal contact for their financial matters.
However, the introduction of Internet banking has diminished this need.
Belgians tend to be rather uncertainty avoidant, meaning that they wish to
be prepared for eventualities. One of the effects is that they accumulate

	Perception	Extension	Conventions	Assessment	Results
Belgium	Quality brand (brand reputation)	Excellent match, innovative	Bonds (kasbons) & savings accounts; Branch offices; Avoid uncertainty	Rather solid; Flexible; Solid	Introduce mutual fund; No sales fee
India	Cosmopolitan brand (brand affinity)	Good match, sophisticated product	UTI, State Banks savings accounts; Branch offices; Thrifty	Rather flexible; Somewhat solid; Solid	Introduce mutual fund; Include branch office distribution; Low transactional cost
Taiwan	Service specialist (brand domain)	Poor match	Stocks; Branch offices; Speculate	Rather solid; Rather solid; Solid	No introduction
Uruguay	Empathy brand (brand affinity)	Excellent match, thoughtful product	Dollars; Branch offices; Personal attention	Solid; Rather solid; Solid	Introduce mutual fund; Dollar-denominated; Branch office distribution; Personalized advice

Figure 11.1 *ABC Bank's proposed extension*

large sums of money in savings accounts 'just in case'. The fear of unforeseen incidents leads Belgians to keep money handy that is earning little interest.

Indian consumers are used to investing their money in state-owned institutions, such as UTI and banks, because of their perceived reliability. In recent years, foreign banks have increasingly been attracting assets from middle-class consumers, as they offered better returns and more modern investment products. The confidence in state institutions has further been eroded by recent problems involving the UTI. Despite the advent of Internet banking in India, most consumers still prefer to buy and sell their investment products in person at a branch office, because of their needs for personal attention and assurances. Indians, even those belonging to the middle classes, tend to be rather careful with their money and will demand a good deal from their financial institutions. This usually translates into wanting free services and low transactional costs.

Taiwanese private investors are addicted to stocks, despite the stock market's poor performance in recent years. The stock exchange is used more for speculative purposes than for long-term investments. This has probably to do with a deep-seated Chinese love of gambling as an instant path to wealth. Gambling is largely illegal in Taiwan. Taiwanese investors still favour the brokerage houses over the Internet as distribution channels. Investors tend to congregate enthusiastically at brokerage firms to track and discuss their stocks. Online share trading accounts for only a few per cent of the total market turnover.

In Uruguay, consumers traditionally invest their money in US dollars, and this has been reinforced by the decline of the peso during the last year. Almost 90 per cent of the private sector's deposits in the private commercial banking system are dollar-denominated. Investment products in Uruguay are sold mainly through bank branch offices, and customers are devoted to their personal contacts at their local office. This is partly because of a need for personal attention and partly because this is the way to get things done efficiently.

The combination of the appraisal of the brand and extension match, and the assessment of the local conventions governing the investment category, led global brand management to decide the following:

▌ In Belgium, the brand and extension match well and are deemed mutually enhancing. The ABC Bank brand is invigorated by the perceived innovativeness of the extension, and the extension benefits from the perceived solidity of the main brand. In addition, the extension meets prevalent needs for secure investments. Direct accessibility of the investments is guaranteed by only levying a purchase fee for the fund and no sales fee. This leaves consumers confident that they can withdraw money whenever they need to. Thanks to the advent of Internet banking, the fund can be distributed entirely online.

▌ In India, the ABC brand and the extension are considered matching. The brand's perceived sophistication is mirrored by an intricate investment product. However, the extension does not appear to further strengthen the ABC brand as a whole. The trail blazed by foreign banks and the recent controversy surrounding state institutions have manifested a need among Indian middle-class consumers for safe modern investment products, and has helped the acceptance of foreign financial institutions. Internet banking is still in its early stages in India, and most banks offer only the basic banking services. Foreign and private banks are at the forefront of these developments. Most consumers still feel strong need for personal attention when it comes to investment products. Therefore, the ABC Bank Capital-Guaranteed Mutual Fund is not solely distributed online, but also through branch offices. Indian consumers are more keenly aware of costs than of returns on their investments. This insight has led to a reduction in transaction fees for India.

▌ In Taiwan, the match between the ABC Bank brand and the Capital-Guaranteed Mutual Fund is poor, because the former is perceived to be a specialist brokerage. Coupled with the speculative nature of private investors in Taiwan, this makes the product ill suited. In addition, distribution through the Internet and through the bank's brokerage offices is not likely to be successful. The combination of these factors leads global brand management to abandon the introduction of the Capital-Guaranteed Mutual Fund in Taiwan altogether.

▌ In Uruguay, the ABC brand and its Capital-Guaranteed Mutual Fund extension are deemed to be an excellent match. The perceived empathetic nature of the brand fits well with the considerate characteristics of the extension, and they are deemed to be mutually reinforcing. The increasing embrace of the US dollar by Uruguayan consumers makes it inevitable that the fund will be dollar-denominated. The limited nature of Internet banking in Uruguay, coupled with a strong need for personal advice and contact, requires the fund to be distributed solely through the bank's branch offices.

This example shows that even a non-harmonized brand can successfully introduce a global extension, albeit with some (minor) local adaptations. In this case, only in Taiwan were the brand and the extension unsuited to each other, because of the very specific nature of the brand locally and the inappropriateness of the product itself to the market.

Brand recognition

Not only can the perception of a brand differ between countries, so can the brand recognition. This has to do with the time that the brand has been present in a country, the position that local brand management has awarded it, the investments made in the brand locally, the positions of other competitive and non-competitive brands in a country, and so on. Differences in brand recognition, be they in comparison with competitive or friendly brands, can have an impact on the brand extension.

Brand discrimination

Figure 11.2 shows the brand discrimination of ABC Bank in the three countries selected for the brand extension, Belgium, India and Uruguay.

In Belgium, ABC Bank is considered one of a generally evoked set of bank brands, all very similar in the eyes of consumers. ABC Bank is one of the banks that most consumers will consider simply because it is so well known, and is hence believed to be dependable. The brand meets security needs on a par with its major competition and that suits the extension well, with its emphasis on 'secure investment'. In both India and Uruguay, ABC Bank is considered distinctive because it is a major foreign bank. In both countries, major foreign banks are considered more modern, efficient, innovative and helpful than the major local banks. This meets local cognitive needs for new experiences, convenience and responsiveness. In Uruguay, foreign banks are also considered a safer place to park one's money. The extension meets these needs for modernity, responsiveness and security, and therefore matches well with the overall brand image.

Brand connections

ABC Bank's brand has varying connections to non-competitive brands in the three countries. In Belgium, the brand has numerous extension brands covering categories such as transactional services, consumer credit, insurance and credit cards. In addition, ABC Bank co-brands credit cards with all major credit card companies, and has a co-branded venture with an

Differentiation	Brand awareness	
	Low	High
High	Niche	Landmark
Medium	Indistinct	Navigation point (India, Uruguay)
Low	Labyrinth	Sanctuary (Belgium)

Figure 11.2   *The brand discrimination of ABC Bank in three countries*

international Internet service provider. None of these relationships contradicts or hinders the new extension. On the contrary, some of them even reinforce the extension. For example, the co-branded Internet service increases the distribution opportunities for the Capital-Guaranteed Mutual Fund. The ABC Bank corporate brand serves to assure consumers that they can expect a minimum level of reliability and service from the various extension brands.

In India, ABC Bank has few brand connections. There are a few extension brands in the areas of mortgages, transactional services and investments. This situation is easy for Indian consumers to understand, and an added extension will not complicate matters. The ABC Bank corporate brand mainly underscores the cosmopolitan nature of this foreign brand.

In Uruguay, the situation is more complex. ABC Bank is obviously a foreign brand, but it has few cosmopolitan connotations for consumers. Apart from a number of extension brands (such as transactional services and mortgages), ABC Bank co-brands credit cards with a local supermarket chain. More important, however, is the fact that ABC Bank Uruguay sells various investment products from other financial institutions, such as mutual funds from Citibank, Chase Manhattan, Deutsche Bank and Robeco. These function as benefit brands to the corporate ABC Bank brand. In a few cases, these branded funds even function as usurper brands, driving the purchase by consumers. The ABC Bank Capital-Guaranteed Mutual Fund is the first of its own fund products that the bank will sell in Uruguay. Communications during the launch will need to be aimed at convincing Uruguayan consumers that ABC Bank is equally capable and experienced in designing mutual funds as other financial institutions.

CONCLUSION

Developing and introducing a brand extension successfully is already a difficult task in one country, but it becomes increasingly complex when more countries are involved. Although the development of the extension my be directed centrally, with the risk of taking on home country and corporate cultural baggage, the introduction can only be conducted by local brand management with the expert guidance of global brand management.

The division of responsibilities for the extension exercise will depend on the degree of harmonization of the brand, and the subsequent opportunities for a standardization of the extension. For globally harmonized brands this means that their extensions equally match the main brand wherever it is available. However, for the majority of brands this is not (yet) the case. The development of their extensions may be centrally guided, but their match with the brand will need to be examined locally. The main brand and the extension may match perfectly even when the main brand differs between countries. Even when the match between these two is perfect, it will often still be necessary to tweak the actual product or service to meet the local consumers' requirements.

12

Creating a new global brand

THE ISSUE

In this age of accelerated globalization and worldwide reach of the Internet, is it possible to launch a global brand: a brand that does not exist in any country and is introduced simultaneously in several or many countries? When launching a totally new global brand, management is faced with a tabula rasa: a brand without any history, intrinsic meaning or direction. Anything and everything is in play, in each and every country. This is precisely the challenge when developing the new global brand.

The key to a successful global brand launch is to develop a new category or subcategory that the brand can claim and sustain, and which provides relevant value to consumers in multiple countries. This single-mindedness of the initial global brand can subsequently evolve into a more rich meaning, but not before the brand has staked out its core territory in the mind of consumers in various countries. A successful example of such a global brand is Yahoo!, which was able quickly to build its brand on the benefit of providing transparency as an Internet guide. Today Yahoo!, in its own words, is 'The only place anyone needs to go find anything, communicate with anyone, or buy anything' (www.yahoo.com).

Because truly new global brands are so rare, this chapter takes a different approach from the one employed in the previous three chapters. It employs less of a 'how to' method to the particular global brand strategy issue, and more of a description of the problems and challenges facing a global brand that is being created (more or less) from scratch.

INTERNAL ANALYSIS

The internal analysis is the most important stage of the global brand creation process. 'Instant' global brands are driven by a strong internal logic, and create entirely new categories or subcategories. This means that the rationale behind these brands needs to be impeccable if one is to avoid spectacular failures. The dot.com years of the second half of the 1990s showed that brands lacking in persuasive visions and business models were able to burn up cash in record time, but were unable to provide value to anyone except for a few lucky company founders and venture capitalists.

The organization

Business strategy

The *inspirational aspects* of the business strategy are especially salient during the global brand creation process. These aspects define how management envisage their yet-to-be-established (sub)category. They must answer the following questions when defining their *vision*:

▌ What technological, social, motivational, legal, economic or political developments form the foundation for the (sub)category?
▌ What sets the (sub)category aside from existing (sub)categories?
▌ What makes this (sub)category sustainable over time?
▌ What are its barriers to entry and exit?

Hotmail was a revolutionary idea envisaged by Sabeer Bhatia and Jack Smith in 1995: e-mail access from any computer anywhere in the world. Hotmail almost single-handedly created an entirely new category of free Web mail services. Sold to Microsoft in 1999, Hotmail had over 110 million subscribers by the end of 2002.

Furthermore, management must delineate the global brand's *mission* as a shaper of the new (sub)category. This means that managers must have a clear idea of how the brand will govern the (sub)category by providing outstanding value to its customers. They must answer the following questions:

▌ What are the critical improvements that we intend to bring to consumers' lives?
▌ How do we make sure that consumers can fully experience these improvements?
▌ How do we ensure that we remain the main provider of these advancements, ahead of future competition?

Jake Burton started making snowboards in 1977 after discovering that the early designs had not progressed much during a decade. In the early years, snowboarding remained pretty much an alternative or underground sport. Jake lobbied hard for ski resorts to open their lifts and slopes to snowboarders. One of the key success factors for Burton was to turn snowboarding not into a recreational pastime but into a true sport. 'Sport first' was Jake's motto from the start. In 1998, snowboarding became a recognized Olympic event. Burton Snowboard's stated mission is to be 'a rider driven company solely dedicated to creating the best snowboarding equipment on the planet' (www.burton.com).

Finally, management must describe its *ambition* for the global brand. Obviously, as the developer of the category, the brand is likely to dominate the category at first. However, the stated ambition must take a longer view and describe the position of the brand in a 5 to 10 year period (usually considered an eternity in new categories). To accurately characterize this kind of ambition, management need to answer questions such as:

▌ How dominant is the global brand likely to be within the new (sub)category in the long run? This is not a superfluous question to ask, because a first mover advantage can quickly wear off if competition can imitate and overtake the brand in terms of the value provided to consumers.

▌ How can we convince consumers that the brand is and will remain superior in both value and prominence? It is crucial to convince consumers that the brand is not only better for them than the competition, but that they can continue counting on the brand as the (sub)category leader.

▌ Which goals can we publicly state to underwrite our ambitions for the brand among consumers, employees and the investment community? Not all organizations will choose to state goals publicly, but it may help to convince stakeholders how serious the organization is about the brand.

Netscape was founded in 1994 on a core vision of the power of networks, the promise of a universal interface to the Internet and the need for open standards. Netscape defined its mission in terms of providing software that would increase the value of networked communications in the broadest sense. Netscape's ambition was for its Navigator Web browser to be the ubiquitous universal interface to the Internet, working on any possible communications device. Market share was therefore a top priority from day one, as Netscape figured that there would be one winner only in the browser category. Whoever got market share first would win the battle and reap the rewards. Netscape set a target of 10 million users after year one. In fact it attracted double that figure. Within four years the stock market valued the company at a half-billion US dollars (Cusomano and Yoffie, 2000).

Microsoft countered with the 'free' Internet Explorer browser, bundled with its Windows operating system. By 1999, Netscape was sold to America Online (AOL) for US $4.2 billion in (hyper-inflated) AOL stock. By mid-2002 Netscape held less than 4 per cent of the worldwide Web browser market by usage share and Microsoft's Internet Explorer held practically the remainder (Websidestory, 2002). In the end, Netscape had paved the way for Microsoft in the same way as Word Perfect, Lotus 1-2-3 and Harvard Graphics had done before. This example shows that a first mover advantage can quickly be lost against a mighty opponent that puts its mind to it, even when it is late to the game.

Correctly defining the strategic objectives and strategic rationale is necessary to ensure that the new global brand will survive. These *objectives* need to define what the organization wants to achieve in terms of changed consumer mind-set and behaviour, and what needs to be done by the organization to bring these changes about. Management must answer the following questions:

■ What will induce consumers to try the brand? For a brand that creates a new (sub)category, generating trial among consumers is probably the most difficult issue. Jaded consumers can easily ignore the brand unless they are pretty sure that it will provide them significant value. An unsuccessful example is Iridium, which tried to build its brand upon worldwide mobile phone access via a system of 66 low-earth orbiting (LEO) satellites. Unfortunately, Iridium management overlooked the fact that most people do not consider 'worldwide' to include vast oceans and deserts, but rather (mostly urban) accessible places. These kinds of places are generally well served by terrestrial mobile networks, which are increasingly accessible through mobile roaming agreements and multi-band handsets. Consequently, Iridium was almost completely ignored by one of its core target markets: international business travellers. After going into receivership in 1999, Iridium was bought for US $25 million (it had cost US $5 billion to establish the company), and now focuses mainly on businesses operating in remote locations.

■ What will change consumers' attitudes, and more importantly their behaviour, permanently? As the brand creates a new (sub)category, the way in which consumers are expected to interact with the brand will often be new. Amazon.com required consumers to buy books and CDs from afar using a relatively newfangled technology called the Internet.

The change in consumers' behaviour was relatively easy because the products involved are homogeneous, and ordering online and home delivery are more convenient than going to a local bookstore.

▌ How many consumers do we expect will try the brand and how many will change their behaviour? Although this is very difficult to estimate for a new (sub)category, it is necessary to set some goals, as this affects both the rationale for and the substantiation of the business strategy. It is very easy to overestimate the figures in a new (sub)category when one uses only rough indicators and rules of thumb. It is very easy to underestimate the figures when using only consumer research, such as a simulated test market.

▌ Where will consumers be located? Even for global brands that are entirely distributed through wide-ranging Web-based or mobile networks, diffusion will differ as a result of the penetration and usage of such networks. This has impacts on various issues such as the brand's business model, allocation of resources, the brand expression, the marketing mix and implementation (for example localization of content, delivery and after-sales services).

The *strategic rationale* for a newly minted global brand must describe how it is going to create and sustain sufficient momentum for the brand. In Chapter 1, seven misconceptions are discussed about the rationale underpinning global strategy. The general notion that can be gleaned from these strategic misconceptions is that 'global' in itself is not sufficient strategy. The strategic rationale needs to focus on why people across various geographies would choose to buy or use the brand: that is, what the relevant value of the brand is to them locally and why they would pay for it.

Google was founded in 1998 and is today widely considered the best Internet search engine in the world. Google receives more than 18 million user queries daily, and has over 62 million unique users a month. Google provides user interfaces in 86 languages and results in 36 languages. More than 50 per cent of Google's traffic comes from outside its home country, the United States (www.google.com). However, none of the users have ever paid a cent to Google. Google's business model is built on Internet portals and providers paying to use the Google technology on their sites, and on a keyword advertising programme that allows businesses large and small to activate so-called sponsored links, which are enhanced text links at the top and right-hand side of the Google results page. These links can be managed by Google's Advertising Operations Group or by the advertisers themselves. The company's Web site lists 10 things Google have found to be true. Among them are:

▌ Focus on the user and all else will follow.

▌ It's best to do one thing really, really well.

▌ Fast is better than slow.

▌ You can make money without doing evil (refers primarily to their non-intrusive advertising solutions).

▌ The need for information crosses borders.

▌ Great just isn't good enough (refers to anticipating and meeting needs that have not yet been articulated).

The *substantiation* of the business strategy is based on the resources, competencies and motivation that the organization can muster for the global brand. Many of the dot.com start-ups required substantial amounts of capital to get off the ground in the first place. Failed e-tailer Boo.com managed to burn up US $185 million during its 18-month existence. Conversely, Debbie Fields launched her Mrs Fields Cookies stores with US $25,000 of private funding in 1977. There were no venture capitalists willing to back a young mother with no business experience and a crazy plan to sell fresh-out-of-the-oven cookies only. Today, Mrs Fields has (franchised) outlets across the United States and in 13 countries overseas. What she lacked in resources, she made up for in resourcefulness, her motto being, 'Good enough never is'. As early as the early 1990s, Mrs Fields' IT philosophy was: 'to put as much decision making and intelligence into the store level PC as is necessary to free the manager to do those things that uniquely people do'. Each store has a computer terminal to access a centralized store management database. A store manager begins the day by inputting that day's characteristics: whether it is a school day, a holiday, the kind of weather, and so on. This causes the system to compute the day's production schedule. Store sales information is entered into the system throughout the day, revising projections.

The new global brand's competencies are its management and employees' shared skills, technologies and talents. These competencies can be decisive in shaping the brand's new (sub)category. Therefore, management must have a very good understanding of how these competencies will affect the formative stages of the (sub)category. Sony's Playstation and Microsoft's Xbox have both introduced online gaming subscription services in 2002. Both services got off to a promising start with 150,000 Xbox Live 'starter kits' sold within a week of the launch and 175,000 subscribers to the Playstation service within six months in the United States. Microsoft's understanding of and experience with computer networking may just give it the edge over Sony in online-console gaming (Economist, 2002e). Only time will tell, but it is clear that Microsoft has a head start over Sony when it comes to experience with Internet software connectivity, online subscription services and online content delivery.

Obviously, all the high-flying global brand success stories are powered by highly motivated people whose best 'just ain't good enough'. However, not only the level of motivation is important, the kind of motivation is too. In 2000, ABN Amro launched MaxTrad, an online international trade portal offering up the bank's insights in and wisdom about international trade, as well as (current) content from sources such as the Economist Intelligence Unit (EIU), Reuters and the International Chamber of Commerce (ICC). In addition, the site offered online access to financial products for international trade, such as letters of credit (L/C). The ultimate ambition was to turn MaxTrad into an 'ecommerce trading community'. One of the major driving motivations behind the portal was ABN Amro's wish to be considered among the leaders of the so-called new economy.

MaxTrad was developed and launched in a record 100 days without consideration for costs. Leo Burnett developed an international television spot (a desperately comical ad warning against MaxTrad giving away trade secrets) which was largely aired during the breaks of the Euro 2000 football (soccer) championships. Unfortunately, ABN Amro's eagerness for the project did not lead to the hoped-for volume of registrations of small and medium businesses on the MaxTrad Web site. Potential clients were scared off by the need for registration, and those that did register considered the site as a handy free news and information tool. Today MaxTrad seems to have found its place as a trade-dedicated Web site offering services such as L/C and payment collection services, cross-border trade management solutions, transactional data tracking and (general) trade information.

Internal conventions

The role of internal conventions depends on whether a new global brand is introduced by an existing organization or by a start-up. In the case of a start-up, these conventions are in a formative stage with stories, symbols, power structures and rituals changing almost daily, and formal organizational structures and control systems being practically non-existent. In the case of an established organization, the brand will be influenced by existing internal conventions.

A new global brand may be hindered by the established organization, because decision-making processes are too slow, structures are too rigid and financial and IT systems are geared towards different kinds of results. On the other hand, the new brand will usually have the advantage of the organization's (worldwide) resources and facilities, such as research and development departments, distribution networks, offices, marketing clout, and the like.

Management may decide to totally divorce the budding brand and its developers from the organization. Raymond Cloosterman founded Rituals in 2000 with the support of Unilever (his former employer) who were looking to support innovation outside of the confines of the corporation. Rituals sells stylish natural cosmetics, beverages and household products online, through catalogues, in its own shops and (more recently) in shop-in-shops. The concept was first launched in the Netherlands, and introduced in Germany and France in 2002. Unilever provided financial, organizational and technical assistance to Rituals. However, despite its best efforts Unilever proved to be too bureaucratic and sluggish for Rituals, and the latter plans to continue unaided.

Internal brand legacy

A brand new brand will be unhindered by historical baggage, but it will have a particular birthright and an (intended) role for its organization. This has to do with how the brand was conceived (for example, as a start-up or by an established organization) and what the aspirations are for it. Swatch was an entirely new watch concept in 1985, developed by the largest Swiss watchmaker SMH out of a desire to rebuild the Swiss watch industry (Hamel and Pralahad, 1994). So from the outset Swatch's birthright and role for the organization were clear.

The brand expression

Once the organizational factors that shape the new global brand have been established, the brand expression can be elaborated. The fact that the brand is establishing an entirely new (sub)category means that it is tremendously focused. The logical consequence is a highly focused brand expression. Enrichments and enhancements to the brand expression can be contemplated once the (sub)category has been established. For the moment, the brand expression needs to concentrate on translating the business strategy into a valuable experience for consumers. Swatch would have been no more than a cheap plastic watch, unable to out-compete its Japanese competitors, if it had not established its stylish yet purposeful brand expression which translated into striking watch designs, highly competitive prices and bold advertising and promotions.

For some new global brands, the brand expression flows so naturally from the business strategy that there is hardly any translation needed. Cisco Systems is the worldwide leader in networking for the Internet. In addition, the company has been a pioneer in using the Internet to provide customer support, sell products, offer training and manage finances.

Finally, the company has set up an Internet Business Solutions Group dedicated to helping business leaders transform their own businesses into e-businesses. Everything about Cisco is so closely tied to the Internet that its positioning is based on its problem-solving abilities for things Internet and Internet protocol (IP) related.

The danger with creating new global brands is that it is not the creation of a new (sub)category that becomes the focus of the brand expression's attempts at crafting a brand experience, but the desire to be considered cool, intelligent, modern or stylish. Letsbuyit.com largely created the co-buying category in Europe by offering consumers the opportunity to jointly purchase products through its Web site and thus obtain bulk purchase discounts. Established in Sweden in 1999, it had expanded rapidly to 14 European countries by the end of 2000. Unable to attract sufficient numbers of 'patient' bargain hunters, it had scaled down its operations to Germany, France and the UK by the end of 2002. Its Swedish business has been franchised to a third party. 'The Letsbuyit.com brand is based on a vision of collective intelligence,' said Soames Hines, the company's Chief Marketing Officer at the brand's zenith in 2000 (Letsbuyit, 2000). He clearly was overstating his case. The brand was based on (presumed) collective bargaining power rather than on collective intelligence. Apparently, not enough consumers were willing to take the trouble to register and wait for bargains for the purchasing model to work sufficiently well.

Marketing

As with the brand expression, the marketing mix is often highly focused on what defines the new (sub)category. New (sub)categories are often defined by certain technologies – such as satellite broadcasting and Internet banking – by certain consumer wants or desires – such as health foods and adventure holidays –and by innovative business models, such as Dell's customized online ordering and NTT DoCoMo's i-mode business partnerships. Such new (sub)categories have an accompanying marketing mix.

Products and services

Products and services are the core of any new (sub)category. CNN invented the 24-hour global news coverage category with an innovative service focusing on continuously updated world news. This was made possible by technological changes (such as handicams, small satellite link-ups and satellite broadcasts) and by changes in consumer wants (instant news any time of day). Perhaps unsurprisingly, CNN's brand expression centred (and still does) on a knowledgeable and reliable brand personality.

Another example is Palm. Despite previous efforts by Apple, Palm largely crafted the personal digital assistant (PDA) category. First launched in 1996, the Palm Pilot has its own unique operating system (OS) which does not treat mobile computing as a miniaturized version of desktop computing. The OS is easy to use, requires limited memory and battery power, and is designed to support a variety of devices from PDAs to smartphones. The efficiency provided by the Palm OS allowed Palm to develop numerous lightweight PDAs which people are able to carry in their pockets. Currently, most handheld devices use the Palm OS. Palm clearly has a brand expression based on a positioning of being simple, wearable, expandable and mobile.

Distribution

The distribution channels chosen by a brand may depend on its newly created (sub)category. A case in point is Dell Computers. The business model it pioneered, of selling direct to consumers and making its computers to order (keeping its inventory near zero), leads inexorably to the use of the Internet and the telephone as distribution channels. Founded in 1985 by freshman college student Michael Dell, the company sold US $50 million worth of computers per day via the Internet alone in 2000 (www.dell.com). Dell's brand expression centres on a positioning of superb value for money and customer focus.

Price

Some brands create new (sub)categories based largely on price. For example, Southwest Airlines was the original low-cost airline and became a model for other such airlines around the world. Southwest started operations in 1971 with flights to Houston, Dallas and San Antonio. The company started with one simple notion, 'If you get your passengers to their destinations when they want to get there, on time, at the lowest possible fares, and make darn sure they have a good time doing it, people will fly your airline.' By 2002, it had become the fourth largest airline in the United States (www.southwest.com). Southwest's brand expression is based firmly on its low-cost positioning, enhanced by its sizeable route network and a love for its customers.

People

Creating a new (sub)category may also induce a brand to adjust its customer service accordingly. Ian Schrager is widely recognized as the creator of the boutique hotel subcategory. His first hotel was a run-down property near Madison Square Gardens in Manhattan. The hotel was named Morgan's, and started a hotel design revolution that became an instant hit among the trendy classes. Since then Schrager has opened another eight boutique hotels in the United States and the UK, and plans for more to follow in the United States and mainland Europe. This focus on design carries through to the staff Schrager hires – he uses a casting agent to pick the service staff – and the uniforms they wear. Apparently, the service can be rather snooty, but then that probably fits well with the Philippe Starck designed surroundings.

Communications

Many newly created global brands rely on publicity to build up recognition and to garner interest and trust among consumers. This is because such brands have something to offer that is newsworthy. Certainly the brands that led the dot.com era received a massive amount of publicity. Those that were followers were unable to get the same kind of coverage, and consequently were forced to use (traditional) advertising. Probably no dot.com brand got as much publicity as Napster. Having irked the Recording Industry of America and associated artists such as Dr Dre and Metallica, Napster founder Shawn Fanning found himself on the covers of music and news magazines across the world. As a result of this attention, the brand's Web site visits grew by 345 per cent during the first six months of 2000 (E-Commerce Times, 2000a). Although Napster lost its court case and had to shut down, and the author would not like to advise using negative publicity, it is clear that publicity is generally more powerful for new brands than other forms of communications.

Marketing implementation

Marketing implementation is often the Achilles heel for new global brands. Precisely because everything is in play, there are few (if any) best practices to apply to the business. TiVo is a prime example of a brand based on breakthrough technology crafting its own new subcategory and having to deal with a multitude of marketing implementation issues. TiVo is essentially a giant hard drive in a box, which hooks up to a television, a cable or satellite feed, and a phone line. Using the phone line, TiVo dials in to a server to collect information about what shows are on when. TiVo can be used to record any of these shows but it also, unlike a conventional VCR, allows users to select shows that should always be recorded, allows them to skip advertising, and allows them to 'pause' in the middle of live broadcasts. TiVo can even track what types of shows you watch frequently and suggest others that you might enjoy.

TiVo is however having difficulties convincing consumers to buy and use the product. On the one hand television watching habits are difficult to influence; on the other hand it is difficult to convince consumers that TiVo offers value over and above a regular VCR. The company's basic advertising statement is that TiVo is like a VCR, except that it digitally records your favourite shows on a hard drive, letting you watch them whenever you want. TiVo tries to foster word of mouth among celebrities and lesser-known mortals. The latter are encouraged to host TiVo parties. TiVo-ware parties give non-users the chance to experience some of TiVo's features, such as pausing the show or rewinding it for an instant replay.

TiVo sometimes creates special content around a big event, such as the Super Bowl or the Oscars, which only TiVo owners can watch. TiVo practises exclusive distribution in the United States, where the product only retails at BestBuy. BestBuy salespeople get special training in how to use TiVo. Unfortunately, some BestBuy stores have a legion of well-trained salespeople, but no TiVo recorders in stock. The TiVo recorder is full of features that elude users, and the set-up is still fairly complex. One key goal has been to reduce the number of steps required to get a new TiVo hooked up to the user's television and phone line, at which point the device dials up to a main server to configure itself and download the latest program guide (Fast Company, 2002b).

By the beginning of 2003, TiVo quit its only foreign market, the UK, because of the lack of take-up there. TiVo's lack of success is attributed to its failure to come up with a simple way of explaining what the machine offers. Nigel Walley of Decipher, a media consultancy, said, 'What you can do with it is astonishing, but it is very hard to sum up the benefits in a few words' (Economist, 2003).

EXTERNAL ANALYSIS

The external analysis for a new global brand is very difficult. Not only does the brand have no previous presence, the (sub)category it creates is also entirely pristine. On the one hand, this means that the brand is free to shape matters. On the other hand, it means that the brand is challenging various (venerable) conventions. A new global brand can be a harbinger of considerable change and may upset many (cosy) arrangements. It is the function of the external analysis to identify what arrangements exactly the brand is supposed to upset, how that provides value to consumers, and how this will offer continuity for the brand.

Conventions

When entering a market with a brand, it is necessary to understand what moves and motivates consumers and will influence their brand perception. Apart from structural factors (category conventions), the factors affecting a brand can be either learnt (cultural conventions) or are motivational (needs conventions). The impact of the three types of convention varies by type of brand, as discussed in the Chapters 5 to 7. The matter to contemplate during market entry is whether to abide by or to challenge prevalent conventions as a way of creating value for consumers and their local communities. A convention is considered to be *solid* when consumers are unwilling to accept an alternative. Then there is little alternative than to adapt the particular aspect of the brand to this convention. A convention is considered to be *flexible* when the convention is undergoing development or erosion in consumers' minds. Then there is an opportunity to challenge such a convention, and to obtain differentiation from competitors and offer distinct value to consumers. Judging the solidity of a convention is dependent upon:

- *Ubiquity.* How widely is something practised by competitors or consumers?
- *Uniformity.* Does every competitor or consumer behave in exactly the same way or think exactly the same about this matter?
- *Stability.* Has the convention changed much over time? Has it begun to show changes recently?
- *Significance.* Does the convention have a particular relevance to competitors or consumers? Do they feel that they could do without it?
- *Depth.* Is the convention rooted in the fabric of the category or in the society? How valuable do competitors and consumers consider it to be to them?

Category conventions

When a new global brand creates an entirely new category, it has no category conventions to contend with. In fact, the brand is in a position to establish most of the key conventions of the category. When Netscape created the browser category it took into account a number of conventions that were prevalent in the business software category (for example, those emanating from operating systems such as Windows), but it was largely able to define the conventions of product experience. The public at large had no experience with Web browsers, so they were willing to accept whatever Netscape developed. The category conventions that Netscape created were later integrated into Microsoft's Internet Explorer, such as the top tool bar with back, forward, and refresh buttons. Therefore, a brand that creates an entirely new category does not need to bother with uncovering category conventions, but needs to determine which conventions it can establish and stake its claim on.

When a brand creates a new subcategory, it usually challenges one or more category conventions from the main category. Ian Schrager's boutique hotels are a deliberate challenge to the predictability of major hotel chain experiences. In such a case, the brand's management already has a good reading of prevalent category conventions. This is because the challenge to these conventions provides the basis for the new brand and its subcategory. It is, however, possible to misread the category conventions and to base the brand on the wrong challenges. Haig (2003) describes how in 1999 Patriot Computers decided to introduce the Hot Wheels PC, a computer aimed at boys and decorated with racing car imagery, and the pink and flowery Barbie PC for girls. This obvious challenge to the drabness of PC design was not only crude, it was also misplaced because it resorted to stereotyping boys and girls, something they evidently did not appreciate.

Needs conventions

A new global brand can meet established needs conventions, but it may also uncover latent needs through a challenge to the conventions. Burton's snowboards were a challenge to the relative sedateness of downhill skiing, and uncovered a pent-up need among younger generations for more excitement and variety on the slopes. Dell Computers, while challenging conventions of distribution, met a very apparent need among consumers for getting the latest technology at affordable prices.

Needs conventions can differ between countries, and can affect the success of the new global brand. The Japanese are well known for their love of gizmos, and Japanese companies have become good at churning out such novelties. Sony's AIBO, introduced in 1999, is a pet robot dog that the company claims is 'the most advanced companion ever created'. AIBOs have 'the capability to communicate with the world around them through the senses of sight, sound and touch. The truly unique artificial intelligence allows each AIBO to decide how it is going to behave based on its instincts, its emotions and these sensory interactions. These interactions with the people they meet, other AIBOs and the world around them will develop your AIBO's unique personality as it learns from every experience' (www.aibo-europe.com). So far AIBO has been successful in Japan, especially among older and elderly consumers (Economist, 2000). Undoubtedly Sony has created a totally new category of 'entertainment robots' which meets needs for (uncomplicated) companionship in Japan. There are indications that other societies do not share the same taste (that is, the emotional and social needs) for such 'ersatz companions', and consider AIBO to be a sophisticated toy rather than a substitute for real pets.

Cultural conventions

A new global brand can easily fall into the trap of believing in a single global culture. Although Starbucks did not create an entirely new category, it did redefine the meaning of coffee houses. Starbucks' rise has been driven mainly by its attention to the consumer experience. With over 4,000 stores in the United States and Canada, Starbucks expanded abroad in the 1990s, first in Asia, later in Europe. In countries that do not have a strong coffee house culture the brand has been an overnight success, and even in some that do have such a culture, such as Austria, Starbucks is considered a young and hip alternative to old-fashioned coffee drinking haunts. However, in Italy – the epicentre of European coffee culture – the notion that locals (even the young and hip ones) will abandon their own coffee bars strikes many as ridiculous. Italian coffee bars are a centre for everyday life in Italy. They serve food as well as coffee (in real cups rather than paper ones) and the prices are way below what Starbucks is asking customers (Business Week, 2002).

A new global brand does not need to treat the world as if it is culturally homogeneous. Some of the most successful ones are very culture-sensitive. Yahoo! is typical of a new global brand, creating its own category, yet being sensitive to local culture. Each local Yahoo! site is tailored to the local consumers, in both language and contents. There is even a regional Yahoo! site for the Spanish region of Catalonia, and ethnic sites for the United States in Chinese and Spanish (www.yahoo.com).

Brand perception

The brand perception of a new global brand is realized in several or many countries within a relatively short timespace. For some brands, their global roll-out may take a decade, while others accomplish this feat in a matter of years or less.

Brand domain

New global brands that are perceived as domain specialists are mainly susceptible to category conventions (see Chapter 5). These are largely absent when a brand creates its own category. The remaining conventions that may affect a domain specialist are cultural conventions (beliefs and customs) and various needs conventions (cognitive, security, transcendence and social). An example of a brand that is currently attempting to create a new category is Segway. Segway is the brainchild of a US inventor, physicist and entrepreneur called Dean Kamen. With the Segway Human Transporter (HT), Kamen aspires to improve upon the most basic form of transportation, walking, by allowing people to go farther, move more quickly, and carry more without separating them from their everyday walking environment. The result is a compact self-balancing electric scooter that moves in tune with the person standing on it. Gyroscopes and tilt sensors in the Segway HT monitor a user's centre of gravity. When a person leans slightly forward, the Segway HT moves forward. When he or she leans back, the Segway HT moves back. This is possible through a proprietary technology the firm calls Dynamic Stabilization. According to the company the Segway is intended to fill the gap that exists between walking and other forms of transportation: cars, buses, trains and the like. There are two models, one for personal use and one for business use (www.segway.com). It is hard not to be impressed by the inventiveness, technological prowess, design skills and dedication of the people who have developed the Segway HT. At the same time, it is difficult to suppress nagging doubts about the usefulness of the Segway HT and the value to consumers worldwide.

When Segway is introduced around the world, one can assume that it will face a number of the cultural and needs conventions. For example, in some countries Segway may face beliefs concerning the healthiness of walking. In other countries, the relevant beliefs may concern the social significance of not having to drive oneself (let alone walk anywhere). In some countries, people may have developed the habit of bicycling to fill the gap between walking and driving and public transport. In other countries, the habits of driving a car are so entrenched that cities largely lack sidewalks (as is the case in many cities in Segway's home country). In some countries, Segway may encounter consumers who consider the brand so novel that they will want one just for the experience. In other countries, consumers may be loath to fork out US $3,000 for that privilege, even if they can afford to. In some countries, consumers may feel that it is dangerous to allow motorized vehicles of any kind on the sidewalk. In fact the San Francisco authorities have banned the Segway HT from the city's sidewalks even before introduction, because of fears about the safety of pedestrians (CNN, 2003). In other countries, consumers think Segway is for indulging their elderly parents. In yet other countries, Segway may appeal to consumers' sense of belonging to an environmentally conscious segment of society. These issues are largely hypothetical, because the Segway HT is currently only for sale in the United States and then only through limited channels. Yet this quick inspection of issues that may face a nascent global domain specialist illustrates the difficulties of attempting such a feat.

Brand reputation

New global reputation specialists are rare because having a reputation implies that a brand has been around for long enough to acquire one. However, it is certainly possible in the case of endorsed brands and personality brands, because these leverage their reputation from other parties with a specific reputation (see Chapter 6). Endorsed brands are mainly susceptible to security needs, because they rely on the expert, knowledgeable reputation of their endorsers. Personality brands are susceptible to a wider range of factors, namely consumers' values and beliefs concerning celebrities and user groups, consumers' self-esteem needs in identifying with celebrities and user groups, and conventions of media, as media choice plays an important role in securing the credibility of the personality brand.

An example of a new global personality brand is Planet Hollywood. The brand is a kind of shrine to Hollywood movies, and is based on backing by Hollywood film stars, such as Bruce Willis, Demi Moore, Arnold Schwarzenegger and Sylvester Stallone. The brand was largely responsible for the creation of the theme restaurant subcategory world-wide. The chain rapidly expanded across the United States, Europe and Asia in the mid to late 1990s. By 1998, Planet Hollywood had some 80 restaurants in some 30 countries. By the end of 2002 Planet Hollywood emerged from bankruptcy for the second time in as many years, and the number of restaurants had declined to 30 in 19 countries. The company claimed it had been hit by the decline in tourist travel following the 11 September 2001 attacks on the USA. However Planet Hollywood had filed for Chapter 11 protection before, in 1999, because of financial problems caused by over-expansion, overtheming and lacklustre cuisine. Visits to the restaurants were one-time events for many consumers: done that, been there, seen it. New customers are generally out-of-towners and tourists who consider the restaurants to be a sightseeing attraction.

Apart from these manifest flaws, Planet Hollywood appears to have encountered a number of external factors that have had a negative influence on the brand. It over-estimated the awe that its Hollywood celebrity backers inspire around the world. While these people may have been the biggest possible cultural icons in the United States, they are not necessarily so elsewhere. Particularly Asia has shown a (renaissance of) strong local film culture during the 1990s. India has its Bollywood stars, Greater China has its action movie stars, as well as a score of acclaimed movie directors. But even in Europe, where US-made films are very popular, their actors are not as revered as they are Stateside. Especially in northern and much of western Europe, where values are predominantly feminine, celebrities are not taken all that seriously, and big egos are not much appreciated (de Mooij, 1998).

Brand affinity

New global affinity specialists are also not common, because an affinity specialist must be able to constantly feel the pulse of its targeted consumer segment. This is difficult to accomplish around the globe. However, brands that are able to read the signs of the time have a chance to bond with consumers the world over. They do face multiple external influences depending on the type of affinity they are able to garner.

Red Bull is an example of a new brand affinity specialist that has created a new beverage category, namely energy drinks. Once a lowly Asian health tonic drunk by tuk-tuk (a noisy three-wheeled motor taxi) drivers in Thailand, it is now the epitome of cool among young people the world over. Red Bull can be found as far afield as Angola, Yemen and Peru. Back in the early 1980s, Dietrich Mateschitz often travelled to Asia on business. There he came across a popular energy drink called Krating Daeng, a syrupy concoction containing substances such as caffeine, taurine, vitamin B and lots of sugar. The drink was dubbed 'the poor man's coffee' and 'amphetamines in a bottle'. Mateschitz has an agreement with the owners of Krating Daeng, the Yoovidhya family, to market Red Bull in all but two Asian markets (Hong Kong and Singapore) so as not to affect sales of the original brand in other Asian countries. However, apparently Krating Daeng is enjoying a halo effect from the success of Red Bull outside Asia (Far Eastern Economic Review, 2000b).

Mateschitz spent three years developing the drink, its distinct silver/blue can and its low-key grassroots marketing strategy. He persuaded students to drive around in Minis and Beetles with a Red Bull can strapped to the roof, and to throw Red Bull parties (Red Bull would contribute a few free cases of the stuff) with weird and wonderful themes. Its (limited) television advertising consists of a series of whimsical cartoons. In addition, Red Bull sponsors events such as Formula One racing, extreme sports, snowboarding and motocross. In 2001 Red Bull sold 1.6 billion cans in 62 countries, an increase of 80 per cent over 2000 (Economist, 2002b). Red Bull has become the drink of choice for ravers, extreme sports fanatics and the Internet generation. It makes sure that it does not dispel any of the mythology that has been built around the brand – such as being made from bulls' testes – as this adds to the mystique of the brand. The challenge for Red Bull is to retain its cool among young consumers, as its original users grow older.

Being an association brand, Red Bull must be sensitive to a number of consumer needs, namely *self-actualization, self-esteem and affiliation needs*, as well as to their *value* systems (see Chapter 7). To start with the last factor, Red Bull is typically a brand that encourages and is aimed at pleasure and excitement, or what Schwartz calls affective autonomy. Not all young people around the world share such 'hedonistic' values, and in the places where they do, particularly northern and western Europe, such values may shift between generations of youngsters. Now it has grown into a mass-marketed brand, it is somewhat doubtful whether the brand can still meet self-actualization and self-esteem needs among 16-year-olds which are largely based on a brand's exclusivity and obscurity. Its street-smart credentials are under pressure from its own ubiquity. Finally, Red Bull was originally a real social drink (pure or mixed) as can be witnessed by Red Bull parties and Red Bull nights at bars. Certainly in Europe, the drink of choice for a teenager's or a student's night out has quickly become Bacardi Breezer instead of Red Bull.

Brand recognition

Brand discrimination

Most new global brands will start life as a niche brand, however, with a (sub)category all to themselves. There is pressure to build up awareness, but mainly to build up distribution. For such novel or innovative brands, word of mouth and free publicity will often suffice to build up awareness and prompt trials. Most of the brands mentioned in this chapter have needed little or no advertising. Word was often out before the brand itself. In such a situation, it is necessary to get the brand into consumers' hands so they can appreciate first-hand the value of the new (sub)category. Differentiation from the competition is therefore also a matter that few of these brands need to put much effort into, at least at the outset.

Various problems may arise when the brand moves into a landmark position. On the one hand, this means that the brand has been so successful that it attracts competition. The case of Netscape shows that a more powerful competitor can destroy a brand. On the other hand, a landmark position may make the brand too omnipresent for consumers' tastes. The case of Planet Hollywood shows what happens if a once-in-a-lifetime experience brand overextends.

Worse still for such a brand is when it slides straight from a niche position into an indistinct one. An indistinct brand is generally stuck in a situation where it does not have the ability to differentiate itself sufficiently, and at the same time lacks the means to increase its awareness. This may be a situation that TiVo and Segway will find themselves in if they are unable to convince sufficient numbers of consumers to use their products, and fail to achieve economies of scale that will allow them to simultaneously lower prices and spend more on promoting their products.

Brand connections

Most new global brands start life as stand-alone product or service brands, simply because they are the heart of the new (sub)category. The brands also usually have the name of the company that spawns them, thus the one brand is the driver of the consumer purchase. However, some new global brands start life differently. The example of the Sony AIBO shows that a new global brand that creates an entirely new category can also be a co-driver. Other new global brands may be better suited to being a component for other brands. Gore-Tex is a prime example of a brand creating an entirely new category, best described as wearable weather protection, without offering the primary consumer product (such as jackets, tents or boots).

CONCLUSION

A truly new global brand is a rare thing, but accelerating technological, economic, motivational and legal changes are likely to make the development of such brands more likely in future. The advent of the Internet at the end of the last century has shown that this occurs in leaps and bounds. Yet it is also clear that creating such brands is no easy task, and success comes only to those who are able to create something so valuable to consumers that the brand can transcend the ever-present differences between societies.

If such brands are to retain their unique positions, they must remain powerful or nimble enough to evade the inevitable competitive onslaught. The case of Hotmail shows that sometimes it is better to surrender the brand while the going is good. The case of Dell shows that staying one or two steps ahead of competition can do wonders for a brand. The cases of Red Bull, Starbucks and Planet Hollywood show that a new global brand cannot rest on its laurels, and must consistently find new ways to appeal to new segments of societies. Finally, it is up to AIBO and Segway to demonstrate that their clever technology and elegant design can provide sufficient value to consumers around the world.

References

Aaker, D A and Joachimsthaler, E (2000) *Brand Leadership*, Free Press, New York

Aaker, J L (2000) *Dimensions of Brand Personality*, Research Paper no 1632, Graduate School of Business, Stanford University, Stanford, CA

Aaker, J L, Benet-Martinez, V and Garolera, J (2001) *Passion and Peacefulness*, Research Paper no 1622, Graduate School of Business, Stanford University, Stanford, CA

AdAge (2002) Rosie rips it out at 'Rosie' magazine, *AdAge*, 18 Sep

Anholt, A (2003) Brand New Justice, Butterworth-Heinemann, London

APM (2002) Asian teen idols: better than western? *Asia Pacific Management News* [Online] www.apmforum.com (accessed 24 Mar 2002)

Asiaweek (2001) Not running smooth as silk, *Asiaweek*, 22 Jun

Automotive Intelligence (1999) Audi TT: production capacity stepped up further, *Automotive Intelligence*, 22 Feb [Online] www.autointell.com

BBC News (2001) Fury over 'benefits of smoking' report [Online] bbc.co.uk (accessed 17 Jul)

Business Week (2002) Planet Starbucks, *Business Week*, 9 Sep

Castle, J W (1995) *The Indonesian Consumer*, SRI/Business Advisory Strategies, Jakarta

CFO (2001) *Going Local*, CFO Asia, Apr

Chevalier, J A (1999) When it can be good to burn your boats, *Financial Times*, Mastering Strategy Supplement, 25 Oct

CNN (2000) President Putin floored by a schoolgirl [Online] www.cnn.com (accessed 5 Sep 2000)

CNN (2003) San Francisco bans Segway [Online] www.cnn.com (accessed 20 Jan 2003)

Cusomano, M A and Yoffie, D B (2000) *Competing on Internet Time: Lessons from Netscape and its battle with Microsoft*, Touchstone, New York

De Mooij, M (1998) *Global Marketing and Advertising: Understanding cultural paradoxes*, Sage, Thousand Oaks, CA

Den Engelsen, B (2002) The Employee as Brand Builder (De medewerker als merkbouwer), *Tijdschrift voor Marketing*, Oct

E-commerce Times (2000a) Napster's priceless publicity, *E-commerce Times*, 13 Sep

E-commerce Times (2000b) Amazon apologizes for pricing blunder, *E-commerce Times* [Online] ecommercetimes.com (accessed 28 Sep)

Economist (1998) Star woes, *Economist*, 9 Apr

Economist (2000) Dr Doi's useless inventions, *Economist*, 21 Dec

Economist (2001) Wal around the world, *Economist*, 8 Dec

Economist (2002a) Big MacCurrencies, *Economist*, 25 Apr

Economist (2002b) Selling energy, *Economist*, 9 May

Economist (2002c) The Japanese are flocking to Britain, thanks to Becks and Beatrix, *Economist*, 29 Aug

Economist (2002d) Cooking Martha's goose, *Economist*, 12 Sep

Economist (2002e) Business bubbles, *Economist*, 12 Oct

Economist (2002f) Strong players, *Economist*, 12 Dec

Economist (2003) Heave ho, TiVo, *Economist*, 6 Feb

Ellis, P (2001) MTV vs. Channel [V], *Asian Case Research Journal*, **5** (2), pp 167–201

Enos, L and Blakey, E (2001) Alternative payment methods get no respect online, *E-commerce Times* [Online] www.ecommercetimes.com (accessed 1 Mar 2001)

Evans, P and Wurster, T S (2000) *Blown to Bits: How the new economics of information transforms strategy*, Harvard Business School Press, Boston, MA

Far Eastern Economic Review (2000a) Pepsi gets street smart, *Far Eastern Economic Review*, 1 Jun

Far Eastern Economic Review (2000b) Bull's-eye, *Far Eastern Economic Review*, 12 Oct

Far Eastern Economic Review (2002a) Elle is for label, in Asia, *Far Eastern Economic Review*, 28 Feb

Far Eastern Economic Review (2002b) Samsung tries to snatch Sony's crown, *Far Eastern Economic Review*, 10 Oct

Far Eastern Economic Review (2003) Small packets, big business, *Far Eastern Economic Review*, **166** (3), 23 Jan, pp 40–41

Fast Company (2002a) Brand marketing: Guinness, *Fast Company*, 58, May

Fast Company (2002b) Can TiVo go prime time?, *Fast Company*, Aug

Fast Company (2003) Calling for a renewable future, *Fast Company*, May

Gad, T and Rosencreutz, A (2002) *Managing Brand Me*, Momentum, Stockholm

Guardian (2000) East not sold on the values of the west, *Guardian*, 3 Oct

Guardian (2002) Cadbury's ad upsets India, *Guardian*, 20 Aug

Haig, M (2003) *Brand Failures*, Kogan Page, London

Hamel, G and Prahalad, C K (1994) *Competing for the Future*, Harvard Business School Press, Boston, MA

Han, J K and Schmitt, B H (1997) The relative importance of product–category dynamics and corporate identity in brand extensions: a comparison of Hong Kong and US consumers, *Journal of International Marketing*, **5** (1), pp 77–92

Hankinson, G and Cowking, P (1996) *The Reality of Global Brands*, McGraw-Hill, London

Haskell, J and Wolf, H (2000) From Big Macs to iMacs, what do international price comparisons tell us? *World Economics*, Mar

Herzberg, F (1987) One more time: how do you motivate employees? *Harvard Business Review*, Sept/Oct

Het Financieele Dagblad (2002a) Philips to collaborate with Ikea (Philips gaat samenwerken met Ikea), *Het Financieele Dagblad*, 30 Oct

Het Financieele Dagblad (2002b) Akzo Nobel gets rid of solvents in car paint (Akzo Nobel rekent af met oplosmiddelen in autolak), *Het Financieele Dagblad*, 3 Dec

Het Financieele Dagblad (2002c) KPN getting under steam with sales of mobile Internet (KPN komt op stoom met verkoop mobiel internet), *Het Financieele Dagblad*, 19 Dec

Het Financieele Dagblad (2002d) ING unleashes revolution in Korean insurance market (ING ontketent omwenteling op Koreaanse verzekeringsmarkt), *Het Financieele Dagblad*, 17 Dec

Het Financieele Dagblad (2003) New Heineken? British beer drinker prefers Stella (Nieuwe Heineken? Britse bierdrinker heeft liever Stella), *Het Financieele Dagblad*, 25 Feb

Hofstede, G (1980) *Culture's Consequences: International differences in work-related values*, Sage, London

Hofstede, G (1991) *Cultures and Organizations: Software of the mind*, McGraw-Hill, London

Ind, N (2001) *Living the Brand*, Kogan Page, London

ING Group (2002) German ING-company DiBa acquires Degussa Bank, ING Group press release, 1 Jul

ING Group (2003) ING Direct welcomes five millionth customer, ING Group press release, 20 Jan

Inglehart, R, Basañez, M and Moreno, A (1998) *Human Values and Beliefs: A cross-cultural sourcebook*, University of Michigan Press, Chicago, IL

Johnson, G and Scholes, K (1993) *Exploring Corporate Strategy*, Prentice Hall, London

Kapferer, J-N (1997) *Strategic Brand Management*, Kogan Page, London

Karolefski, J (2003) *The Sport of Naming* [Online] www.brandchannel.com (accessed 13 May 2003)

Kinnear, T C (2000) Brave new horizontal world, in *Mastering Strategy*, Pearson Education, Upper Saddle River, NJ

Koehn, N F (2001) *Brand New: How entrepreneurs earned consumers' trust from Wedgwood to Dell*, Harvard Business School Press, Boston, MA

Kotler, P (1999) *Kotler on Marketing: How to create, win and dominate markets*, Free Press, New York

Kunde, J (2000) *Corporate Religion*, Financial Times Prentice Hall, London

Letsbuyit (2000) Letsbuyit.com launch campaign adjudged a success, corporate press release [Online] www.letsbuyit.com (accessed 14 Nov 2000)

Levitt, T (1983) The globalization of markets, *Harvard Business Review*, May–Jun

Lindstrom, M (2003) *Brandchild*, Kogan Page, London

Macrae, C (1996) *The Brand Chartering Handbook*, Addison-Wesley, Boston, MA

Maslow, A (1954) *Motivation and Personality*, Harper, New York, NY

Milavanovi, G (1997) Marketing dimensions of global advertising, University of Nis, *Scientific Journal Facta Universitatis, Series: Economics and Organization*, **1** (5)

Morgan, A (1999) *Eating the Big Fish*, Wiley, Chichester

OECD (2002) *Financial Market Trends*, no 81, OECD, Paris

Peters, T (1999) *The Brand You 50*, Knopf, New York

Pinto, D (2002) *Intercultural Communication: A three-step method for dealing with differences,* Maklu, Antwerp

Pringle, H and Gordon, W (2001) *Brand Manners*, Wiley, Chichester

Rangan, S (1999) Seven myths to ponder before going global, *Financial Times*, Mastering Strategy Supplement, 29 Nov

Rangan, S and Adner, R (2001) Profits and the Internet: seven misconceptions, *MIT Sloan Management Review* (Summer), pp 44–53

Ries, A and Trout, J (1981) *Positioning: The battle for your mind*, McGraw-Hill, New York

Rokeach, M (1973) *The Nature of Human Values*, Free Press, New York

SAM (undated) MTV – how to stay hip forever; an interview with Christina Norman, *SAM Magazine* [Online] www.sammag.com (accessed 17 Dec 2002)

Schmitt, B H and Simonson, A (1997) *Marketing Aesthetics: The strategic management of brands, identity and image*, Free Press, New York

Schwartz, S (1999) A theory of cultural values and some implications for work, *Applied Psychology*, **48** (1), Jan, pp 23–47

SME IT Guide (2001) Cookie business, *SME IT Guide* [Online] www.smeit.com.sg (accessed Sep 2001)

Temporal, P (2000) *Branding in Asia*, Wiley, Chichester

Treacy, M and Wiersema, F (1995) *The Discipline of Market Leaders*, HarperCollins, London

Watson, J L (ed) (1997) *Golden Arches East: McDonald's in East Asia*, Stanford University Press, Stanford, CA

websidestory (2002) The incredible shrinking browser [Online] www.websidestory.com (accessed 28 Aug 2002)

winespectator (2002) *Burgundy and its Enemies* [Online] www.winespectator.com (accessed 10 Oct 2002)

Write News (2002) Reuters launches revised website targeting consumers, *Write News* [Online] www.writenews.com (accessed 29 Nov 2002)

ZDNet (2002a) Compaq Australia faces lawsuit over one cent laptops, ZDNet Australia [Online] www.zdnet.com.au (accessed 6 May 2002)

ZDNet (2002b) Compaq issues refunds for one-cent PCs, ZDNet Australia [Online] www.zdnet.com.au (accessed 9 May)

Index